T0400272

Military Occupations in First World War Europe

Our view of the First World War is dominated by the twin images of the fronts and the home fronts, yet the war also generated a third type of 'front', that of military occupation. Vast areas of Europe experienced the war under a military regime. This book deals with the occupations by the German and Austro-Hungarian empires. Their conquests ranged from Lille in the West to the Don River in the East, and from Courland in the North to Friuli and Montenegro in the South. They encompassed capital cities such as Brussels, Warsaw, Belgrade and Bucharest, as well as areas of crucial economic importance. Millions of people experienced military occupation and, even though they were civilians, the war had a deep impact on their lives. Conversely, occupied territories influenced the states that had conquered them and the way these states waged war.

The chapters in this book analyze military occupation in 1914–1918 both from the point of view of the occupied and from the point of view of the occupier. They study counter-insurgency warfare, forced labour, food regimes, underground patriotism, and cultural policies. They demonstrate that military occupation was an essential dimension of the Great War.

This book was originally published as a special issue of *First World War Studies.*

Sophie De Schaepdrijver teaches Modern European History at Penn State University, USA. She has published widely on military occupations in the First World War in general, and on the German occupation of Belgium in particular. Her latest book is *Gabrielle Petit: the Death and Life of a Female Spy in the First World War* (London: Bloomsbury Academic, 2014).

Military Occupations in First World War Europe

Edited by
Sophie De Schaepdrijver

LONDON AND NEW YORK

First published 2015
by Routledge
2 Park Square, Milton Park, Abingdon, Oxon, OX14 4RN, UK

and by Routledge
711 Third Avenue, New York, NY 10017, USA

Routledge is an imprint of the Taylor & Francis Group, an informa business

© 2015 Taylor & Francis

All rights reserved. No part of this book may be reprinted or reproduced or utilised in any form or by any electronic, mechanical, or other means, now known or hereafter invented, including photocopying and recording, or in any information storage or retrieval system, without permission in writing from the publishers.

Trademark notice: Product or corporate names may be trademarks or registered trademarks, and are used only for identification and explanation without intent to infringe.

British Library Cataloguing in Publication Data
A catalogue record for this book is available from the British Library

ISBN 13: 978-1-138-82236-8

Typeset in Times New Roman
by RefineCatch Limited, Bungay, Suffolk

Publisher's Note
The publisher accepts responsibility for any inconsistencies that may have arisen during the conversion of this book from journal articles to book chapters, namely the possible inclusion of journal terminology.

Disclaimer
Every effort has been made to contact copyright holders for their permission to reprint material in this book. The publishers would be grateful to hear from any copyright holder who is not here acknowledged and will undertake to rectify any errors or omissions in future editions of this book.

Contents

Citation Information	vii
Notes on Contributors	ix

1. Introduction: Military occupation, political imaginations, and
   the First World War
   Sophie De Schaepdrijver   1

2. *Mauvaise conduite*: complicity and respectability in the occupied Nord,
   1914–1918
   James E. Connolly   7

3. *Sursum Corda*: the underground press in occupied Belgium, 1914–1918   23
   Sophie De Schaepdrijver and Emmanuel Debruyne

4. Between recruitment and forced labour: the radicalization of German
   labour policy in occupied Belgium and northern France   39
   Jens Thiel

5. 'A kind of Siberia': German labour and occupation policies in
   Poland and Lithuania during the First World War   51
   Christian Westerhoff

6. Warsaw University under German occupation: state building and
   nation *Bildung* in Poland during the Great War   65
   Jesse Kauffman

7. The fruits of occupation: food and Germany's occupation of
   Romania in the First World War   81
   David Hamlin

8. Norms of war and the Austro-Hungarian encounter with Serbia, 1914–1918   97
   Jonathan E. Gumz

9. Misconceived *realpolitik* in a failing state: the political and
   economical fiasco of the Central Powers in the Ukraine, 1918   111
   Wolfram Dornik and Peter Lieb

Index   125

Citation Information

The chapters in this book were originally published in *First World War Studies*, volume 4, issue 1 (March 2013). When citing this material, please use the original page numbering for each article, as follows:

Chapter 1
Introduction: Military occupation, political imaginations, and the First World War
Sophie De Schaepdrijver
First World War Studies, volume 4, issue 1 (March 2013) pp. 1–5

Chapter 2
Mauvaise conduite: *complicity and respectability in the occupied Nord, 1914–1918*
James E. Connolly
First World War Studies, volume 4, issue 1 (March 2013) pp. 7–21

Chapter 3
Sursum Corda: *the underground press in occupied Belgium, 1914–1918*
Sophie De Schaepdrijver and Emmanuel Debruyne
First World War Studies, volume 4, issue 1 (March 2013) pp. 23–38

Chapter 4
Between recruitment and forced labour: the radicalization of German labour policy in occupied Belgium and northern France
Jens Thiel
First World War Studies, volume 4, issue 1 (March 2013) pp. 39–50

Chapter 5
'A kind of Siberia': German labour and occupation policies in Poland and Lithuania during the First World War
Christian Westerhoff
First World War Studies, volume 4, issue 1 (March 2013) pp. 51–63

Chapter 6
Warsaw University under German occupation: state building and nation Bildung *in Poland during the Great War*
Jesse Kauffman
First World War Studies, volume 4, issue 1 (March 2013) pp. 65–79

CITATION INFORMATION

Chapter 7
The fruits of occupation: food and Germany's occupation of Romania in the First World War
David Hamlin
First World War Studies, volume 4, issue 1 (March 2013) pp. 81–95

Chapter 8
Norms of war and the Austro-Hungarian encounter with Serbia, 1914–1918
Jonathan E. Gumz
First World War Studies, volume 4, issue 1 (March 2013) pp. 97–110

Chapter 9
Misconceived realpolitik *in a failing state: the political and economical fiasco of the Central Powers in the Ukraine, 1918*
Wolfram Dornik and Peter Lieb
First World War Studies, volume 4, issue 1 (March 2013) pp. 111–124

Please direct any queries you may have about the citations to
clsuk.permissions@cengage.com

Notes on Contributors

James E. Connolly, Department of History, University of Manchester, UK

Emmanuel Debruyne, Institute of Civilizations, Arts and Letters (INCAL), Université Catholique de Louvain (UCL), Belgium

Sophie De Schaepdrijver, Department of History, The Pennsylvania State University, USA

Wolfram Dornik, Ludwig-Boltzmann-Institut für Kriegsfolgen-Forschung, Austria

Jonathan E. Gumz, Department of History, University of Birmingham, UK

David Hamlin, Department of History, Fordham University, USA

Jesse Kauffman, Department of History and Philosophy, Eastern Michigan University, USA

Peter Lieb, Department of War Studies, Royal Military Academy Sandhurst, UK

Jens Thiel, Institut für Geschichtswissenschaften, Humboldt-Universität zu Berlin, Germany

Christian Westerhoff, Bibliothek für Zeitgeschichte, Württembergische Landesbibliothek Stuttgart, Germany

INTRODUCTION
Military occupation, political imaginations, and the First World War

Sophie De Schaepdrijver

This theme issue presents a selection of the latest scholarship on the military occupations of the First World War in Europe. It demonstrates the significant recent expansion in our knowledge of this aspect of the war. Recent monographs, some of them by contributors to this issue, also testify to this leap in scholarship.[1] This progress has, very fruitfully, included work on Bulgarian, Italian and Russian military occupations.[2] The articles in this issue, as it happens, all deal with the military occupations by the German and Austro-Hungarian empires. At their height, these encompassed territories stretching from Lille in the west to the Don River in the east, and from Courland in the north to Friuli and Montenegro in the south. These occupied territories were both separate from and central to the war. They were separate from the war in that they had a different statute: they were neither fronts nor home fronts. Conquest had made them into hinterlands of the armies that had conquered them. In that sense, they had been placed outside of the war. But in other senses, the occupied territories were very much drawn into the war. First, their populations were mobilized by the war; second, they impacted the mobilizations of the states that had conquered them.

To turn to the first point: the occupied populations were deeply touched by the war in many ways; Annette Becker aptly describes their situation as one of 'internal siege'.[3] If the world war era, as Hannah Arendt has written, looked as if 'mankind had divided itself between those who believe in human omnipotence (who think that everything is possible if one knows how to organize masses for it) and those for whom powerlessness has become the major experience of their lives',[4] then it is clear on what side of the line the occupied of the era's first conflict stood. Of course, their powerlessness was, as the contributions to this issue indicate, neither uniform nor continuous. Many had experienced, at the start of the war, a period of extreme violence, at the hands of either retreating armies or invading armies, or both. During the time of occupation that followed, the spectre of massacres of civilians receded, many (if not all) refugees returned and spaces of routine activity opened up again. But violent repression and coercion were never far away. Tens of thousands of Serbians wound up in Austro-Hungarian prison camps. Workers from the Baltic, Poland, France and Belgium were forced into labour camps and work gangs in Germany, at the fronts and in the occupied territories. Exploitation was intense. Romanian and Ukrainian grain was hauled off in massive quantities to the Austro-Hungarian and German home fronts. The occupied territories paid for, lodged and fed the occupying armies, and, in addition, suffered crippling collective fines for even minor infractions. Many among the occupied were, then, 'mobilized' for the needs of the conquering power; some coerced to work or deliver goods at gunpoint, others forced by material hardship to work. Others – policemen, mayors, shopkeepers – found themselves squeezed in between the needs of the occupied and the requirements of the occupiers. Yet others took the new opportunities offered by occupation regimes, as commercial middlemen, police informers, journalists for the censored press, providers of entertainment or other services or sympathetic community spokesmen. Occupied civilians could also mobilize in that they withheld resources from the occupying power in self-defence, wielding various weapons of despair, such as the Romanian farmers hiding their grain in pretend burials (mentioned in David Hamlin's contribution), or the Baltic workers mutilating themselves to get out of labour camps (mentioned by Christian Westerhoff). Some of this withholding of resources – manpower, food or legitimacy – was done in more systematic, collective, deliberate and public ways. Railroad workers went on strike in Belgium and Ukraine (the latter are mentioned by Wolfram Dornik and Peter Lieb); there was armed resistance in southern Serbia; in northern France and even more in Belgium, the underground press attempted to undermine the legitimacy of occupation rule (see the contribution by Emmanuel Debruyne and myself). Some among the occupied offered active support to their own or allied armies through offering escape help to trapped soldiers from the other side, or spying on the conquering troops. Resulting large-scale repression by occupation forces, fuelled by what Isabel Hull has pertinently called 'latitudinarian suspicion', made life even harder on all of the occupied.[5]

Even those among the occupied who were not 'mobilized' in any of these ways, but managed to maintain a modicum of routine in their lives, then, found themselves drawn into the war. The remit of 'normal' lives and livelihoods shrank beyond recognition. It was impossible to escape the war, whether in work and trade or in other daily activities (buying food, clothing, fuel or anything else; commuting and travel; communications; staying informed; child-raising, education, sociability, entertainment, the privacy of home). In addition, as the contributions by James Connolly and others show, the occupations profoundly influenced how the occupied saw, judged and – frequently – condemned one another, often along dimensions of class, gender or ethnicity. To say that the occupied could not escape the impact of the war is not to say that they felt the hand of the occupier everywhere; as Jesse Kauffman writes, one should not ascribe to occupying authorities powers that they did not have. Several contributions testify to these limits of power: the Polish Government-General could not always get hold of workers targeted for forced labour, as Christian Westerhoff shows; no censorship could be imposed in Ukraine, as Wolfram Dornik and Peter Lieb demonstrate; in Romania, as David Hamlin writes, control over the food supply was undermined both by locals and occupation troops in favour of a flourishing black market. But, of course, if this black market testified to the limit of the occupiers' power, it also showed how desperately 'normal' lives and livelihoods had shrunk.

The second point to be made is that the occupied territories impacted the mobilizations of the states that had conquered them. For those states-at-war, the occupied territories were more than just a by-product of having been able to push their armies so far forward. Once these territories were conquered (and, in the case of Romania and possibly Ukraine, even before actual conquest), they became war aims in their own right. The possession of these territories recrystallized, so to speak, the occupying societies' engagement with the war. They did so on three counts: with regard to resources, to perspectives on the war, and to war effort. First, the resources of the conquered territories – wheat, oil, workers, taxes – were, unsurprisingly, keenly counted on. (Equally unsurprisingly, these resources and their accessibility were often overestimated: policy-makers, lobbyists and editorialists referred to occupied territories as so many 'great granaries', 'bread baskets' or 'basins of people' just waiting to be tapped into.) Second, conquest also changed outlooks on the war in the occupying states. In its most ambitious form, the new fact of conquest gave rise to fantasies of waging war to redraw the map. Thus, policy-makers in the Austro-Hungarian Empire envisioned a new role on the Balkans; Germans considered Ukraine the 'key' to unlocking regional dominance; schemes emerged for permanent control over the Belgian coastline. In its least ambitious form, the new fact of conquest still offered reassurance: at the very least, the conquered territories could serve as securities to ensure a satisfactory exit from the war, or so it was hoped. A third impact of conquest was that it called for a new war effort, one eagerly proffered, often mobilizing those who could not enlist. Germany and Austria-Hungary sent occupying troops (often territorials too old to be sent to the front), governors, bureaucrats, policemen, doctors, military judges, censors, labour recruiters, boy-scouts and tens of thousands of women working as secretaries or in other ancillary – or sometimes less ancillary – capacities. Some experts rotated between occupied territories. As the articles in this issue show, an important distinction must be made between those territories under exclusive military control, such as the northern French and western Belgian operations and staging areas or the militarily-ruled northern Polish and Baltic territory known as Ober Ost, on the one hand, and, on the other hand, the civilian-military hybrids that were the Governments-General of Belgium and Poland. Coercive labour, as Jens Thiel and Christian Westerhoff show, was implemented very differently in both types of territory. Military rulers in Serbia, as Jonathan Gumz shows, at least initially made much of the difference between their kind of rule and the 'civilian' rule on the home front. (The greater vigour ascribed to unfettered military rule was, as we know, constitutive of the Ludendorff mystique.)[6]

For all that, occupation regimes everywhere faced the same two priorities: first, to keep order in the occupied territories to permit the armies to fight and exploitation to proceed; second, precisely, exploitation – the channelling of resources to the front and the home front. Over and above this, a more ambitious perspective emerged: that of permanent domination through structural changes to be made in the conquered territories. Examples are the attempted 'de-nationalizing' of elites in Serbia; the co-opting or marginalizing of landowners, intellectuals or other groups; and attempts to establish indirect rule through polonization, lithuanization, flemishization or ukrainization. All of these endeavours constituted, of course, another face of conquest, and they happened in a context of repression and exploitation. At the same time, the claim to permanent domination – at least the way this claim was made in *this* war – introduced interstices in between the violence, spaces of earnest – or almost earnest – endeavour.

The military occupations, then, must be seen not only as extensions of the domain of war, which they were, but also as extensions of the domain of political imaginations, a domain that is central to our understanding of the First World War. How the military occupations were set up, how they functioned, how they were experienced by occupiers and occupied alike, all shed light on the political imaginations at play. The article by Jonathan Gumz, which explores the shifting sway of international norms of war through the lens of the Austro-Hungarian occupation of Serbia, and the article by Jesse Kauffman, which charts the balance between consent and coercion in the Government-General of Warsaw, both address the question of political imaginations most directly. But the question runs through all of the articles. James Connolly charts the 'moral-patriotic framework' within which the occupied French passed judgment on each other. Emmanuel Debruyne and I discuss how, in Belgium, both occupiers and occupied linked the invasion-era transgression of norms of war to the legitimacy of the occupation regime. The articles by Jens Thiel and Christian Westerhoff on coercive labour in West and East, respectively, highlight the dismissive stereotyping of the working-class occupied as 'work-shy', while showing the moderating influence of norms of war and of schemes for indirect rule. David Hamlin shows how the rituals of food gifts in rural Romania indicated relations of propitiation, hence of power, while at the same time establishing a sense of mutual obligations. And, finally, Wolfram Dornik and Peter Lieb identify anti-Bolshevism as a mainspring of German violence in Ukraine – at least against armed opponents. As all of these articles show, the question of the containment of war suffused discourses and practices, even if answers differed. As Alan Kramer has written, while the era of the First World War meant a decisive step towards total war, especially as regards the erosion of the distinction between combatants and non-combatants, the 'dynamic of destruction' was 'man-made [and] capable of infinite variation'.[7]

All of this, of course, played out against the backdrop of military mobilization and of the ongoing hecatomb at the fronts. That backdrop was continuously referred to by occupiers and occupied: French women were accused by their fellow occupied of betraying their menfolk at the front, as James Connolly shows; the deliberately brutal treatment of Belgian deported labourers, highlighted by Jens Thiel, betrays a vindictive resentment of unmobilized, military-age, able-bodied men. The military backdrop could justify long-term plans for domination, with attendant emphasis on 'sensible rule' (such as the plans harboured by Governor-General von Bissing for Belgium). But it also could – and, in the second half of the war, increasingly did – lead to the impatient dismissal of long-term plans in favour of immediate, sometimes even punitive, exploitation. However, as several articles show, there was no unequivocal brutalizing turn across occupations. Coercive labour, introduced in 1916, was partially rescinded, as Jens Thiel and Christian Westerhoff point out; occupied Serbia from 1917 even enjoyed a 'gradual de-escalation' of repression, as Jonathan Gumz shows; and Wolfram Dornik and Peter Lieb document the absence of violent collective repression in the Ukraine in 1918. A certain shared sense of mutual obligation among European belligerents and vis-à-vis civilians seems to have endured – at least compared to the Nazi occupations in the East. Admittedly, these constituted such a nadir of normlessness as to make the transgressions of the First World War appear more minor than they were. Still, the authors who directly address the Nazi occupations – viz. Jens Thiel, Christian Westerhoff, Jesse Kauffman, Wolfram Dornik and Peter Lieb – all conclude that whatever 'horizons of experience' the first occupation era made available to the occupiers of the Second World War, the differences in the approach to occupation were fundamental. They were also deliberate: as Christian Westerhoff points out with regard to the East, the Nazi leadership expressly rejected the expertise of occupation personnel of the First World War.

As a last reflection, one might suggest that this rejection of the occupations of the First World War was linked to the military hecatomb of that war, or, at least, to the way the hecatomb was interpreted among the defeated. One of the ways in which the First World War 'brutalized the postwar imagination' (as Jesse Kauffman writes) was the extreme right's progressive appropriation of the memory of the war dead. The occupations of the First World War were retrospectively dismissed (not least by Ludendorff) as unworthy of the allegedly sublime sacrifices made at the military fronts. They were unworthy because they had been too bureaucratic, too hesitant, too lenient – in a word, too civilian. And so they had been, to a point. As the articles in this issue show very well, the military occupations of the First World War were steeped in the political imaginations of the early twentieth century. These imaginations shifted even during the war; civilians suffered hitherto unimaginable violences (at least, unimaginable vis-à-vis Europeans), and yet some degree of circumspection, some notions of a shared moral space, of an international (or, for that matter, a national) court of public opinion, endured. The ultimate, paradigm-altering shift in notions of war and occupation happened afterwards – and it was at least partly due to the way the erstwhile conquerors chose to remember the military occupations of the First World War.

Notes

1. The years 2010–2012 alone saw the publication of monographs by Annette Becker and by Philippe Nivet on occupied northern France, Laurence Van Ypersele and Emmanuel Debruyne on civilian resistance in Belgium, Christian Westerhoff on coercive labour in Poland and the Baltic, Wolfram Dornik and Peter Lieb on the Ukraine, and others. In addition, Tammy Proctor's *Civilians in a World At War, 1914–1918* (New York: New York University Press, 2010) devotes ample attention to occupied populations. Forthcoming dissertations include the work of Heiko Brendel (Mainz), on the Austro-Hungarian occupation of Montenegro, of Julie Jacoby (Cornell University) on the Austro-Hungarian occupation of Poland, and of Larissa Wegner (Düsseldorf) on the German occupation of northern France, among others.
2. For example, Björn Opfer-Klinger's 2005 monograph on the Bulgarian occupation of Vardar-Macedonia, Petra Svoljšak's work on the Italian occupation of parts of Slovenia (e.g. 'The Social History of the Soča Region in the First World War,' *Mitteilungsblatt des Instituts für soziale Bewegungen* 41 (2009): 89–109), and Christoph Mick's 2010 monograph on the successive occupations of Lemberg/Lvov/L'viv, reviewed here.
3. Annette Becker, *Les cicatrices rouges. France et Belgique occupées, 1914–1918*, Paris: Fayard, 2010, 13.
4. *The Origins of Totalitarianism*, new ed., New York: Harcourt Brace Jovanovich, 1973, VII (preface to the first edition, written in the summer of 1950).
5. Isabel V. Hull, *Absolute Destruction: Military Culture and the Practices of War in Imperial Germany* (Ithaca, NY: Cornell University Press, 2005), 247.
6. Even the American critic H.L. Mencken expressed a – possibly flippant – preference for the firm Ludendorffian approach to occupation over that of the 'hordes of frockcoated and bespatted *Beamten*' elsewhere, with their 'inextricable complex of bureaux' and their ladling out of 'the blessings of *Kultur*.' H.L. Mencken, 'Ludendorff,' *The Atlantic Monthly* 119:6 (June 1917), 823–32.
7. Alan Kramer, *Dynamic of Destruction: Culture and Mass Killing in the First World War*, Oxford: Oxford University Press, 2007, 329.

Mauvaise conduite: complicity and respectability in the occupied Nord, 1914–1918

James E. Connolly

King's College London

This article examines the occupied war culture of the Nord in 1914–18, focusing on various forms of behaviour met with opprobrium and disdain by many among the occupied population, which flood archival documents. An argument is put forward for a new conceptual category to understand such actions and the wider culture – what is termed *'mauvaise conduite'* or misconduct, in some senses a forerunner to the notion of collaboration. This concept covers actions which comprised both illegal and legal misconduct – behaviours that were forbidden by French law, and those which were permitted but frowned upon by fellow inhabitants. This conflation of different forms of misconduct – illegal and legal, sexual and non-sexual, friendly and political – was central to the culture of the occupied population, who occasionally expressed outrage at certain actions via physical and verbal attacks on suspect individuals. In doing so, they upheld a moral-patriotic framework based on the notion of respectability. Breaches of this framework were also punished by the French authorities after the war, but only on a small scale, and *mauvaise conduite* was eventually replaced in the memory of the occupation by the other aspect of the occupied war culture: resistance.

In 1914, the department of the Nord was one of France's most productive agricultural and industrial regions, famed for its sugar beet, textile and mining industries.[1] Its highly urbanized population represented a bastion of French socialism.[2] Yet, Catholicism also remained strong, especially in the capital, Lille.[3] This specificity would be significant for the occupation. From October 1914 to November 1918, the German army occupied two-thirds of the department. Trenches ran a few kilometres west of Lille, cutting off the north-western territory, and trapping a population of 1,176,000 in what became a militarized area.[4] Large towns such as Lille-Roubaix-Tourcoing, Douai and Cambrai, were never less than 25 km from the front for most of the war.[5]

The Germans divided the area into different staging zones (*Etappen*), each controlled by an *Etappeninspektor*, charged with providing soldiers with food, accommodation and transport. Below him was an *Etappenkommandant*, the highest authority to which French people could appeal. Each *Kommandant* and his *Kommandantur* controlled 1–40 French communes, and possessed wide-ranging personnel, including their own administrative staff. Members of the army of occupation and front-line troops *en route* to or on leave from the trenches often billeted with French civilians, much to the chagrin of the latter. Three German police forces existed: gendarmes, sometimes including *Landsturm* (reservists); a military police formed of soldiers exempt from front-line service; and the secret police, involved in counter-espionage.[6] The French municipal police and judiciary were permitted to deal exclusively with French-on-French crime,[7] reflecting a wider trend: French authorities were sidelined at all but the municipal level. The prefect could and did criticize German policy but had no formal authority.[8] Instead, the Germans engaged with French mayors and municipal councillors, using them as middlemen both to inform the population of German demands, and to fulfil such demands. Thus, local notables were often left in an impossible situation.[9]

Life for *all* occupied French was extremely difficult. They were isolated and faced severe restrictions, with travel and correspondence between communes by and large forbidden.[10] Almost every aspect of life was regulated, from the imposition of German time to public hygiene measures.[11] Thousands of posters informed the population of the numerous rules, and the punishments for any infractions – often inevitable, given the wide-ranging nature of regulations which criminalized previously acceptable acts.[12] The Germans exploited the human and material resources of the occupied territory, initially via searches and requisitions, but from 1916 onwards through forced evacuations and forced labour (including building trenches).[13] Yet, the greatest concern was food, which was in extremely short supply, partly due to German requisitions and the near-complete collapse of local economies.[14] Many would have died were it not for the intervention of Herbert Hoover's Commission for Relief in Belgium, and the French Committee for Feeding Northern France (CANF).[15]

In this environment, there emerged a form of 'war culture'[16] the expressions of which are primarily accessible via wartime diaries, police reports and interviews with repatriated individuals. The central element of this moral–patriotic framework concerned interaction with the hundreds of thousands of German men living alongside the occupied population. This 'occupied war culture' (what I will call the *culture de l'occupé*) called for the strict enforcement of distance[17] – for instance, refusing to shake the hand of a German.[18] Distance alone could uphold occupied civilians' sense of respectability, and, because the upholders of the framework were overwhelmingly bourgeois, civil servants or other *lettrés*, respectability loomed large in their worldview. These occupation–time mores were upheld by types of collective or self-imposed surveillance similar to what occurred among civilians in unoccupied France,[19] but with a unique occupied twist. Perceived breaches of the limits of respectability were criticized by compatriots. The hardening of the regime from 1916 may have both increased the likelihood of such breaches (as people struggled to survive) and of attendant criticism.

This article is about infractions against this moral–patriotic framework, from general contact with the Germans (which was legal but frowned upon) to harming fellow *occupés* (such as informing). Much of what we know about 'incorrect behaviour' is passed on to us through the eyes of the upholders of the framework – few sources allow for a grasp of how much 'incorrect behaviour' actually occurred, although they demonstrate a belief that this was commonplace.

Sources must be understood in context: liberation and post-war investigations/trials, usually based on denunciations of compatriots, may represent a settling of scores. Repatriated members of the occupied population, interrogated by the military *Service de Renseignements*, may have been particularly severe towards those who had stayed behind – or may have felt pressurized to respond to questions about suspect persons. Occupation diaries and letters are perhaps less problematic. At any rate, the aggregate documentation suggests a genuinely shared culture born of the experience of occupation.

I will study perceived breaches of this moral–patriotic framework, broadly defined. Occupied life allowed for a variety of responses to the Germans, despite the restrictions the French faced. Forms of resistance have received ample scholarly attention in recent years.[20]

This article concentrates on less well-known experiences such as denunciations, relationships with Germans and profiteering.[21] Some works dealing with this topic have tended to adopt a legalistic definition of collaboration (in 1914–1918 comprising 'intelligence' or 'commerce with the enemy').[22] Others study sexual relations, but separately from legal collaboration.[23] In this article, I have made the conceptual choice to group all forms of 'misconduct' together, from consensual sexual relations to intelligence with the enemy, because this amalgam – tellingly – corresponded to many (if not all) contemporary perceptions.

These perceptions provide a doorway into the *culture de l'occupé* and its definitions of what constituted good and bad behaviour. As to the distinction between perceived and actual misconduct, I will not deal with it here except to say that some misconduct really did occur.[24] This article will highlight perceived misconduct, and argue that forms of behaviour criticized were not necessarily illegal. These do not fall into the remit of 'collaboration' insofar as this term suggests a distinct set of clearly defined or ideological actions. (Nor did contemporaries use the term.) Historians use 'collaboration' in reference to 1914–1918 regarding the most extreme actions such as informing, usually defined as illegal; this legal definition was not the basis of the occupied population's understanding of misconduct, which amalgamated different forms, especially the sexual and the legal.

Defining *mauvaise conduite*

On 8 November 1918, the Applancourt sisters from Prisches (between Caudry and Fourmies) were under investigation for their conduct under the occupation. They were accused of denouncing their father to the Germans, and of having German lovers – in other words, both of actual treason (which was illegal) and of sexual misconduct (which was not). One of the sisters freely admitted that she had a German lover with whom she had a child; the other denied ever having relations with Germans. Each blamed the other for denouncing their father.[25] Both the truth of the matter and the sequel of the investigation remain unknown.

Whatever the reality, the witnesses interviewed did not approve of the actions of the sisters; and the investigating gendarme stated that he was examining their 'mauvaise conduite' (misconduct or bad behaviour).[26] This term does not relate uniquely to occupation behaviour – *mauvaise conduite* existed as a concept before the war[27] – and the term was not employed all that frequently. Nevertheless, people from the occupied area did occasionally use the term *mauvaise conduite* to describe behaviour that was, to them, deplorable from a moral–patriotic standpoint.[28] It was interchangeable with the word 'inconduite',[29] but I opt for *mauvaise conduite*, partly echoing 1920s historian Georges Gromaire's notion of 'mauvais éléments' (bad elements).[30] Its antithesis was *belle conduite*, for which individuals were praised after the war.[31]

This notion provides a springboard from which to launch a new conceptual category. I use *mauvaise conduite* as an umbrella term to describe forms of behaviour not all labelled explicitly under this rubric at the time, but perceived in a negative light by occupied, and occasionally non-occupied, compatriots. It refers to any kind of complicity, not just to actions that were illegal or harmed compatriots, although the multiple forms of misconduct were intertwined, in perceptions and possibly in practice. Certainly, all actions viewed as misconduct received similar opprobrium whether in diaries, interviews with repatriated individuals or post-war police reports or trials. Sexual relations were blamed as much as denunciations; friendly relations were scorned as much as commerce with the Germans.

The 'respectable' behaviour against which *mauvaise conduite* was placed involved comportments such as refusing to work for the Germans, remaining hostile to and avoiding all forms of intimacy with the enemy, and staying 'dignified' despite daily privations. Against this framework, perfectly legal actions such as sexual or friendly relations with Germans, or leading a lifestyle considered overly lavish, could only be perceived as betraying the community. Misconduct also veered into the illegal, although legal, semi-illegal and illegal misconduct were often conflated – complicity never came alone, because of the need to redefine the community as one of suffering, both for the occupied population and the fighting French soldiers. Any affront to the community of suffering, whether sleeping with Germans or actively spying for them, suggested further complicity; the abandonment of the local community for the enemy could never be purely symbolic.

What forms did *mauvaise conduite* take, and what were the reactions of occupied compatriots to these real or imagined breaches of respectability? How did it tie into the *culture de l'occupé*?

The female specificity: sexual *mauvaise conduite*

The population of the Nord, as in the other nine occupied departments, had become overwhelmingly female.[32] Many men had fled the Germans in August–October 1914 to join the French army, and those who remained were often removed from their communes to carry out forced labour. It is thus perhaps unsurprising that *mauvaise conduite* was conceived of by occupied and non-occupied French alike as a fundamentally female phenomenon. Indeed, as Philippe Nivet has demonstrated, this was the cornerstone of the non-occupied French view of the occupied 'Boches du Nord'.[33]

The primary form of this misconduct involved intimate relations between French women and Germans. Nivet and Le Naour have highlighted the perception of such women as 'bad Frenchwomen' or 'women of the Boches' by occupied and unoccupied compatriots.[34] Although not illegal, intimate relations were viewed as a moral crime, a transgression of what Le Naour calls 'the patriotic taboo'.[35] Sexual misconduct was seen as occurring on a large scale: the police commissioner of Comines, interviewed at Évian in December 1917, estimated that 8 of 10 women had 'frequented' the Germans, bourgeois women as much as working-class women.[36] Repatriated inhabitants from Valenciennes believed that 60% of women engaged in 'debauchery' with the Germans.[37] Even if the reality was less dramatic, the belief that this was the case and the contempt in which such women were held were central to the occupied 'war culture'. Nivet describes this ubiquitous belief as an obsession.[38] Accusations of sexual misconduct flood the testimony of repatriated or liberated people from all occupied departments, and *Nordistes* feature prominently.[39] Those repatriated from January to April 1917 alone highlighted 1566 suspect individuals, of whom at least 1237 were *Nordistes*. Among these were at least 928 women, the majority (690) accused of sexual misconduct.[40]

In lists of suspects across the entire occupied area compiled by the British Intelligence Service 'I(b)' in July–October 1918, 797 individuals listed were identifiable by gender, of which 702 were women. Of the 416 women from the Nord, 362 were signalled as the mistresses of Germans, prostituting themselves or family members to the Germans, having intimate relations with Germans, having been treated for venereal disease, having children born of German fathers, or being on 'good' or 'friendly' terms with Germans (usually implying sexual intimacy).[41] French *Deuxième Bureau* suspect lists also contain many women accused of intimacy with the Germans, although files specifically devoted to the Nord are lacking.[42] However, in some parts of the Nord, post-liberation investigations were carried out by French gendarmes attached to the British army – and the related documentation has been preserved.[43] These inquiries concentrated on almost 500 women, all accused of having engaged in sexual misconduct (mainly prostitution) with Germans.[44] Other sources hint at potential prostitution: by the liberation, 6200 women had been treated for venereal disease in the *lazaret* of Lille – although not all were prostitutes, the *Commissaire de Police* of Lille provided these statistics in the middle of a paragraph about prostitution, which had 'taken considerable proportions since the arrival of the Germans'.[45] In Tourcoing, just one *lazaret* had treated 410 women by 31 December 1916.[46] Sexual misconduct was scrutinized more frequently than others, perhaps due to the French authorities' fears of the 'venereal peril',[47] although actual investigations were minimal. Thus, there was a strong *perception* of widespread sexual misconduct, shared among many *Nordistes*; actual sexual misconduct is impossible to verify.

The difficulty in disentangling informal and formal prostitution from genuine companionship and love is evident, as is arriving at the motives behind such actions. However, evidence of mutual, consensual relationships does exist.[48] Mme Lenoy of Anstaing was reported to have frequently 'joked with German officers and soldiers'. Public rumour claimed that she had intimate relations with a German Sergeant Major, whom she allegedly married. 'She publicly declared: "Love does not have a mother country [*Patrie*]."'[49] Surprisingly, the investigating gendarme concludes with: 'Despite this, her behavior does not appear to have been scandalous.'[50] He drew similar conclusions for other women, irrespective of whether they married their German lovers. This indicates that there were exceptions to the opprobrium. Yet, for most of the local population, the very existence of the amorous relationship in which Mme Lenoy engaged would have been scandalous, even if she had married the German. Friendships with Germans could be exaggerated into romantic/sexual relations, glances embellished as friendships and obligatory encounters perceived as willing rapports – all in all, anything less than a hostile attitude towards the Germans was frowned upon as undignified and unrespectable, disregarding the accepted norms of the *culture de l'occupé*.

This is clear in the language used to denounce such women. Hundreds of women were accused by neighbours and refugees of leading a 'life of debauchery', 'frequenting/being frequented by' or 'receiving' Germans, visiting or running places of 'ill-repute' known for debauchery and 'bad company', and generally engaging in 'scandalous' behaviour.[51] Many were said to have been prostitutes,[52] although this may have simply been a way to insult them, or to render their transgression of social norms more palatable. The outrage is explicit: Séraphine Descamps from Trélon was said to live a 'scandalous life with German officers'.[53] In the commune of Lys-lez-Lannoy, according to the mayor, one Mme Terrasse had always behaved 'correctly' before the war, but during the occupation demonstrated 'deplorable conduct'. Although she was not a prostitute, 'her house was frequented by many German soldiers', one of whom had been her lover, with whom she often walked in the street. She was consequently expelled from her home by her father-in-law, moving in with her aunt in Leers, where her conduct was 'very reprehensible' – her 'house was the *rendez-vous* of enemy policemen, and a lot of goods and merchandise seized by them were bought by her then re-sold to her benefit'.[54] The negative judgement of her behaviour is palpable – again, sexual and other misconduct are linked – and is closely tied to wider social mores carried over from pre-war times. For example, in July 1915, a woman from Tourcoing who had left 'the maternal domicile to live in concubinage' with a Frenchman was refused the allowance to which she had been entitled whilst living with her mother, because the municipality thought that this would encourage '*l'inconduite* of this girl' and would be 'contrary to all moral principles'.[55] In this instance, misconduct had nothing to do with the occupation, since the man was French, though there was an occupation element to the matter, viz. the allowance. Thus, pre-war, predominantly (but not exclusively) Catholic moral-sexual mores criticizing concubinage endured under the occupation; they combined with patriotism to form the backbone of the *culture de l'occupé*.

In this context, many women engaged in sexual misconduct were seen as betraying not only their country but also their husbands at the front. Often the extra detail 'her husband is at the front/mobilised/a prisoner' was added without commentary by those interrogated at Évian, and post-war investigators.[56] This detail spoke for itself, its concise phrasing full of the restraint seen as lacking in these occupied women. Overall, at least 270 married women from the Nord were suspected by interrogated refugees of intimate relations with the Germans[57] – although a wartime French intelligence report concerning Lille suggests that such relationships may have been attempts to ameliorate the situation of husbands, brothers and sons who were prisoners-of-war.[58] The lengthy 1925 work by Georges Gromaire, a professor at the prestigious Parisian Lycée Buffon, also attempted to justify such relations.[59] Nevertheless, the view expressed by refugees was blunt: 'The wives of mobilised men prostitute themselves shamelessly.'[60]

Women who 'lived it up/partied',[61] danced, sang and/or listened to music with the Germans were also considered to be morally suspect.[62] Extravagant expressions of pleasure were perceived as anti-patriotic, just as in unoccupied France.[63] Pleasure shared with the Germans was doubly treasonous. Mme Thibaux from Solre-le-Château raised suspicions about Mme de Metz, because she had relations 'with German soldiers and principally with gendarmes, many of whom were her lovers. There were constantly, both night and day, parties at her house, they danced and played music.'[64] In a post-war document regarding a woman who allegedly prostituted herself during the occupation, the following damning sentence was underlined: 'She feasted with them and got herself drunk.'[65] Thus, just as in Belgium, feasting and partying became 'injustice *par excellence*, the very image of the betrayal of common misfortune, the inversion of grief and hunger'.[66]

A repatriated woman from Hestraud mentioned in January 1917 that Mme Cottret and her daughter not only engaged in 'debauchery' but, worse, they 'did not hide their affections, and dressed in luxury finery, which they did not wear before the war, they walked daily with German soldiers'.[67] Other women were suspected because they 'led a joyous life' with the Germans.[68] Men were also accused of being 'familiar' with the Germans and partying with them – such as a Justice of the Peace of Douai – though this was rare.[69] Simple pleasures were equally frowned upon; in Lille, female workers of the textile mills (*filatures*) displayed no sense of economy: they 'look to satisfy their desire for gluttony [...] buying sweets and chocolates from the *pâtisseries*, whereas the rich people deprive themselves of these'.[70] Public displays of joy and extravagance were unfitting during wartime, when the occupied population believed it was engaged in unified, dignified suffering for France – a 'Calvary' according to many in the pious Nord.[71] This flaunting of luxury was merged with sexual misconduct, itself merged with patriotic misconduct, forging a triumvirate betraying both the *petite patrie* and the *grande patrie*.

The male specificity: abusing power

Men were also believed to have carried out unrespectable (non-sexual) acts during the occupation, although the understanding was that this was rarer: 310 suspect *Nordiste* men are mentioned in January–April 1917 Évian interrogations,[72] 54 in I(b) files[73] and at least 33 were the object of post-war investigations in the Nord.[74] The diminished male population may explain why men were more seldom named. There is no evidence of relationships with Germans, despite French insinuations of homosexuality among German soldiers who liked to cross-dress,[75] or the presence of German women in the occupied area fulfilling administrative and, purportedly, policing roles.[76] Yet, the more in-depth examinations into suspect men and the conclusions of various post-war trials suggest that male *mauvaise conduite* was treated more seriously by French authorities.[77] This was because the men investigated were in formal positions of authority: all 33 investigated from late 1918 until late 1919 were mayors, mayoral secretaries, municipal councillors or local constables. They were accused by compatriots – although not always unanimously, as some witnesses defended the accused – of abusing their power during the occupation, of complicity with the Germans.[78] It was alleged that they were directly responsible for the punishment of compatriots, had 'sold out' to the Germans or had been on 'friendly' terms with them – 'proved' by photographs in which mayors and their families appear next to Germans.[79]

The full details regarding these investigations and their sequel are often missing, but some accusations held true, such as those concerning the mayoral adjunct (M. Debrime) and mayoral secretary (M. Pamart) of Catillon-sur-Sabre. This case also demonstrates the strength of the *culture de l'occupé*, which outlasted the occupation itself. On 7 August 1919, a petition signed by 55 inhabitants was sent to the prefect of the Nord, complaining about the suppression of daily allowances allotted by the municipality to those who 'did their duty' during the occupation, whereas those who had 'openly welcomed the invader' were still receiving funds. This was the fault of the municipality, 'guilty of grave acts' during the occupation.[80] In fact, Debrime and Pamart were already under investigation, suspected of intelligence with the enemy, embezzlement and fraud. Both were arrested and imprisoned in Lille's Citadel; Debrime was eventually sentenced to a month's imprisonment and suspended from his functions for three months. The ramifications for Pamart are unclear.[81]

Some accusations appear to have been the result of misunderstandings of the difficult position in which the accused found themselves during the occupation. In the 'affaire Berteaux', the mayoral secretary (a member of the CANF) was accused of friendly relations with the Germans. He was said to have spent much time with officers, with whom he exchanged gifts, and was further accused of fraud and embezzlement. His defence was that he was simply 'oiling the machine' of relief operations: without a certain degree of complicity with the Germans, the entire relief effort would have failed – a judgement with which the president of the relief committee wholeheartedly agreed.[82] Gromaire acknowledged some mayoral 'connivance' with the Germans, but diminished its importance and drew a distinction between these 'repugnant acts' and full-blown 'treason' – a distinction not held by the occupied population.[83]

A few post-war accusations were proven to be the result of personal–political scheming, such as attempts to discredit the mayor of Bachy by Jules Samain, a 'systematic complainer' of 'doubtful morality' who desired to play a role in municipal politics.[84] However, whether born of misunderstandings, political scheming or genuine cases of abuses of power, these accusations demonstrate the strength of the *culture de l'occupé*, according to which close relations with the Germans were forbidden, and unity with compatriots was essential. Any breaches of these mores, whatever the circumstances, were viewed as unpatriotic and unrespectable – as *mauvaise conduite*. Claims that such breaches had taken place could be exploited in the post-war period, but these claims drew their potency from the very real fears and beliefs of the occupation.

General *mauvaise conduite*

Nivet distinguishes between 'rapprochement' with the Germans and more explicit forms of 'collaboration'.[85] Whilst these are useful categories, reflecting the opinion of the Allied militaries,[86] they represent a demarcation not always representative of the *culture de l'occupé* which saw all forms of *mauvaise conduite* as equally morally repugnant and reprehensible.

There was a widespread belief among the occupied population that denunciation was rampant.[87] Men were suspected of this,[88] but the majority of informers were said to be women also engaging in sexual misconduct,[89] in the usual blurring of illegal and legal wrongdoing. Informers were alleged to denounce their compatriots for hiding goods due for requisition or Allied soldiers,[90] or avoiding forced labour.[91] Denunciations did take place, with some occupied people openly admitting responsibility[92] – they were so commonplace (refugees claimed) that the Germans were shocked and amused.[93] A summary of an interview with 469 repatriated people from the Nord underlined both the belief in frequent denunciations and the difficulty in assessing the truth behind this belief:

> The Germans constantly carry out searches, and the public is wrong to think that these are the result of denunciations, there are many fewer than what is believed and said; any individual who is seen entering the *Kommandantur* for what is usually a personal affair is immediately suspected of being a denunciator and those who are victims of searches immediately accuse a neighbour of being responsible.[94]

But when people really were denounced, the consequences were serious: fines, imprisonment or even execution.[95] It is true that denunciation was not a practice solely linked to occupation: war profiteers were denounced across unoccupied France.[96] Yet, denouncing suspect French people to French authorities was arguably a civic duty; denouncing Frenchmen to Germans represented the betrayal of compatriots to the enemy, a transgression of the duty enshrined in the *culture de l'occupé*.

So too was engaging in espionage for the Germans, representing legally defined misconduct. A poem written in Lille in August 1915 attacked 'Bochartes', those 'women without honour, monsters without decency' who 'betray their blood, their flag' by spying for the Germans.[97] A handful of women reappear in the testimony of repatriated people from Lille. They are mentioned as potential spies, mistresses of Germans who had allegedly moved freely within and outside the occupied area.[98] Overall, though, few people were accused of full-blown espionage, even if they were seen as informers or 'in the pay of the Germans'.[99] *Mauvaise conduite* retained at its core a blurring of illegal and legal misconduct.

Many male suspects were believed to have engaged in commerce with the enemy, the other form of legally defined treason: at least 200 *Nordistes* (52 women and 148 men), plus the majority of the 33 men mentioned above, were suspected of this.[100] They were perceived as war profiteers, buying goods from the Germans and selling them at exorbitant prices to the French, or providing the Germans with goods and money, for a fee.[101] The former directly affected occupied compatriots, whereas the latter provided the enemy with resources that could be used against Allied troops – both were deemed undignified and scandalous by the occupied population. The special commissioner of Évian remarked in April 1917 that numerous complaints about such behaviour had been made, with calls for justice after the war.[102]

Others were accused of working voluntarily for the Germans in industry or agriculture, as cleaners or cooks or even for the German police forces.[103] The number of *actual* volunteers appears to have been extremely low – for example, just 157 French civilians were working for the Germans in Tourcoing in late June 1915,[104] and, moreover, the very nature of the Germans' 'voluntary' labour system renders it impossible to know whether these were genuine volunteers.[105] Some people admitted to working voluntarily for the Germans,[106] but most refused to work until forced.[107] The very logic behind such refusals fuelled the disgust felt towards volunteers: patriotic respectability meant not aiding the enemy in any form, whatever the personal or collective cost. To do so was treason. Most occupied French would have agreed and shared the sentiments of Mlle Munch, who wrote a song in Pérenchies in 1916 'against French and Belgian civilians digging trenches for the Germans of their own free will'. In the song, 'red with rage', she addresses the workers directly: 'You are making tombs for your brothers [...] For money, oh!' She promised post-war revenge for the 'foul wound' that would remain in her heart, and signed off 'A Frenchwoman at heart' [*Française de coeur*].[108] Although this feeling was widely held, one may also detect a certain class bias. M. Blin, a retired teacher from Auchy-les-Orchies, wrote in September 1917 that 'bourgeois opinion is not favourable to the workers from Roubaix, voluntarily responding to German demands [...] Besides their daily salary of 7 fr, they are getting wood, beans, potatoes etc. which they sell at a good price. humanity [*sic*], conscience, patriotism, honesty, all the sentiments which make man dignified are erased in the face of such narrow selfishness!'[109]

Popular punishment: reinforcing respectability?

During the occupation, popular revenge occasionally occurred, comprising physical, textual and verbal abuse, emphasising the importance and limits of respectability in the *culture de l'occupé*. These incidents also highlight that notions of moral-patriotic respectability were not confined to the *bourgeoisie* – and breaches of respectability were not necessarily dealt with in a 'polite' manner, which might feasibly fit within the context of 'respectable' behaviour. One example is the anti-*mauvaise conduite* tracts that appeared in Lille-Roubaix-Tourcoing throughout the occupation. Evidence exists of three such tracts – *La Vérité*, *La Liberté* and *Les Vidanges* – the first two usually seen as part of the *Patience/L'Oiseau de France* clandestine publication.[110] All contained impassioned attacks on women who slept with Germans ('Vile females!!'), people engaging in commerce with the Germans and other 'Traitors and cowards'. They implored the population to 'Boycott and desert the cafés and houses that fraternise with the enemy', used misogynistic language ('A putrid person full of infection for the boches [*sic* ...]' remarkable for her ugliness'), and ended with mock adverts naming and shaming people and places involved in *mauvaise conduite*.[111]

Furthermore, there are many reports of local populations hurling insults at those engaging in *mauvaise conduite*, especially women – 'Bocharte' and 'femme à Boches' used most frequently, plus variations such as 'Bochette' or 'Bochesse'.[112] This seemed to happen so frequently that the Germans put up posters detailing the punishment of those insulting French people working for the Germans,[113] punishments that were enforced.[114]

Women as well as men took out their rage on those working voluntarily for the Germans. In Denain in 1914, there were 'veritable battles of women', with those recruited in German workshops 'hit and threatened with having their hair cut'. From then on, few worked for the Germans.[115] This was the first of many mass incidents: in February 1915, a crowd of about 100 people threw stones through the window of an *estaminet* in Lille, run by a Belgian man believed to have denounced hidden French soldiers. The demonstration lasted for three hours before the French police dispersed the crowd.[116] On 4 March, Mme Delvidre of Lille was booed by a crowd of 500 people, who threw stones at her and called her a whore. The German police had to rescue her, firing shots in the process. She had also been attacked the previous day.[117] This was a precursor to what became known as the 'Sandbag Affair', a series of strikes in textile factories from April–July 1915, primarily in Lille-Roubaix-Tourcoing. The traditional narrative states that these workers and their employers decided to stop producing sandbags for patriotic reasons.[118] Actually, the strikes started with crowds of outraged (seemingly working-class) people refusing to allow the workers to enter the factories, launching verbal and physical attacks including pulling hair and beatings. Many victims and perpetrators seem to have been women.[119] On 18 April 1915, a 'French woman of middle-class background' was 'mistreated by numerous women' – 'her clothes and hair were ripped, she was kicked' and 'cries such as "She's with the dirty Boches" could be heard'.[120] Thus, it was not just working-class women who worked for the Germans, and the mention of her class suggests that the German authors were shocked by this attack, perhaps expecting assaults on working-class women. Further attacks occurred in Roubaix in June 1915.[121]

German measures to restart factory work, punishing people who obstructed or attacked those working for the Germans, soon quelled the disorder, but discontent remained, with some calling for post-war revenge.[122] Indeed, in March 1916, the chief commissioner of Lille was concerned about the settling of scores after the liberation, involving 'acts of violence, pillage, or even summary executions'.[123] Clearly, the various assaults on suspect individuals were themselves infractions of respectable social relations, but they were carried out in defence of a perceived 'duty' to the community, thus justified within the *culture de l'occupé*.

The post-war revenge desired by so many never manifested itself on a large scale as in Belgium,[124] neither in official nor unofficial punishments of *mauvaise conduite*. Some trials took place, as Renée Martinage has demonstrated: of the 83 people charged with intelligence or commerce with the enemy at the *cour d'assises* of Douai from 1919 to 1925, 43 were condemned and 40 acquitted. Punishments ranged from minor correctional sentences to up to 20-year imprisonment outside the national territory.[125] Furthermore, war councils and the judicial system of the Nord dealt with hundreds of such affairs in 1919–1920, although not all ended in a trial. The public prosecutor of Valenciennes led 24 affairs of intelligence with the enemy in July 1923 alone.[126] However, overall, punishments for *mauvaise conduite* were relatively rare – precisely because this conception extended beyond legal notions of collaboration.

It should be noted that popular retaliations were comparatively rare after the war. Few attacks on the property and persons of those suspected of *mauvaise conduite* occurred in October 1918 in Lille.[127] In some rare instances, women had their heads shaved, but this happened on a smaller scale than in Belgium, and certainly on a far smaller scale than in 1944–1945, probably because of the primacy of legal repression and the Allied military presence.[128] Overall, there was surprisingly little popular retribution considering the strength of the occupied population's disdain for people accused of misconduct. Letters sent by liberated *Nordistes* during the Allied reoccupation deplored the lack of official punishment of these individuals, especially women.[129] The intertwining of illegal and legal misconduct therefore did not endure after the war: people were only punished for actual harm done to compatriots, not ordinary contacts with the Germans – much to the dissatisfaction of locals.

Soon after the liberation, another aspect of the *culture de l'occupé* dominated the local memory of the occupation: resistance, which had existed in various forms. *Mauvaise conduite* was largely forgotten in favour of a more acceptable patriotic vision of the occupation. The *culture de l'occupé* thus outlasted the occupation itself, but the notion of *mauvaise conduite* faded away by the mid-1920s: it would reappear and be reconfigured in the crucible of the Second World War, when it became collaboration *tout court*.

Acknowledgements

I thank the Arts and Humanities Research Council and the Institute of Historical Research for funding the research behind this article. Special thanks to Sophie De Schaepdrijver for her many useful comments, suggestions and questions concerning the early drafts of this article, and my thesis in general.

Notes

1. Hilaire, *Histoire du Nord*, 58–83.
2. Ibid., 168.
3. Ibid., 138.
4. Molina, 'Femmes', 3.
5. Nivet, *France*, 5.
6. Gromaire, *L'occupation*, 41–56.
7. Commissaire de police de Condé, Vieux-Condé, Fresnes, Escautpont and Crespin, to Sous-Préfet at Valenciennes, 28 November 1918, 9 R 512, Archives départementales du Nord (ADN).
8. Hélot, *Cinquante Mois*, 163.
9. Debarge, 'Fourmies', 292.
10. Poster, Valenciennes, 7 November 1914, 9 R 756 (ADN).
11. Becker, *Cicatrices*, 174; Poster, Tourcoing, 9 January 1918, 9 R 748 (ADN).
12. See 9 R 702–75 (ADN).
13. See 9 R 841 (ADN) for letters of protest regarding forced labour and deportation; Basdevant, *Déportations*; Wallart, 'Déportation'.
14. Gromaire, *L'occupation*, 86–206.
15. Becker, *Cicatrices*, 140; Nivet, *France*, 150–85; McPhail, *Long Silence*, 55–90.
16. The 1990s saw a historiographical shift to the study of *culture de guerre*, a broad-based system through which belligerent populations made sense of the war and persuaded themselves to continue fighting it: Winter and Prost, *The Great War*, 159; Smith et al., *France*, xv; Audoin-Rouzeau and Becker, *Retrouver*.
17. Rousseaux and van Ypersele, *La Patrie*, 27; Nivet, *France*; Becker, *Cicatrices*; McPhail, *Long Silence*; De Schaepdrijver, *La Belgique*.
18. Valenciennes, Condamnation de M. Louis, Inspecteur primaire, July 1917, 9 R 313 (ADN).
19. Le Naour, *Misères*, 14.
20. Of particular note are Becker, *Cicatrices*, 256–70; Olivier Forcade, 'L'espionnage'; Nivet, *France*, 207–64.
21. Though some have studied this: Nivet, *France*, 265–300; Le Naour, *Misères*, especially 276–300; Gromaire, *L'occupation*, 61, 84, 158, 203, 208, 247–8, 266, 334–7, 444.
22. Martinage, 'Collaborateurs'.
23. Nivet, *France*, 279–2; Becker, *Cicatrices*, 240.
24. See documents in 3 U 281/31–78, 2 U 1/444–8, 2 U 1/571, 2 U 2/515, 3 U 274/174, 3 U 303/6–7 (ADN).
25. Prisches, Lotard, report no. 231, 8 November 1918, 9 R 1197 (ADN).
26. Ibid.
27. Lys, Bailly, report no. 142, 30 October 1918, 9 R 1196 (ADN).
28. See, for example, Sûreté Générale, 3ᵉ Armée Britannique, État-Major, Procès-verbal 21 December 1917, 17 N 433, Service Historique de la Défense (SHD) testimony of Henri Duquenne (Courchelettes); 4 M 513 Archives départementales de la Haute-Savoie (ADHS): Évian, Rapatriés, report no. 1264, 28 April 1917; no. 675, 5 February 1917.
29. See, for example, G.Q.G., État-Major-Général, 2ᵉ Bureau, S.R.A., Note pour les S.R. d'Armée, 14 August 1916, 19 N 547 (SHD); Mission Française de Sûreté Générale attachée à la 4ᵉ Armée Britannique, Procès-verbal no. 238, 7 February 1918 (Auby), 17 N 433 (SHD).
30. Gromaire, *L'occupation*, 334.
31. Montay, response to question 34 of the *Commission Historique du Nord* questionnaire, 1923, 15 J 87 (ADN).
32. Nivet, 'Femmes', 275.
33. Nivet, *Réfugiés*.
34. Ibid., 387–421; idem., 'Femmes'; idem., *France*, 279–92; Le Naour, *Misères*, 276–300.
35. Le Naour, *Misères*, 290.
36. Commissariat d'Évian, interrogatoire no. 3362, 20 December 1917, 4 M 519 (ADHS), cited in Le Naour, 'Femmes tondues', 152.

MILITARY OCCUPATIONS IN FIRST WORLD WAR EUROPE

37. Report no. 356, 19 December 1916, 4 M 352 (ADHS), cited in Nivet, *Réfugiés*, 388.
38. Nivet, *Réfugiés*, 387.
39. See 4 M 513, 517–20 (ADHS); 17 N 433, 19 N 547, 19 N 1571 (SHD).
40. 'At least', because often the suspect's gender and crime is unclear, and I have yet to analyse the statistics of all Évian interrogations, 4 M 513 (ADHS).
41. Record Group 120: entry 198, and Record Group 165, National Archives of the United States of America (USNA). Thanks to Tammy Proctor for sending me these files.
42. See, for example, 17 N 207 (SHD) for lists of suspects in Meurthe-et-Moselle.
43. 9 R 1196 (ADN), regarding Croix, Flers, Lannoy, Leers, Lys, Mouvaux, Roubaix, Toufflers, Wasquehal and Wattrelos.
44. Ibid.
45. Report of Commissaire de Police de Lille, 12 November 1918, 9 R 584 (ADN).
46. Refuge de Femmes, Boulevard Gambetta 270, 15 January 1917, H 4 A 30, Archives municipales de Tourcoing (AMT).
47. See Le Naour, *Misères*, 127.
48. Nivet, *France*, 285–90.
49. Lannoy, Ghesquier, proce's-verbal no. 29, 15 November 1918, 9 R 1196 (ADN).
50. Ibid.
51. Ibid., Croix, Dupuis, procès-verbal no. 199, 7 November 1918, and Poreaux, procès-verbal no. 237, 8 November 1918; Lannoy, Huilliez, procès-verbal no. 18, 14 November 1918, et passim; 4 M 513 (ADHS): Notice Individuelle, Hélène Lemaitre and Reine Covin (Fourmies), 28 Febraury 1917, and Bertha Dissy (Maubeuge), 6 February 1917; Report no. 999, 12 March 1917 (Lille); no. 791, 22 February 1917 (Denain); no. 899, 7 March 1917 (Trélon), et passim.
52. 182 prostitutes, 9 R 1196 (ADN); 130 prostitutes, 4 M 513 (ADHS); Record Group 165: 63 prostitutes (USNA).
53. Report no. 899, 7 March 1917 (Trélon), 4 M 513 (ADHS).
54. Croix, Cousinet, procès-verbal, 17 November 1918, 9 R 1196 (ADN).
55. Mairie de Tourcoing, Bureau de Bienfaisance, 20 July 1915, H 4 A 27 (AMT).
56. See documents in 4 M 513 (ADHS), such as report no. 477, 12 January 1917 (Cambrai); 9 R 1196 (ADN).
57. 4 M 513 (ADHS); other documents do not record the marital status efficiently.
58. Ibid. report no. 1140, 19 April 1917.
59. Gromaire, *L'occupation*, 444.
60. Report no. 496, 17 January 1917 (Valenciennes), 4 M 513 (ADHS).
61. 9 R 1196 (ADN): Croix, Dupuis, procès-verbal no. 203, 7 November 1918; Croix, Duhain, procès-verbal no. 253, 8 November 1918; Roubaix, report of Paris, n.d. (between 25–27 October 1918).
62. Ibid., Croix, Dupuis, procès-verbal no. 245, 8 November 1918; Lannoy, Mignot, procès-verbal no. 9, 10 November 1918; Wasquehal, Fleury, procès-verbal no. 156, 7 November 1918.
63. Le Naour, *Misères*, 50–66, 79–83.
64. Solre-le-Château, procès-verbal concerning Mme de Metz (Duschamps), 16 November 1918, 9 R 1197 (ADN).
65. 9 R 1196 (ADN): Croix, Dupuis, procès-verbal no. 192, 7 November 1918.
66. Rousseaux and van Ypersele, *La Patrie*, 204.
67. Report no. 494, 17 January 1917 (Hestraud), 4 M 513 (ADHS).
68. See, for example, ibid., Notice Individuelle of Louise Carpentier and Berthe Dupret (Courrières), 21 March 1917; report no. 1225, 25 April 1915 (Tourcoing).
69. Ibid., report no. 1075, 21 March 1917.
70. Ibid., report no. 989, 14 March 1917.
71. Mlle Munch to mayor of Lille, 9 November 1918, 4 H 241, Archives municipales de Lille (AML).
72. 4 M 513 (ADHS).
73. Record Group 165 (USNA).
74. 9 R 1193, 1229 (ADN).
75. Report no. 953, 12 March 1917 (Lille). See also: Crouthamel, 'Cross-dressing'.
76. 4 M 513 (ADHS): Report no. 519, 18 January 1917 (Sous-le-Bois); no. 756, 16 February 1917.

MILITARY OCCUPATIONS IN FIRST WORLD WAR EUROPE

77. See 9 R 1193, 1229 (ADN); Martinage, 'Collaborateurs'.
78. 9 R 1193, 1229 (ADN).
79. 9 R 1193 (ADN): Gognies-Chaussée, Affaire Libert, passim; Denain; Crèvecoeur-sur-l'Escaut, postcard sent to Préfet du Nord, n.d.; Neuville-en-Ferrain, Affaire Walcke, Commissaire spécial de Lille to Préfet, 21 June 1919.
80. Catillon, petition to Préfet, 7 August 1919, 9 R1229 (ADN).
81. Ibid., Sous-Préfet de Cambrai to Préfet, 8 September 1919; Commissaire Divisionnaire, Chef de la 2ème Brigade de police to Procureur de la République in Cambrai, 28 April 1919; idem. to Préfet, 17 October 1919; Ville de Lille, Commissariat de Police du 1er arrondissement, report no. 366, 8 November 1919.
82. Fourmies, Affaire Berteaux documents, 9 R 1193 (ADN).
83. Gromaire, L'occupation, 61–2.
84. Bachy, Commissaire Spécial de Lille to Préfet, 11 August 1919, 9 R 1193 (ADN).
85. Nivet, France, 279–300; idem., 'Femmes', especially 299–309.
86. See the distinction between sexual and patriotic misconduct in 17 N 393 (SHD): G.H.Q. "I", Brigadier-General, General Staff, Intelligence, I(b).4908, Memorandum on C-E During an Advance, 6 April 1917, Devoirs des interprètes en cas d'avance.
87. Nivet, France, 298–300; Gromaire, L'occupation, 335–7.
88. See report no. 474, 12 January 1917 (Cambrai), 4 M 513 (ADHS).
89. Nivet, France, 292.
90. 2 U 1/445 (ADN): Cour d'assises du Département du Nord, no. 12, 15 January 1921, concerning Mme Blancpain; no. 50, Arrêt du 23 Avril 1921, concerning Mme Monniez.
91. Cour d'assises du Département du Nord, no. 71, Arrêt du 16 Octobre 1922 concerning Mme Honoré, 2 U 1/446 (ADN).
92. Ibid., Notice Individuelle, Irma Lemaire (Fourmies), 28 February 1917. For a letter of denunciation, see Vercruysse to the Kommandant, 17 June 1918, H 4 A 30 (AMT).
93. 4 M 513 (ADHS): report no. 493, 17 January 1917 (Nord, Maubeuge); no. 1074, 21 March 1917(St-Amand and Rennegies).
94. Ibid., report no. 788, 22 February 1917.
95. See, for example, ibid., report no. 511, 18 January 1917 (Louvroil); Cour d'assises du Département du Nord, no. 28, 23 February 1921, concerning Mme Rappé, Mlle and Mme Delhaye, 2 U 1/445 (ADN).
96. Flood, France, 125.
97. Labbé, A la Guerre, 47.
98. 4 M 513 (ADHS): report no. 971, 18 March 1917; no. 927, 9 May 1917; no. 894, 7 March 1917; no. 953, 12 March 1917, all regarding Lille.
99. See, for example, ibid., report no. 791, 22 February 1917 (Denain). A further 17 men in this carton were suspected of espionage.
100. 4 M 513 (ADHS) (40 women and 118 men); Record Group 165 (USNA) (12 women and 30 men).
101. 4 M 513 (ADHS): report no. 1158, 20 April 1917 (Lille); no. 476, 12 January 1917 (Escarmin); Nivet, France, 2935; Gromaire, L'occupation, 84, 334–5.
102. Ibid, report no. 1268, 28 April 1917 (Douai).
103. 4 M 513 (ADHS): report no. 721, 12 February 1917 and no. 894, 24 February 1917 (Valenciennes); La Dépêche du Nord, 21 December 1918, H 4 A 282 (AML); Croix, Dupuis, procès-verbal no. 291, 9 November 1918, 9 R 1196 (ADN); Nivet, France, 342; Gromaire, L'occupation, 208, 247–8.
104. Kommandant Von Tessing to mayor, 24 July 1915, H 4 A 32 (AMT).
105. Becker, Cicatrices, 178–9.
106. Notice Individuelle, Céline Blinette (Denain), 9 February 1917, 4 M 513 (ADHS).
107. Becker, Cicatrices, 171.
108. Mlle Munch to mayor of Lille, 9 November 1918, 4 H 291 (AML).
109. Journal de M. Blin, instituteur en retraite à Auchy-les-Orchies (1914–1918), 20 September 1917, 74 J 225 (ADN).
110. See Becker, Cicatrices, 262–3.
111. 3 U 281/77 (ADN): La Vérité (Lille), no. 1, 15 December 1915; Les Vidanges: Bulletin concernant le chapitre de la malpropreté à Bruxelles, Lille, Roub-Tourcoing, 1 January 1917,

MILITARY OCCUPATIONS IN FIRST WORLD WAR EUROPE

no. 1, édition B; *La Liberté – Organe n'ayant passé par aucune censure. Bulletin de propagande patriotique*. 15 November 1915.

112. Report no. 1167, 21 April 1917 (Lille), 4 M 513 (ADHS); Nivet, *France*, 339.
113. Report no. 1168, 21 March 1917, 4 M 513 (ADHS).
114. Ibid., report no. 494, 17 January 1917 (Hestraud); Directeur de la Circonscription Pénintentiaire de Loos to Préfet, 19 September 1915, 9 R 795 (ADN).
115. Report no. 705, 9 February 1917, 4 M 513 (ADHS).
116. Report of Commissaire Central du 5e arrondissement, cited by the Commissaire Central de Lille to Préfet, 12 February 1915, 9 R 581 (ADN).
117. Report of Commissaire de police du 7e arrondissement, 4 March 1915, 4 H 273 (AML).
118. Nivet, *France*, 227–9; Becker, *Cicatrices*, 176.
119. There is much documentation on these events. See 9 R 716, 726, 735, 753 (ADN); H 4 A 32 (AMT); 4 H 121 (AML).
120. Kleeberg to Chef de la Police Civile de Lille, 19 April 1915, 4 H 274 (AML).
121. Commissaire Central to mayor of Roubaix, 5 July 1915, 9 R 726 (ADN).
122. Nivet, *France*, 342–4.
123. Commissaire Centrale intérimaire de Lille, 'Mesures à prendre', 24 March 1916, 9 R 580 (ADN).
124. Rousseaux and van Ypersele, *La Patrie*, especially 51–2; Becker, *Cicatrices*, 247–8.
125. Martinage, 'Collaborateurs', 97–111.
126. Nivet, *France*, 352.
127. Duhain, procès-verbal no. 394, 9 November 1918, 9 R 1196 (ADN).
128. Tuohy, *Occupied*, 18; Le Naour, 'Femmes tondues', especially 154; Nivet, *France*, 343–5; Rousseaux and van Ypersele, *La Patrie*, 45–51.
129. 16 N 1462 (SHD): Commission de contrôle postal de Lille, 16 November 1918, 5–7; 16 December 1918, Extraits, 2–4; 1 January 1919, Extraits, 2–3.

References

Archival sources

Primary sources collected from the following archives:

Archives départementales du Nord (ADN).
Archives départementales de la Haute-Savoie (ADHS).
Archives municipales de Lille (AML).
Archives municipales de Tourcoing (AMT).
Service Historique de la Défense (SHD).
National Archives of the United States of America (USNA).

Published sources

Audoin-Rouzeau, Stéphane, and Annette Becker. *Retrouver la guerre 14–18*. Paris: Gallimard, 2000.
Basdevant, Jules. *Les Déportations du Nord de la France et de la Belgique en vue du Travail forcé et le Droit International*. Paris: Recueil Sirey, 1917.
Becker, Annette, ed. *Journaux de combattants et de civils de la France du Nord dans la Grande Guerre*. Villeneuve d'Ascq: Presses Universitaires du Septentrion, 1998.
Becker, Annette. *Les cicatrices rouges 14–18: France et Belgique occupées*. Paris: Fayard, 2010.
Crouthamel, Jonathan. "Cross-Dressing for the Fatherland: Sexual Humour, Masculinity and German Soldiers in the First World War." *First World War Studies: Journal of the International Society for First World War Studies* 2, no. 2 (2011): 195–215.
Debarge, Sébastien. "Fourmies occupée pendant la Grande Guerre." *Revue du Nord* 80, no. 325 (April–June 1998): 285–309.
De Schaepdrijver, Sophie. *La Belgique et La Première Guerre Mondiale*. Bern: P.I.E.-Peter Lang, 2004.
Flood, P. J. *France 1914–1918: Public Opinion and the War Effort*. London: Macmillan, 1990.

Forcade, Olivier. "L'espionnage féminin ou un nouvel héroïsme au combat en 1914–1918." In *Les femmes et la guerre de l'antiquité à 1918*, edited by Philippe Nivet, and Marion Trévisi, 361–72. Paris: Economica, 2010.

Gromaire, Georges. *L'Occupation allemande en France (1914–1918)*. Paris: Payot, 1925.

Hélot, Jules. *Cinquante Mois sons le joug allemand. (L'occupation allemande à Cambrai et dans le Cambrésis)*. Paris: Payot, 1919.

Hilaire, Yves-Marie, ed. *Histoire du Nord Pas-de-Calais de 1900 à nos jours*. Toulouse: Éditions Privat, 1982.

Labbé, Auguste. *A la Guerre comme à la Guerre: les Boches A Lille – Recueil de chansons lilloises écrites pendant L'Occupation Allemande, par Auguste Labbe alias César Latulupe, ex-prisonnier civil du bagne d'Anrath et d'Holzminden*. Lille: Édition Populaire, 1919.

Le Naour, Jean-Yves. "Femmes tondues et répression des 'femmes à boches' en 1918." *Revue d'histoire moderne et contemporaine* 47, no. 1 (January–March 2000): 148–58.

Le Naour, Jean-Yves. *Misères et tourments de la chair durant la Grande Guerre: les mœurs sexuelles des Français, 1914–1918*. Paris: Aubier, 2002.

Martinage, Renée. "Les collaborateurs devant la cour d'assises du Nord après la très Grande Guerre." *Revue du Nord* 77, no. 309 (January–March 1995): 95–115.

McPhail, Helen. *The Long Silence: Civilian Life under the German Occupation of Northern France, 1914–1918*. London: I.B. Tauris, 1999.

Molina, Isabelle. 'Les femmes dans le Nord occupé pendant la première Guerre Mondiale', mémoire de maîtrise sous la direction de R. Vandenbussche, Lille III 1999.

Nivet, Philippe. *La France occupée 1914–1918*. Paris: Armand Colin, 2011.

Nivet, Philippe. "Les femmes dans la France occupée (1914–1918)." In *Les femmes et la guerre de l'antiquité à 1918*, edited by Philippe Nivet, and Marion Trévisi, 275–324. Paris: Economica, 2010.

Nivet, Philippe, and Marion Trévisi, eds. *Les femmes et la guerre de l'antiquité à 1918*. Paris: Economica, 2010.

Rousseaux, Xavier, and Laurence van Ypersele, eds. *La Patrie crie vengeance! La Répression des 'inciviques' belges au sortir de la guerre 1914–1918*. Brussels: Le Cri, 2008.

Smith, Leonard V., Stéphane Audoin-Rouzeau, and Annette Becker. *France and the Great War, 1914–1918*. Cambridge: CUP, 2003.

Tuohy, Ferdinand. *Occupied 1918–1930: A Postscript to the Western Front*. London: T. Butterworth, 1931.

Wallart, Claudine. "Déportation des prisonniers civils au 'camp de concentration' d'Holzminden novembre 1916 – avril 1917." *Revue du Nord* 80, no. 325 (April–June 1998): 417–48.

Winter, Jay, and Antoine Prost. *The Great War in History: Debates and Controversies, 1914 to the Present*. Cambridge: CUP, 2005.

Sursum Corda: the underground press in occupied Belgium, 1914–1918

Sophie De Schaepdrijver[a] and Emmanuel Debruyne[b1]

[a]*Department of History, The Pennsylvania State University, Weaver Building, University Park, PA, USA; [b]Institute of Civilizations, Arts and Letters(INCAL), Université catholique de Louvain(UCL), Place BlaisePascal 1, bteL3.03.21, Louvain-la-Neuve, Belgium*

Sursum Corda studies the underground press in occupied Belgium during the First World War. No other European occupied territory, in 1914–1918, produced such an intensive underground discourse. The article links this exceptional proliferation to the circumstances of Belgium's entry into the war, viz. the violation of neutrality and the civilian massacres of 1914. These issues, which galvanized a sense of national identity, were stressed by the underground press to deny legitimacy to the German occupation regime. This underground press was sustained by ad hoc networks of people from the urban middle classes, most of them Catholic. The German occupation regime, in its quest for legitimacy, spent considerable effort dismantling these networks. Underground press activity, at its most intense in 1915, sank to a very low pitch in 1917–1918. This was not only due to hardened repression and material difficulties but also due to a sense, among the occupied population, of the diminished (though never completely expired) relevance of the message of the underground press.

Around noon on 14 April 1916, in the city of Charleroi in Belgium, a prison van drove towards the German jail. Among the arrestees was an exhausted-looking *bourgeoise* in a lace hat; the incongruous sight drew aghast glances from passers-by. They would have been even more appalled had they known that the woman was expecting her sixth child and had had to leave her five young children – including a baby of seven months – with a nanny who was herself arrested within hours of her employer. The woman's name was Maria Van Doren; her husband, Eugène, the 40-year-old owner of a small cardboard factory, was at that very moment wandering the streets of Brussels in search of shelter, after a night spent on a rooftop hiding from the German police. Eugène Van Doren was then arguably one of the most wanted men in occupied Belgium. He was the main organizer behind *La Libre Belgique* (Free Belgium), the country's best-known underground paper. From 13 April, the *Polizei* had rounded up dozens of members of the network. But Van Doren, taken in by a succession of friends to the cause, would escape them. His wife was effectively taken hostage for two months, but, as she later wrote, 'I had decided to play the role of (. . .) the woman who knows nothing and I think I have played this role well'. Unable to charge Madame Van Doren, the authorities released her on 17

June. She did not see her husband again until the Armistice and had to face a series of hardships – the death of parents, children's grave illnesses and the theft of most of her furniture – alone.[2]

To be sure, other mothers in occupied Belgium, more deeply implicated in 'illegal' activities or affected by deprivation, fared much worse and so did their children. Still, Maria Van Doren's brush with the occupiers' police is significant. Her difficulties and her husband's tribulations – which no doubt provided picaresque excitement only in the retelling – indicate how far some of the occupied were willing to go for the sake of uncensored expression.

The underground press that emerged in Belgium and northern France under German occupation constitutes a textbook example of what scholars of the First World War have called 'self-mobilization' – civil society rallying behind the national cause in wartime, with the support but not on the initiative of the state apparatus.[3] The expression 'self-mobilization' is particularly apposite here, since the underground press was created not only in the absence of a supporting state but also against actively hostile authorities. It was a vast collective effort, relying on networks of editors, authors, typesetters, printers, couriers and distributors, as well as purveyors of paper, ink, machinery, storage space, safe houses and documentation. This collective effort produced altogether 80 clandestine periodicals. Almost all of them, 77 titles, were produced in Belgium. The reason for this disproportion was that, in the Belgian Government-General, after the trauma of the massacres and mass flight of 1914, a modicum of routine was reinstated that allowed for types of civilian endeavour out of reach to the occupied French, who suffered closer proximity to the front with a concomitant heavier military presence, as well as deeper material scarcities and the absence of many more adult men.[4]

Seen from a more general European perspective, too, the proliferation of underground papers in occupied Belgium was exceptional.[5] Nowhere else in occupied Europe during the First World War was clandestine discourse so intense. This conclusion can be drawn even if occupied Eastern Europe still needs further research. In Serbia and Montenegro, low literacy rates and the fierce persecution of the educated elites seem to have precluded the emergence of an underground press.[6] In the Polish Government-General and in Ober Ost, by contrast, some clandestine discourse emerged – with what seem to be tellingly different accents. In militarily occupied Ober Ost, clandestine publications in Lithuanian criticized the occupation regime.[7] In the Government-General of Warsaw, by contrast, the underground press seems to have been less concerned with condemning the occupation regime than with debating Poland's political future.[8]

In occupied Belgium, the self-appointed mission of the underground press was to assert and, by its very existence, enact a sense of national independence. This sense of the national – which was more robust in early twentieth-century Belgium than later perspectives would acknowledge – was rooted in notions of classic liberalism widely if not uniformly established.[9] The very circumstances of Belgium's entry into war – the German ultimatum to a neutral country, the invasion, the short spell of extreme civilian vulnerability and, ultimately, the imposition of an occupation regime – had convinced many that this was a conflict over the core values of liberalism, viz. the rule of law, limitations to military power and freedom of speech. Belgium, as a state, was considered to have bravely stood for those values; international praise deepened a sense of a Belgian community of fate.[10] The start of the war, then, was not conducive to Belgians' acceptance of an occupation regime. But at the same time, occupation, as it did elsewhere in Europe, represented a return to a kind of normalcy after the panic of mobile warfare and invasion. It was precisely here that the underground press came in: by working to keep alive the original outrage, it kept reminding audiences that the state of occupation was not normal. Over four years of occupation, this reminder would elicit enthusiasm as well as exasperation.

When censorship was introduced in the Belgian Government-General on 13 October 1914,[11] most newspapers stopped publication in protest. To fill the void, the Press Department (*Pressestelle*) of the Government-General launched censored dailies, such as *Le Bruxellois* in late October, followed by *La Belgique* in November; newspapers in Dutch, aimed at Flemish audiences, soon followed. These were entirely new ventures, with new editors and journalists. Though readers resented their censored status, these so-called *emboché* ('fritzified'[12]) papers were much more widely read than post-war accounts would concede.[13] With their local news, commercial and personal ads, recipes and letters to the editor, they re-established a sense of normalcy; the *Pressestelle* granted them the favour of publishing lists of Belgian POWs; readers starved for news from the fronts attempted to read between the lines of the military communiqués. Meanwhile, these papers, while avoiding open praise for the German Empire, legitimized occupation rule by criticizing the Belgian government in exile and highlighting injustices in Belgian society before and during the war.[14]

The first weeks of the occupation had brought an immediate sense of being cut off from the world. As the defending armies were beaten back, some Entente papers still reached the cities, where they fetched fantastic prices. In reaction, small groups, concerned that disinformation and the black market in news sapped civilian morale, formed to spread uncensored information cheaply. More or less daily bulletins offered readers a mix of uncensored news items. The first such publication, the short-lived *La Vedette*, appeared in Hasselt in the eastern province of Limburg, one of the first Belgian cities to be occupied, on 8 August 1914.[15] No copy has survived. (This corresponds to a more general pattern. Of the 80 known clandestine periodicals, as many as 25 have not left a trace except their name: because of the circumstances of the war – small print-runs, inferior paper quality and destruction for safety reasons – not a single issue remains, at least in the public domain.) Among other such publications were one nameless daily named *Le Bulletin* by its readers, put together by a postal employee in Brussels from 23 August 1914 (three days after the city was taken) until his arrest in May 1915, and totalling 213 issues[16]; the prolific *La Soupe*, published in Brussels to the tune of more than one issue a day during its one year's existence (from September 1914 to September 1915), and which, next to military news, offered its readers extracts from particularly objectionable German self-justifications[17]; and *Les Dernières Nouvelles*, launched in November 1914 in hard-hit Leuven by an eyewitness to the massacres of August, and totalling 203 issues until its demise in June 1915.

Shortly into 1915, as the landscape of the war in the West had changed – the front had set, and the occupation regime was settling in – the landscape of the clandestine press changed too. A new type of clandestine periodical emerged: published at weekly or longer intervals, it offered readers a more judicious selection of Entente news, and more context in which to interpret events. In Leuven, the editor of *Les Dernières Nouvelles* began a new journal, the *Revue Hebdomadaire de la Presse Française* (later *Revue de la Presse*), on 5 January 1915; its intention was still to publish excerpts from the Entente press, but in a more firmly editorialized manner so as to 'form public opinion'.[18] In Antwerp, a 55-year-old owner of a printing business named Jozef Buerbaum launched a series of polemic brochures under the pseudonym 'Janus Droogstoppel'; the first of these *Droogstoppels*, as they were called, appeared in mid-January 1915. It was a lengthy indictment of the German conduct of war.[19] In Brussels, the *Libre Belgique*, which called itself not just an information journal but 'a fighting journal', its name an explicit rebuke to the censored *La Belgique*, burst on the scene on 1 February 1915.[20]

What we call the 'interpretive turn' in the clandestine press was linked to the appearance of a major text: Cardinal Mercier's pastoral letter *Patriotism and Endurance*. Presented at the New Year 1915, amidst mounting apprehension that the war might not be a short one, it enjoined the occupied to think of the occupying regime as temporary. 'Occupied provinces are not conquered provinces', declared Mercier; 'Belgium is no more a German province than Galicia is a Russian province'.[21] After this pointed reference to the unacceptability of all military occupations, the letter went on to state that 'the Power that has invaded our soil and now occupies the greater part of our country (. . .) [has] no lawful authority. Therefore in soul and conscience you owe it neither respect, nor attachment, nor obedience. The sole lawful authority in Belgium is that of our King, of our Government, of the elected representatives of the nation'. An occupying regime only interested in order might have tolerated such statements, for Mercier preached patience, not revolt, and reminded his audience of the massacres of the preceding summer. But this reference, precisely, was seen in the upper echelons of the Government-General as a slur on the imperial army; and calling German rule temporary counteracted plans to gain a permanent foothold in the conquered country. Mercier's letter was promptly banned; printers were arrested and copies seized from parish priests.[22] The ban proved singularly counter-productive: it galvanized underground patriotic culture. If the letter had passed unobtruded, wrote Buerbaum, only 'the odd intellectual' would have recognized its relevance; as it was, 'its brutal seizure in all parishes got the general public involved, and so the Germans wound up giving the Pastoral Letter a great deal of resonance both with the faithful and with others'.[23] The pastoral letter's impact on the underground press was both practical and discursive. On the practical side, an entire clandestine cottage industry sprang up to copy and distribute the text, causing the practice of *samizdat* to penetrate deeper into civil society. On the discursive side, expressing faith in the restoration of Belgian independence and reminding fellow citizens to not 'resign themselves to the so-called inevitable'[24] and to keep on 'elevating their souls to the level of the Ideal'[25] were now firmly defined as civilian war efforts in their own right and for the long run.

The interpretive turn in the underground press was further stimulated by the occupation regime's divide-and-conquer effort. Called *Flamenpolitik* ('Flemish policies'), this strategy aimed to deepen the discontent of the majority Flemish population with a state in which French was still the dominant language, in the process questioning Belgium's claim to nationhood.[26] From 1915, the *Pressestelle* launched newspapers designed to portray the Belgian state as essentially hostile to Flemings.[27] Flemish spokesmen condemned these papers and their contributors (called 'activists') for serving the occupation regime; open letters of protest were sent to the Governor-General. One *Droogstoppel* brochure called *Flamenpolitik* a scam with reference to the fate of Polish culture in Prussia.[28] Next to his brochures, in August 1915 Buerbaum had started a periodical, *De Vrije Stem* (The Voice of Freedom), which critiqued the occupation regime and its recruits in a deliberately folksy tone. The more highbrow *De Vlaamsche Leeuw* (The Lion of Flanders) was launched in the fall of 1915; addressed to militant Flemish elites, it set out to explain why they should reject what it saw as the instrumentalizing of the Flemish cause by the occupation regime. In the same fall of 1915, a group of Brussels priests and magistrates launched *L'Âme Belge* (The Soul of Belgium), which, among other messages of national unity, informed its readers of the position taken by loyal Flemish militants.[29]

These delineations of the national interest in times of enemy occupation were carried largely by the kind of people who, since the nineteenth century, had been mainstays of the imagined national community, in Belgium as elsewhere: viz., the educated middle- and lower-middle classes of small business owners, teachers, civil servants, journalists, professionals and their families. Most of them lived in cities: of the 61 underground papers of which the provenance is known, 37 were produced in Brussels, 8 in Antwerp, 4 in Ghent and the rest in smaller cities, most of them in Flanders.[30] Most of them wrote in French: only 14 of the underground papers were in Dutch, another 2 in both Dutch and French. This preponderance of French was not a function of region: outside of Brussels, most of the underground papers came from the Flemish provinces. Rather, it indicates that educated Belgians' public culture in the early twentieth century was still largely couched in French, including in Flanders. The Flemish networks were linguistically intertwined: in Antwerp, for instance, the French-language periodical *Patrie*, launched by the bank manager Gustave Snoeck, was printed by Buerbaum together with his own Dutch-language periodicals.[31] For all that, Buerbaum would later grouse that the intellectuals of Antwerp had taken their time rallying to the underground press[32]; and the preponderance of French in underground discourse does indeed suggest that those Flemish elites who in the early twentieth century had already opted for Dutch were more reluctant than their francophone counterparts to join a movement so suffused with ardent Belgian patriotism. Yet those who did, wrote with conviction: the Dutch-language underground papers' criticism of *Flamenpolitik* generated some of the corpus' most fundamental arguments against the political culture of occupation.[33]

If the underground press in occupied Belgium did not bear a distinctive ethnic stamp, it did bear a distinctive political one: all but one of the major periodicals were produced by Catholic milieux. It is true that the vagaries of conservation have not favoured the two other 'political families' of Belgium. The country's first clandestine paper, *La Vedette*, was of Liberal bent; Socialist milieux produced two underground periodicals, *Le Révolté* (The Rebel) et *Les Petites Nouvelles* (roughly, *Little Reports*); only the titles of these three publications remain. It is also true that, after the war, more documentation was assembled and more memoirs were published on the major Catholic papers and the networks that produced them. Yet, given the post-war (and international) lionizing of Belgian civilian resistance and the lessened clout of political Catholicism in post-war Belgium, it is highly unlikely that major non-Catholic efforts would have remained unacknowledged. We should, therefore, conclude that the underground press in occupied Belgium did indeed possess a Catholic bent (with one late exception, to which we will return), perhaps unsurprisingly, given the impact of Mercier's pastoral letter. The question of what this means cannot be explored in full here. But it will be well worth inquiring how engagement in the underground press meshed with 'lived religion', in the sense of 'the totality of [people's] ultimate values, their most deeply held ethical convictions, their efforts to order their reality, their cosmology'.[34] For now, all we can wield is the coarse yardstick of political programmes; thus measured, the underground press does not reveal itself to have been a party press. It contained no calls for de-secularizing measures. (Nor was it suffused with confessional prejudice: one finds little anti-Lutheran rhetoric, and occasional anti-Semitic slurs were not exclusive to the Catholic press.[35]) The Catholic bent of the underground press meant, rather, the mobilization of a particular segment of the urban middle classes, whose social lives were arranged less along linguistic than confessional lines in dense arrays of organizations – reading circles, lending libraries, mutual-aid societies, labour unions, primary schools, Jesuit colleges, choral societies, gymnastic clubs and so on.[36] This tight-knit world, with its cadre of committed clerics, proved receptive to self-mobilization – perhaps all the more so as Belgium's Catholics, before the war, had been vocal in praising the Wilhelmine Empire as the most politically sound and trustworthy of the Great Powers.[37]

It was the Catholic milieux that created the longest-lived papers. More in general, of the 70 periodicals of which the lifespan is known, 28, or two-fifths, existed for at most one

MILITARY OCCUPATIONS IN FIRST WORLD WAR EUROPE

month; another 26 for up to a year; and only 16, or one-fifth, endured for longer than a year. The longest-lived ones were the *Revue de la Presse* (161 issues between February 1915 and the Armistice), the *Libre Belgique* (170 issues between February 1915 and the Armistice), *De Vrije Stem* (91 issues between September 1915 and March 1918), *De Vlaamsche Leeuw* (37 issues between November 1915 and the Armistice) and the *Âme Belge* (55 issues between November 1915 and the Armistice). These major papers, all of them emanating from Catholic milieux, were borne by dense and intricately ramified networks spanning several provinces. A post-war memoir on the *Libre Belgique*, published in early 1919, mentioned 539 names of collaborators; it sold 35,000 copies in a short time and was reissued in an updated version, this time naming 667 people, since a further 128 had come out of the shadows in the meantime.[38] Another memoir mentioned 710 collaborators.[39] These papers had the largest print-runs. The *Libre Belgique*, at its height, reached 20,000, the *Droogstoppels* 10,000. *De Vlaamsche Leeuw* printed 5000 copies per issue; the *Revue de la Presse*, 4500. Minor journals, like the Ghent *Het Nachtlichtje* (The Little Night-Light), a handwritten bulletin, stencilled some 500 copies per issue, others even less – the Brussels *Zievereer-Excelsior*, a joke journal, had a print-run of about 70. Resonance often exceeded print-run, since issues went from hand to hand. That is why *De Vrije Stem* was published in a small format. But it did fill, at its height, 16 pages.[40] The other long-lived journals too offered heft.

Much of their commentary centred on the theme of veracity – less with regard to military events as with regard to the events of 1914. Military news, increasingly baffling, was more and more often summarized under exhortations to keep on hoping. 'Sursum Corda!' (Lift Up Your Hearts) wrote *De Vlaamsche Leeuw* in the disheartening month of June 1916, and defined impatience as unpatriotic.[41] Because a war so heinously unleashed could not but end in the vindication of the wronged party, the underground press kept returning to '1914'. Between October 1915 and March 1916, for instance, the *Libre Belgique* network took considerable risks to issue a serial supplement: an anonymous book-length pamphlet entitled *J'accuse, von einem Deutschen* (J'accuse, By A German), a banned indictment of Germany's entry into war as imperialist.[42] Another prohibited text followed in early 1916: the Belgian bishops' refutation of the 'German White Book', the official publication that accused Belgian civilians of having sniped at the invading troops in 1914.[43] Issuing these texts put considerable pressure on the fragile machinery of the underground press. (More in general, post-war reports detailing these and other bottlenecks highlight the bluntly material side of the work: poring over tiny photographs of smuggled newspapers, muffling the noise of the presses, maximizing cramped storage space, frantic cutting and folding of brochures, lugging heavy packages in public and other, sometimes insurmountable difficulties.) But highlighting '1914' was considered essential: acknowledging these truths meant re-establishing a measure of justice, it was a reminder of the enduring sway of international norms. And from this, all else would flow – for the idea that an authority based on an original breaking of norms could endure in their own time was, quite simply, inconceivable to the men (and not a few women) who kept the clandestine press going, steeped as they all were in the grand historical narrative of ineluctable justice. 'The truth', then, was a *Leitmotiv*; the *Libre Belgique*, in 1915, devoted 89 major articles over 55 issues to German mendacity regarding the start of the war, Belgium's neutrality, civilian sniping and occupation measures. These articles bore titles such as 'What German Promises are Worth', 'Belgian Honor Withstands the Assault of German Lies', 'German Bluff', 'How They Conduct Surveys', 'Mendacity Fair', 'Feldgrau Fabrications', 'More on the German Lies', 'Another Brazen German Lie', 'The Imperial Liar', 'Teutonic Hairsplitting', 'The Brigands' Plea', 'What Truth Means in Germany' and 'Dirty Hypocrite!'.

The point of all this effort escaped even some sympathetic observers. Calling *La Libre Belgique* 'a useless piece of bravado', the US envoy Brand Whitlock wondered why the occupation government went after it so fiercely.[44] Whitlock, well acquainted with the vicissitudes of securing food relief to the Belgians, saw the position of the occupied in a 'Grotian' perspective, to borrow a term coined by the occupation scholar Karma Nabulsi: civilians were entitled to protection but had to refrain from joining the fray. By contrast, the world of the clandestine press was imbued with what Nabulsi calls a 'Republican' sense of an occupied population's task: that of rallying to the fatherland's aid in times of crisis, using the methods available to civilians.[45] Denying legitimacy to the occupiers was one such method, combated with equal resolve (to Whitlock's bafflement) by the Germans. It is no coincidence that the only notes of frustration in the usually sanguine reports of the head of the German Political Department in Brussels, Baron Von der Lancken, concern the clandestine press.[46] From mid-1915, police services in the Government-General geared up to eradicate it. In Brussels, Police Department B (*Polizeistelle B*), in charge of chasing down both escape networks and forbidden publications, employed dozens of high-ranking professional policemen sent in from Germany and Germans who had been living in Belgium before the war, as well as Belgian informers.[47] The underground-press section was led by an infantry lieutenant who before the war had worked in Belgium as a sales representative for a perfume house. A special unit, employing both men and women, was devoted to the *Libre Belgique* alone.[48]

This grim determination originated in the occupying bureaucrats' and officers' awareness of the importance of '1914' to their authority, an awareness that mirrored that of the clandestine press. Efforts at persuasion therefore hinged on a reinterpretation of the outbreak of the war. In early January 1915, for instance, inhabitants of Brussels found flyers stuck under their doors with allegations of secret Belgian–British agreements, implying that Belgium had not been neutral at all at the start of the war.[49] This attempt to convince with diplomatic arguments, however one-sided, awkward and mendacious, translated a desire on the part of Governor-General Moritz von Bissing and his administration to couch German rule in Belgium in something other than blunt military superiority.

This endeavour, though inspired by a wish to step back from destruction,[50] entailed the fierce repression of a harmless endeavour. This is no paradox. The occupation regime's ardent wish to establish legitimacy – an achievement that was hoped to transcend the violence of the invasion, for Belgians and Germans both, and to give meaning to the ongoing loss of German lives at the front – precluded tolerance for an underground discourse bent on denying the regime legitimacy by referring to past and enduring violences. And yet such tolerance could have been envisioned in theory (as with Mercier's pastoral letter), for the underground papers did not represent an active threat. Far from championing armed resistance, they condemned it as 'forfeiting national honor'.[51] (This very reticence was a rebuke to the invaders: as Annette Becker has perceptively pointed out, it was a way to condemn the escalation of the war of which the 1914 massacres had been an example.[52])

Although the underground press condemned violent action, many of its contributors combined their engagement in this form of unarmed resistance with others. For instance, the young architect Philippe Baucq, head of distributions for the *Libre Belgique*, was also involved in a network helping trapped Entente soldiers escape occupied Belgium; he was, for that reason, executed in October 1915 together with Edith Cavell. Others worked as spies. Only in the second half of the war did secret intelligence services instruct their agents to relinquish their work for the clandestine press as being 'less useful to the Fatherland'.[53] But until then, resisters' multitasking had made clandestine networks more vulnerable to information circulating within *Polizei* departments. These departments had reached full strength by early 1916 and the first large-scale raids on underground papers took place in April of that year. ('A true disaster', wrote a *Libre Belgique* organizer, adding he was sure the operation had been betrayed.[54]) A first major trial of the *Libre Belgique* followed in July 1916. Other periodicals were hit too: in that same summer, the *Âme Belge*, the *Droogstoppel* brochures, *De Vrije Stem* and the *Revue de la Presse* all lost their editors-in-chief and dozens of printers, couriers and distributors. In Ghent, *L'Antiprussien* (The Anti-Prussian) emerged, lost its editor-in-chief and disappeared all in the same month of July 1916.[55] Although no one was condemned to death over press activities proper, punishment could be harsh, because German military justice defined press crimes as *Kriegsverrat* (war treason) instead of mere offences against censorship. The Jesuit Dubar, for instance, was sentenced to 12 years over his *Libre Belgique* work. The lawyer Paillot, accused of having distributed the pamphlet *Une nuit de Guillaume II* (A Night of Wilhelm II), received a four-year sentence for having insulted the emperor. A frail man, he died in prison.[56]

The intense repression of 1916 coincided with worsened material difficulties. Paper became so scarce that the *Libre Belgique* had to limit its print-run from 20,000 to 10,000 copies, and sometimes even 5000.[57] The *Droogstoppels* went from 10,000 to 6000. *De Vrije Stem* cut its number of pages from 16 to 8.[58] Eventually, Buerbaum's son Ernest, who from his hiding place in a shed on a building lot had resumed the paper after his father's arrest, would be forced to give up in March 1918 because of the dearth of paper and because his associate, the 18-year-old Gustaaf Lava, was shot dead while resisting arrest.[59] Overall, from 1916, underground press activity plummeted. When measured month by month, in terms of overall number of issues produced, it is clear that by the end of 1916, the 'golden age' of the underground press was over; 1917 and 1918 were slump years (Figure 1).

But repression and scarcity were not the only forces explaining this decline. Wartime diaries attest to an exhaustion of the very élan behind the clandestine press, linked to a lessening of the urgency to point out what the war was about. The ineluctable justice hoped for in 1915 was a long way in coming. The *Libre Belgique*, for one, no longer stressed the issue of veracity to the same extent. (The 89 articles over 55 issues mentioned above amounted to a ratio of 1:6 for the year 1915; the importance of the theme dropped subsequently – the comparable figures for the next three years were 0:8, 0:5 and 0:6.) The great morality play of the invasion lost its contours in the context of the occupation, a lower-intensity but lengthier ordeal not easy to interpret. For one thing, 'the enemy' was not always foreign. Some writers for the clandestine press urged the occupied to practise solidarity. Others however went after fellow citizens with venom, occasionally lapsing into slander. One extreme case was the one-time Lille publication *Les Vidanges* (Garbage)

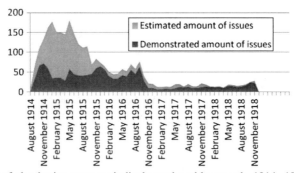

Figure 1. Issues of clandestine press periodicals produced by month, 1914–1918 ($n = 77$).

of January 1917, consisting of a two-page 'complete and exact list of filthy sluts and disgusting characters who engage in trade – and worse – with our enemies'.[60] While other periodicals did not go as far, several went for the *ad hominem*. *De Vrije Stem*, for one, denounced 67 people as informers; among them figured one man who was actually working for British intelligence and would be executed in June 1917.[61] Others pillorized entire groups. The Brussels *Satirische Zeitung* (Satirical Journal; the title only was in German) called the unemployed layabouts coddled by public charity – only a few months before they would be brutally deported to forced labour in Germany.[62]

Those very deportations ended what prospects of unforced acceptance the occupation regime might have had.[63] Though eventually rescinded, at least in the Government-General, they heralded what one might call a 'Ludendorffian turn' in the occupation regime, marked by intensified exploitation, mounting impatience on the side of the German military with the occupation regime's 'civilian' priorities, and a *de facto* relinquishing, on the part of the occupation regime, of claims to couch German rule in anything but force. (As if on cue, Von Bissing died in April 1917.)

This 'Ludendorffian turn' in German rule coincided with a weakening of the 'interpretive turn' in the underground press – almost as if both parties were simultaneously abandoning the discourse of moral credit and national honour. Many among the occupied had started to consider the clandestine papers as a nuisance. The Catholic Brussels journal *Ca et Là* (Here and There) wrote in December 1917 that 'if in 1915, when the authors and the editors of the forbidden papers were surrounded by nothing but warm feelings, someone would have told them that the day would come when they would not only have to defend themselves against the *Boches*, which is an honor, but that they would have actual Belgians as their enemies, they would have been very surprised indeed'. The long-drawn-out ordeal of occupation had caused many to bitterly retreat from public engagement. *Ca et Là* pinpointed four reasons for the clandestine papers' disfavour. Some held them responsible for the Germans' hardening of restrictions. Others thought they had usefully fought the censored press at the start of the war, but now brought only 'tears'. A third argument was that the length of the war had rendered them irrelevant. And, finally, they were accused of being too quick to condemn and insult. *Ca et Là* considered these criticisms unwarranted, or at least highly exaggerated. In no way did they detract from the role the underground press had to play even now – indeed, had to play more than ever, for war-weariness had rendered German propaganda even more insidious, and it was therefore essential to 'publish, as much as possible, that which cannot be said out loud'.[64]

This last call did not go altogether unheeded. In spite of the crisis, the underground press did endure, albeit on a much diminished basis, around the basic, non-negotiable programme of the occupying regime's unacceptability. There was even a modest regrouping.[65] *Ca et Là* was, after all, launched in the slump year of 1917. So was another high-profile periodical, *De Vlaamsche Wachter* (The Flemish Guardian), which threw itself into philippics against *Flamenpolitik* and its champions, and especially against the new Flemish university of Ghent, which fulfilled a long-held Flemish wish but was deemed unacceptable in a context of deportations and forced labour.[66] The last year of the war would see another small revival. In Brussels, in mid-April 1918, to combat the anxieties caused by the peace of Brest-Litovsk and the German spring offensive in the West, an important new periodical was launched. This was the high-brow *Le Flambeau: revue belge des questions politiques* (The Torch: Belgian Review of Politics), the only major underground publication of occupied Belgium not created by Catholic milieux. Its main organizer was the brilliant Byzantologist Henri Grégoire, who before the war had made a name as a member of the commission sent to investigate atrocities in Congo, and whom Robert Graves, not known to gush over other men's intellect, would describe after the war as 'tough, witty, and capable', having 'acquired a certain slyness and adaptability (...) as a Belgian civilian in the German occupation'.[67] Even the much-battered *Libre Belgique* held on, although a rival, in late March 1918, remarked tartly that the 'varied and well-documented content' of the *Revue de la Presse* was 'far more interesting these days than the often heavy and monotonous articles offered by its patriotic competitor'.[68] But by the summer, the *Libre* was back to offering more than just uplifting homilies: it observed the German opposition closely and applauded its position on the war.[69] More in general, while underground discourse often engaged in a wholesale rejection of all things German – if need be by means of crude cartoons or puns – another, never-relinquished priority was that of looking for 'communities of truth' within Germany.[70] The major clandestine papers made a point of seeking out congenial German opinions. This reflected hopes of an eventual resumption of dialogue.

It would be a mistake, then, to define the underground press in occupied Belgium as solely an expression of a war culture bent on demonizing the enemy. While some of its outbursts fit that image, much of the clandestine discourse remained, ultimately, bounded by its own message, that of the unacceptability of occupation. Because this was a concrete and finite credo, it could coexist with some measure of antimilitarism and with appeals to reason. The clandestine discourse of occupied Belgium, then, for all its scattered brutalizing notes, contained its own paths to cultural demobilization.[71]

By way of epilogue, we may note that the search for 'communities of truth' did not stop in November 1918. Ten years after the Armistice, *Le Flambeau*, one of two underground publications to continue after the war,[72] commissioned the leading German journalist Carl von Ossietzky to write an article about Weimar public opinion. The resulting essay, which sharply condemned the stab-in-the-back legend as sapping the Republic, would further contribute to making Von Ossietzky *persona non grata* with the German right.[73] His eventual, terrible fate at the hands of the Nazis testified to the closing off of all dialogue concerning the Empire's past war.

Notes

1. For a more elaborate version of Emmanuel Debruyne's contribution to this article, see 'Véridiques, antiprussiens et patriotes'.
2. Van Doren, *Les tribulations*, 149–62 (quotation 158), 181–5.
3. A term first defined by Horne: 'Introduction: Mobilizing for "total war"'.
4. Conditions similar to those in France existed in the Belgian operations and staging areas (*Operationsgebiet* and *Etappengebiet*, respectively) in East and especially West Flanders, in the southern and western extremities of Wallonia, as well as in the territory occupied by the German Marine Corps.
5. In addition, next to the periodical press, one-time underground publications (documents, open letters, caricatures, songs) thrived, especially in 1915. It should be noted that the underground press in Nazi-occupied Belgium (and, of course, France) would be even more abundant.
6. Nationalist guerrillas in southern Serbia may have organized, or at least planned, a rudimentary system of fliers (Jonathan Gumz, personal communication, with thanks), but there are no signs that occupied Serbia generated a full-fledged underground press: Gumz, *The Resurrection*; Knezevic, *The Austro-Hungarian Occupation*; Mitrovic, *Serbia's Great War*. Neither did Montenegro (Heiko Brendel, personal communication, with thanks) nor the parts of Slovenia occupied by Italy (Petra Svoljšak, personal communication, with thanks). There was no 'underground' press in occupied Ukraine because the occupying authorities failed to establish censorship (see the contribution by Wolfram Dornik and Peter Lieb to this issue).
7. Liulevicius, *War Land*, 183.
8. With thanks to Jesse Kauffman and Stephan Lehnstaedt.
9. Stengers and Gubin, *Histoire du sentiment national*.

MILITARY OCCUPATIONS IN FIRST WORLD WAR EUROPE

10. De Schaepdrijver, 'Occupation, Propaganda'.

11. The 13 October decree was followed by a 4 November 1914 order, reminding the Belgian population that all printed matter (including photos and sheet-music) and public representations (lectures, plays, poetry readings and so on) not expressly *authorized* by the Governor-General were expressly *banned*. Huberich and Nicol-Speyer, *Deutsche Gesetzgebung*, vol. I, 21–2; Von Köhler, *Die Staatsverwaltung*, 25–7; Pirenne and Vauthier, *La législation*, 138–40; *The German Police System*, 224–7; Boghaert-Vaché, *La Presse*, 17–24.

12. Since emboché is a play on the words 'boche' (Fritz, Hun) and 'embauché' (recruited), a more complete but too complex translation would read 'taken hun'.

13. Van Den Dungen, 'Les milieux de presse'; *La Vérité*, 70 (23 November 1914), 7.

14. A rare expression of self-defence is the 1920 book *Malgré tout!* by the editorialist of *La Belgique*, Ray Nyst.

15. *La Vedette*, the brainchild of the Liberal publisher François Olyff, seems to have lasted only two or three weeks. De Keyser and Lipkens, *Drukkend Hasselt*, 27–8.

16. Lucien Laudy, 'Le Bulletin', *La Gazette*, 24 August 1924. (Clipping from HIA, VP.)

17. Massart, *La Presse Clandestine*, 6–7 and passim.

18. *Histoire de La Revue de la Presse clandestine*, undated report [early 1921], BSA, ASP, file 81 folder 505, p. 10. This report also mentions the earlier launching of *Les Dernières Nouvelles* in Leuven, *supra*.

19. 'Droogstoppel' (Dead-wood) was a character from the classic 1860 Dutch novel *Max Havelaar*; Buerbaum had chosen the name to make readers and the *Polizei* think the brochures were smuggled in from the Netherlands. Buerbaum, *Gedenkschriften*, vol. 1, 27.

20. Gille et al., *Cinquante mois*, vol. 1, 287–9 (9 March 1915). See also Delandsheere, *La 'Libre Belgique'*; De Moor, *Mes aventures*; Goemaere, *Histoire*; Millard, *Uncensored*; Van De Kerckhove, *L'histoire merveilleuse* and Van Doren, *Les tribulations*.

21. The English translation can be consulted on the website of the German *Zentrale für Unterrichtsmedien im Internet*: http://www.zum.de/psm/1wk/ww1/mercier.php3

22. De Schaepdrijver, 'L'Europe occupée'. See also Horne and Kramer, *German Atrocities*, 271.

23. Buerbaum, *Gedenkschriften*, I, 18; in more detail, Buerbaum, *Hoe ik er toe kwam, de brochuren-Droogstoppel te schrijven*, n.d. [late 1919], BSA, ASP, file 80, p. 1.

24. *Het Nachtlichtje*, 'Number 000 [sic], year 1915', p. 1.

25. *Histoire de La Revue de la Presse clandestine*, undated report [early 1921], BSA, ASP, file 81 folder 505, p. 84.

26. De Schaepdrijver, 'Belgium'.

27. The first of these papers were *De Vlaamsche Post* (The Flemish Mail), launched in the university city of Ghent in February 1915, and *Het Vlaamsche Nieuws* (Flemish Tidings), launched in Antwerp in June 1915.

28. 'Droogstoppel' (Jozef Buerbaum), *De oorlog der Vlamingen en de taalstrijd in Duitsch-Polen* [The Flemings' War and the Language Struggle in German Poland], n.d. [mid-January 1916]. See also *Gedenkschriften*, vol. 1, 115–38.

29. As appreciated by *De Vlaamsche Leeuw*, 3:19 (October 1917), p. 4.

30. To be precise: of the 61, 3 came from northern France, 37 from Brussels, 8 from Antwerp, 4 from Ghent, 5 from other Flemish cities and 4 from small Walloon cities. In addition, as the files show (BSA, ASP, file 194, folder 502), the major cities, Liège especially, evolved vast networks distributing the papers from Brussels, such as the *Libre*, which was harder to obtain in Antwerp, at least in early 1915: Buerbaum, *De Geschiedenis van 'De Vrije Stem'*, BSA, ASP, file 80, p. 4.

31. BSA, ASP, file 81 folder 502. Snoeck was also a major distributor of the *Libre Belgique*.

32. Buerbaum, *Gedenkschriften*, vol. 1, 283.

33. For example, those of the medievalist Alfons Fierens, who skewered the use of *völkisch* terminology in 'activist' discourse. De Schaepdrijver, 'That Theory of Races'.

34. Definition in Orsi, *The Madonna*, xvii. We thank William S. Cossen for alerting us to the notion of 'lived religion'. A deeper exploration of the link between the underground press and lived religion must build on Annette Becker's work on faith in the war, starting with her assertion that, to the extent that the war was about 'a certain way to view the world', it was a war of religion by definition (*La Guerre et la foi*, p. 15).

35. One *Libre Belgique* article of October 1915 vilified, in heavily anti-Semitic terms, the lawyer Fritz Norden, a German established in Belgium who had published an essay questioning

MILITARY OCCUPATIONS IN FIRST WORLD WAR EUROPE

Belgium's pre-war neutrality. 'Fidelis' [Albert Van De Kerckhove], 'Une Saleté' (A Piece of Dirt), *La Libre Belgique* 49, p. 3. But non-Catholic journals did not shrink from anti-Semitism either. (For example, *Satirische Zeitung* 22, 20 October 1916, p. 1, against the editor-in-chief of *Le Bruxellois*.)

36. On this world, see the French sociologist Henri Charriaut's survey *La Belgique Moderne*, p. 190.
37. Bitsch, *La Belgique*, 397 and passim.
38. Goemaere, *Histoire*, appendix 'Livre d'Or'.
39. Van de Kerckhove, *L'histoire merveilleuse*, 275–89.
40. Buerbaum, De Geschiedenis van 'De Vrije Stem', BSA, ASP, file 80, p. 5.
41. *De Vlaamsche Leeuw*, 6, June 1916, p. 2. This Christian liturgical phrase was a trope in Catholic Belgian resistance culture: it comes back repeatedly, for instance, in the last letters written by the brothers Louis and Antony Collard, two young men who had worked for British intelligence, before their execution in Liège in July 1918. Debruyne and Van Ypersele, *Je serai fusillé demain*, 111.
42. The book was by Richard Grelling, a German lawyer and pacifist living in Switzerland. Published anonymously in the spring of 1915, it was translated into eight languages by 1916. It was banned in Germany and in the Austro-Hungarian Empire. Dreyer and Lembcke, *Die deutsche Diskussion*, 42–5; biographical information in Luchins and Luchins, 'Kurt Grelling'.
43. BSA ASP file 81 folder 502, *Rapport sur la Libre Belgique*, unsigned [Albert Dankelman], n.d. [September 1921]. See also Gille et al., *Cinquante mois*, vol. 2, 61. On the 'White Book' and the Belgian bishops' reponse, Horne and Kramer, *German Atrocities*, 237–47, 272–3.
44. Whitlock, *Journal*, p. 170 (22 June 1915). Whitlock kept this verdict to himself after the war and wrote a glowing preface to a *Libre* organizer's memoir, Van De Kerckhove's *L'histoire merveilleuse*.
45. Nabulsi, *Traditions*.
46. Amara and Roland, *Gouverner*, pp. 157 (August–October 1915) and 372 (February–July 1918). On both occasions, Von der Lancken lamented the *Libre Belgique*'s counteracting of the Government-General's propaganda among Catholics.
47. With 70 people on duty (not counting Belgian informers), *Polizeistelle B* was 'in many ways the most important security organization in Belgium'. *The German Police System*, 216.
48. BSA, ASP, file 196, *Rapport Ball*, Report 1, pp. 29–33; Report 2, pp. 3, 14, 52; Report 3, p. 64. (This was a report drafted in December 1918 by Fritz Ball, a former agent of the German police.) Also Gille et al., *Cinquante mois*, vol. 3, 90.
49. Gille et al., *Cinquante mois*, vol. 1, 222 (7 January 1915).
50. On the notion of 'stepping back from destruction', and on the implicit maintenance of international norms by occupation regimes in the First World War, see Jonathan Gumz' *The Resurrection*.
51. 'Justicier Criminel', by 'Belga' (the Jesuit Peeters), *La Libre Belgique*, 61 (January 1916), p. 1. The article condemned the January 1916 killing of a Belgian informer by a patriot. So did 'À propos d'un drame', *L'Âme Belge*, 1st series nr 5 (January 1916) which blamed the Germans for having introduced such 'corruption'.
52. Becker, *Les cicatrices*, 261.
53. BSA, ASP, file 194, folder 'Province de Liège', report by Emma Weimerskirch of Liège, 13 August 1920, p. 10. She and her two sisters were instructed to cease working for the *Libre Belgique* in February 1918 by the head of the *Dame Blanche*, a network operating for the War Office (by then the dominant secret service behind the Western front: Van Ypersele and Debruyne, *De la guerre de l'ombre*, 83–6). The *Polizei* were aware of this development: BSA, ASP, file 196, *Rapport Ball*, Report 3, p. 2.
54. BSA, ASP, file 81 folder 502, *Rapport sur la Libre Belgique*, unsigned [Albert Dankelman], n.d. [September 1921].
55. The first issue came out on July 7, the second one on July 21; the editor-in-chief, Pierre Verhaegen, was arrested on the 29th. BSA, ASP, file 82.
56. Kirschen, *Devant les conseils*, 339–68, esp. 356 on *Kriegsverrat*. The original German list of accused with the definition of their crimes is in BSA, ASP, file 193 folder 502, Chaudron report. On the application of *Kriegsverrat* to occupied populations, Hull, *Absolute Destruction*, 125 and 231. On *Majestätsbeleidigung* (insulting the Emperor) in occupied Serbia, see the contribution by Jonathan Gumz to this issue.
57. Van De Kerckhove, *L'histoire merveilleuse*, 132.

58. Buerbaum, De Geschiedenis van 'De Vrije Stem', BSA, ASP, file 80, p. 9.
59. Lava (identified as 'Emiel August' in some sources, as 'Gustaaf' by Buerbaum) had worked for the Buerbaums from the start. He had been arrested a first time, together with Buerbaum senior, in August 1916, was imprisoned until April 1917 and had returned to work for the *Vrije Stem* after he was freed. In May 1919, declared a 'martyr' of the underground press, he was given a state funeral in Antwerp. Buerbaum, *Gedenkschriften* vol. 1, 271, 282–5.
60. *Les Vidanges*, 1 (1 January 1917), p. 1. With thanks to James Connolly (see also his contribution to this issue).
61. *De Vrije Stem* 16 (Spring, 1916), p. 13. *De Vrije Stem* had been launched expressly to identify informers: Buerbaum, *De Geschiedenis van 'De Vrije Stem'*, BSA, ASP, file 80, pp. 3–4. After the war, Buerbaum apologized in his memoirs (*Gedenkschriften*, vol. 1, 264), and in the press: 'Eene Eerherstelling' (A Rehabilitation), *Het Handelsblad van Antwerpen*, 4 March 1921, p. 3. The man in question, the 39-year-old contractor Frans Vergauwen, had been one of the best 'escape agents' of Belgium before joining secret intelligence. Kirschen, *Devant les conseils*, 265, 268, 276–83, 291.
62. *Satirische Zeitung*, 5 (23 June 1916), p. 3.
63. See Jens Thiel's contribution to this issue.
64. *Ça et Là* [number 3], December 1917.
65. This development is not comparable to the remobilizations that took place on other home fronts, because these were mainly driven by states (Horne, 'Introduction', 14–16).
66. On *De Vlaamsche Wachter,* BSA, ASP, file 81 folder 504, letter by Constant Eeckels, 25 July 1920.
67. Robert Graves, *Goodbye*, 267. Grégoire was Dean of Letters at Cairo University during Graves' tenure there in the later 1920s. On Grégoire's role in the Congo commission, see Stengers, 'Le rôle de la Commission'. The two other editors of *Le Flambeau* were Anatole Mühlstein, who would be named councillor at the Polish embassy in Paris in 1930 and who would work together with Grégoire again in New York in 1943–1945, and the classical philologist Oscar Grojean, who would work with Grégoire in Cairo in 1925–1928, and who would, under the Nazi occupation of Belgium, use his contacts in high civil service to protect several Jewish high-school teachers and pupils. Bots, *Bibliographie*.
68. Tytgat, *Bruxelles*, 453 (31 March 1918).
69. Witness the articles written by the journalist and war chronicler Louis Gille on the Independent Social Democratic opinions expressed in the *Leipziger Volkszeitung* in the summer of 1918: 'Un député rend, au Reichstag, hommage aux magistrats belges persécutés', *La Libre Belgique* 153 (1 June 1918); 'Un discours d'un député allemand écrasant pour l'Allemagne', *La Libre Belgique* 157 (13 July 1918); and 'L'oppression allemande dans les provinces baltiques et en Ukraine d'après un député allemand', *La Libre Belgique* 158 (15 July 1918). The *Leipziger Volkszeitung* was prohibited in the occupied territories with an eye to keeping order among the occupying troops and the troops passing to and from the front.
70. On 'communities of truth', Horne and Kramer, *German Atrocities*, Chapter 7.
71. On this concept, see *Démobilisations culturelles*.
72. *Le Flambeau* continued to appear until 1976 as a political magazine. *La Libre Belgique* is still one of the major daily newspapers of Belgium.
73. Carl von Ossietzky, 'Où va l'Allemagne? Questions et réponses par un Allemand', *Le Flambeau* 11:11, 1 November 1928, pp. 235–44.

References

Unpublished sources

Belgian State Archives, Brussels (BSA): *Archives des Services Patriotiques* (ASP), files 80, 81, 82, 193, 194, 196.
Hoover Institution Archives (HIA), Stanford, CA: *Verbouwe Papers* (VP).

Underground papers

Consulted at (in addition to the archives mentioned above):

- Lille, France: Archives Départementales du Nord.
- Belgian Royal Library, Brussels: Archives et Musée de la Littérature; Rare Books Collection; General Reading Room.
Centre d'Études Guerre et Société, Brussels, Belgium: collection of underground papers.
- Mons, Belgium: Mundaneum.
Ca et Là.
De Vlaamsche Leeuw.
De Vlaamsche Wachter.
De Vrije Stem.
Droogstoppel (brochures 1 through 28).
Het Nachtlichtje.
L'Âme Belge.
L'Antiprussien.
L'Autre Cloche.
L'Écho (De Ce Que Les Journaux Censurés N'Osent Ou Ne Peuvent Pas Dire).
La Libre Belgique.
La Revue de la Presse.
La Soupe.
La Vérité.
Le Courrier de France.
Le Journal de Von Bissing.
Les Dernières Nouvelles.
Les Dernières Nouvelles de la Guerre.
Les Vidanges.
L'Oiseau de France/La Patience.
Patrie.
Recueil de Poésies et Nouvelles publiées pendant la guerre de 1914–1915.
Revue bi-hebdomadaire des Nouvelles de la Guerre.
Satirische Zeitung.

Other published sources; scholarship

Démobilisations culturelles après la Grande Guerre, theme issue of *14/18. Aujourd'hui. Today. Heute. Revue annuelle d'histoire* 5. Péronne: Historial de la Grande Guerre, 2002.

Amara, Michaël, and Hubert Roland, eds. *Gouverner en Belgique occupée. Oscar von der Lancken-Wakenitz – Rapports d'activité 1915–1918. Édition critique.* Brussels/Frankfurt: P.I.E.-Peter Lang, 2004.

Becker. Annette. *Les cicatrices rouges. 14–8. France et Belgique occupées.* Paris: Fayard, 2010.

Becker, Annette. *La guerre et la foi. De la mort à la mémoire 1914–1930.* Paris: Armand Colin, 1994.

Bitsch, Marie-Thérèse. *La Belgique entre la France et l'Allemagne 1905–1914.* Paris: Publications de la Sorbonne, 1994.

Boghaert-Vaché, Arthur. *La presse pendant l'occupation,* 3rd revised ed. Brussels: Brian Hill, 1919.

Bots, Marcel. *Bibliographie des revues libérales: Le Flambeau (1918–1976),* http://www.liberaalarchief.be/Flambeau-inl.pdf (accessed 3 March 2012).

Buerbaum, Jozef. *Gedenkschriften door Janus Droogstoppel uit den Duitschen bezettingstijd 1914–1918.* 3 vols. Antwerp: Buerbaum-Vander Goten, n.d., 1921.

Charriaut, Henri. *La Belgique Moderne: Terre d'Expériences.* Paris: Flammarion, 1910.

Debruyne, Emmanuel, and Laurence Van Ypersele. *Je serai fusillé demain. Les dernières lettres des patriotes belges et français fusillés par l'occupant 1914–1918.* Brussels: Racine, 2011.

Debruyne, Emmanuel. ""Véridiques, antiprussiens et patriotes". Les journaux prohibés en pays occupé. 1914–1918." In *La résistance en France et en Belgique occupées (1914–1918),* edited by R. Vandenbussche, 77–97. Villeneuve d'Ascq: CEGES-IRHiS, 2012.

De Keyser, Bart, and Myriam Lipkens. *Drukkend Hasselt.* Hasselt: Stedelijk Museum Stellingwerff-Waerdenhof, 2003.

Delandsheere, Paul. *La 'Libre Belgique'. Histoire des origines de la 'Libre Belgique' clandestine.* Brussels: Albert Dewit, 1919.

De Moor, Vincent (abbé), writing as 'Lieutenant Marcel', *Mes aventures et le mystère de la 'Libre Belgique'*. Brussels/Paris: Vromant, 1919.

De Schaepdrijver, Sophie. "Occupation, Propaganda, and the Idea of Belgium." In *European Culture in the Great War: The Arts, Entertainment, and Propaganda, 1914–1918*, edited by Aviel Roshwald, and Richard Stites, 267–94. Cambridge: Cambridge University Press, 1999.

De Schaepdrijver, Sophie. "L'Europe occupée en 1915: entre violence et exploitation." In *Vers la guerre totale: le tournant de 1914–1915*, edited by John Horne, 121–52. Paris: Tallandier, 2010.

De Schaepdrijver, Sophie. "Belgium." In *A Companion to the World War I*, edited by John Horne, 386–402. London: (*Blackwell Companions to World History* series) Wiley-Blackwell, 2010.

De Schaepdrijver, Sophie. ""That Theory of Races": Henri Pirenne on the Unfinished Business of the Great War." *Revue Belge d'Histoire Contemporaine* XLI (2011): 3–4, 533–52.

Dreyer, Michael, and Oliver Lembcke. *Die deutsche Diskussion um die Kriegsschuldfrage 1918/19*. Berlin: Duncker & Humblot, 1993.

The German Police System as Applied to Military Security in War. Great Britain, War Office, General Staff, 1921. (Copy from Durham Constabulary Library, with thanks to Clive Emsley and Benoît Majerus.).

Gille, Louis, Alphonse Ooms, and Paul Delandsheere. *Cinquante mois d'occupation allemande*. 4 vols. Brussels: Albert Dewit, 1919.

Goemaere, Pierre ('Istoricos'). *Histoire de la Libre Belgique clandestine*. Brussels: La Libre Belgique, n.d., 1919, two editions.

Graves, Robert. *Goodbye to All That: An Autobiography*. London: Penguin, [1929] 1960.

Gumz, Jonathan. *The Resurrection and Collapse of Empire in Habsburg Serbia, 1914–1918*. Cambridge: Cambridge University Press, 2009.

Horne, John. "Introduction: mobilizing for "total war", 1914–1918." In *State, Society and Mobilization in Europe during the First World War*, edited by John Horne, 1–18. Cambridge: Cambridge University Press, 1997.

Horne, John, and Alan Kramer. *German Atrocities 1914: A History of Denial*. New Haven: Yale University Press, 2001.

Huberich, Charles Henry, and Nicol-Speyer, Alexander, eds. *Deutsche Gesetzgebung für die Okkupierten Gebiete Belgiens*. 21 vols. The Hague: Nijhoff, 1915–1919.

Hull, Isabel V. *Absolute Destruction. Military Culture and the Practices of War in Imperial Germany*. Ithaca/London: Cornell University Press, 2005.

Kirschen, Sadi. *Devant les conseils de guerre allemands*. Brussels: Rossel & Fils, 1919.

Knezevic, Jovana. "The Austro-Hungarian Occupation of Belgrade during the First World War: Battles on the Home Front." PhD diss., Yale University, 2006.

Liulevicius, Vejas Gabriel. *War Land on the Eastern Front: Culture, National Identity and German Occupation in World War I*. Cambridge: Cambridge University Press, 2000.

Luchins, Abraham S., and Edith H. Luchins. "Kurt Grelling: Steadfast Scholar in an Age of Madness." *Gestalt Theory* 22 (4/2000): 228–281, An expanded version of this article is available online at http://gestalttheory.net/archive/kgbio.html (accessed 7 April, 2012).

Massart, Jean. *La presse clandestine dans la Belgique occupée*. Paris/Nancy: Berger-Levrault, 1917.

Millard, Oscar E. *Uncensored: The True Story of the Clandestine Newspaper 'La Libre Belgique'*. London: Robert Hale, 1937.

Mitrovic, Andrej. *Serbia's Great War, 1914–1918*. London: Hurst, 2007.

Nabulsi, Karma. *Traditions of War: Occupation, Resistance, and the Law*. Oxford: Oxford University Press, 1999.

Nyst, Ray. *Malgré tout! Complément et examen des débats du procès du journal 'La Belgique'*. Brussels: self-published, n.d., 1920.

Orsi, Robert Anthony. *The Madonna of 115th Street: Faith and Community in Italian Harlem, 1880–1950*. New Haven, CT: Yale University Press, 1985.

Pirenne, Jacques, and Maurice Vauthier. *La législation et l'administration allemandes en Belgique*. Paris: Les Presses Universitaires de France, New Haven, CT: Yale University Press n.d., 1925.

Stengers, Jean. "Le rôle de la Commission d'enquête de 1904–1905 au Congo." In *Mélanges Henri Grégoire. Annuaire de l'Institut de Philologie et d'Histoire Orientales et Slaves* X (1950): 701–26.

Stengers, Jean, and Éliane Gubin. *Histoire du sentiment national en Belgique des origines à 1918, Volume 2: Le grand siècle de la nationalité belge, de 1830 à 1918*. Brussels: Racine, 2002.

Tytgat, Charles. *Bruxelles sous la botte allemande. (De la déclaration de la guerre de la Roumanie à la délivrance.) Journal d'un journaliste*. Brussels: Charles Bulens, 1919.

Van De Kerckhove, Albert('Fidelis'). *L'histoire merveilleuse de la Libre Belgique. Préface de Son Excellence M. Brand Whitlock, Ministre des États-Unis à Bruxelles*, 2nd ed. Paris: Plon-Brussels: Albert Dewit, 1919.

Van Den Dungen, Pierre. "Les milieux de presse bruxellois pendant la Grande Guerre." *Les Cahiers de La Fonderie, 32* (theme issue *Bruxelles en 14–18: La Guerre au Quotidien*) (2005): 15–20.

Van Doren, Eugène. *Les tribulations du 'manager' de la Libre Belgique clandestine, 1914–1918*. Brussels: L'Édition Universelle, 1947.

Van Ypersele, Laurence, and Emmanuel Debruyne. *De la guerre de l'ombre aux ombres de la guerre. L'espionnage en Belgique pendant la guerre de 1914–1918. Histoire et mémoire*. Brussels: Labor, 2004.

Von Köhler, Ludwig. *Die Staatsverwaltung der besetzten Gebiete, Volume I: Belgien*. Stuttgart: Deutsche Verlags-Anstalt, 1927.

Whitlock, Brand. *The letters and journal of Brand Whitlock*, edited by Allan Nevins. 2 vols. New York/London: D. Appleton-Century Company, 1936.

Between recruitment and forced labour: the radicalization of German labour policy in occupied Belgium and northern France

Jens Thiel

Institut für Geschichtswissenschaften, Humboldt-Universität zu Berlin, Germany

Translated from the German by Sophie De Schaepdrijver

The deportation and forced labour of Belgian and northern French civilians in the fall and winter of 1916/1917 is one of the darkest chapters of the history of the German occupation regime behind the Western Front. The forced conscription of civilian labourers was part and parcel of the radicalization of labour policies in the occupied Eastern and Western territories – albeit a radicalization which was subsequently rescinded. Only the exceptional circumstances of war explain this shift from a labour policy centred on voluntary enrolment to ever-more coercive practices. The forced mobilization of civilian labour in the occupied territories, but also its failure, can be interpreted in the context of the First World War's 'totalizing' tendencies.

1. Preliminary remarks

'Poor little Belgium' had been a trope in world public opinion since the start of the war. The German armies' invasion of a small, neutral neighbouring state – a violation of international law – and the imposition of an occupation regime allowed Entente propaganda to portray the German enemy's conduct of the war and policies of occupation as exceptionally brutal and inhumane. The theme of Belgian civilians' fate at the hand of the Germans loomed especially large.[1] By the fall of 1916, just as the campaign around the 'German Atrocities' of the summer of 1914[2] and the solidarity drive with the occupied Belgians had somewhat flagged, indignation reached new heights. In that season, the German military and civilian authorities started to deport Belgian and northern French workers, both employed and unemployed, to forced labour in Germany or behind the Western Front, which raised a worldwide storm of outrage. Not just in Entente states – sharp protests were voiced in neutral countries as well. The measures came in for blame even in Germany. It should be noted that indignation centred mainly on forced labour in the West, not so much on similar measures in the occupied East.[3] Forced labour under the German occupation regime in Romania in 1917/1918 – now uncovered by new scholarship – went practically unnoticed.[4]

For all the outrage, there was actually nothing exceptional about the deportations of French and Belgian workers. Forced labour and deportation have been part of the history of war, and for that matter also of peacetime, through millennia.[5] The era of the world wars, admittedly, constitutes a particularly low point in this long history, but nothing indicates that forced labour and deportation will disappear any time soon.[6]

A further preliminary remark is in order. The deportations of workers in Belgium and France from 1916 were strictly deportations for the purpose of forced labour; they were not meant to redraw the map. Plans to forcibly and permanently evacuate entire ethnic or social groups barely figured in the occupation policies of 1914–1918 in Belgium and France.

By way of further clarification, we should note that German labour policies in the occupied territories during the First World War were influenced by three main elements. The first one was the German Empire's existing policy of recruitment of foreign labourers, which up to the outbreak of the war was limited mainly to the hiring of agricultural seasonal labourers from Russian Poland.[7] The second one were German colonial experiences with 'foreign' labour – even if their importance should probably not be overestimated.[8] The third one was the war itself, which, from its outbreak, had presented the military, economic interests, the state and the administration with unfamiliar problems and challenges.

For reasons of space, it is impossible to describe this context in detail here, but it is important to highlight two dimensions. The first is that of the new experience of administering conquered territories in the West and the East, and especially of maximizing all available resources, including labour. The second is constituted by developments on the Home Front, where, as some scholars have argued, an incipient 'totalization' took place,[9] especially after the takeover of Supreme Army Command by Paul von Hindenburg and Erich Ludendorff in September 1916. But the hubris of the first months – manifested in the so-called 'Hindenburg Program' – soon yielded to more sober perspectives, which allowed for a return to a wartime 'normalcy' of sorts. This shift away from radicalization impacted labour policies as well. As a result, deportation and forced labour were partially rescinded in the occupied territories, while in Germany, far-reaching plans for the regimentation of German workers were effectively abandoned. In both cases, civilian 'total mobilization' in the service of warfare proved to be a failed conceit.

One additional remark: the imposition of forced labour on foreign workers during the First World War was not a German specialty, in contrast to statements made in Entente propaganda (and occasionally in scholarship today). Germany's allies, the Habsburg Empire, Bulgaria and the Ottoman Empire, coerced civilians into labour as well, both in the territories they occupied and vis-à-vis allegedly hostile national minorities on their soil. The recruitment of civilian labourers in Habsburg military occupation regimes in Italy, Albania, Rumania, Montenegro and Serbia, for example, bore definite coercive elements.[10] In Bulgarian-occupied Vardar-Macedonia, civilians were deported for forced labour.[11] In the Ottoman Empire, Turkish military authorities aligned Armenians, Greeks and Syrian Christians into 'Workers' Batallions' of an estimated 25,000–50,000 people, deployed in constructing military infrastructure.[12] In the Entente, at least in France and the UK, foreign labourers were not coerced to work. These states did not have an occupied labour reservoir at their disposal. Like all belligerents, they put prisoners of war to work, but this was in accordance with international law. Whatever the arguments of German propaganda, or of some Flemish nationalists, neither the regime imposed on interned German civilians by the Entente nor the recruitment of free Belgian workers in France or the UK was at all comparable to the labour coercion inflicted on Belgian civilians. Like the labour required of prisoners of war, these measures were in accordance with international law and, as in the case of Belgians working in England, with customary national arrangements.[13] In the UK and France, the response to labour shortages was a reliance on domestic labour reservoirs, foreign labour, especially from colonies and other overseas suppliers such as China[14] and of course prisoners of war.[15] One exception among Entente states was tsarist Russia, which inflicted forced labour on civilians in occupied Galicia. This is an as-yet underexplored episode.[16] Moreover, in general, the recruitment of free or coerced 'foreign' labour during the First World War needs a more systematic analysis that is able to map out the differences, but also the similarities between the various labour regimes, and bring into sharper focus the 'grey areas' where coerced labour shaded into free contractual labour.[17]

2.   German labour policies up to the start of the 'Belgian deportations' in the fall of 1916

From the summer of 1914, when Germany invaded and occupied most of Belgium and established a civilian administration in the new Belgian Government-General, the question of what to do about the mass of Belgian workers and unemployed had stood at the centre of German occupation policies. The problem of feeding the unemployed was largely resolved with the help of the US-led 'Commission for Relief in Belgium' with its Belgian pendant, the 'Comité National'. But the German civilian administration could not diminish the mass of unemployed, which soon rose to half a million people in the Government-General. Apart from food and economic issues, the workers' question also touched on other realms of policy, such as the Flemish and the social question. Social policy plans, such as the promise to introduce social and labour protection legislation after the German example, were means to at least rhetorically co-opt the Belgian working class, which was seen as a potential threat. In addition, German business lobbies hoped that heightened social costs would permanently diminish the global competitive power of the Belgian economy, or, in the best of cases, even spell the end altogether of unfair competition from laissez-faire Belgium.[18]

But the main goal of German labour policies in occupied Belgium and northern France was the recruitment of as many workers as possible, both for the German war economy and for the immediate needs of the army and of the military administrations in the front areas (*Operationsgebiet*) and the staging areas close behind the front (*Etappengebiet*), both of which, unlike the Government-General, were under exclusive military rule. However, the initial recruitment policy – complemented with the not-quite-voluntary enrolment of civilians in so-called emergency public relief works (*Notstandsarbeiten*) – was not very successful. In the German war economy, acute and ever-increasing labour shortages had been palpable as early as the fall of 1914. Military mobilization had severely diminished the workforce in industry and agriculture, as well as in small businesses and handicrafts, a state of things further aggravated by the shift to armaments production. Neither the use of prisoners of war[19] nor the increased employment of women and young workers[20] could resolve these shortages. Inevitably, to decision makers in the military, the state and the war economy, the occupied territories in East and West loomed ever larger as potential labour recruitment areas. The vast mass of skilled workers in Belgium rendered unemployed by the war was especially coveted by leaders in the neighbouring western German mining and heavy industries. Belgium appeared to be one vast, wide-open reservoir of labour, indeed a 'basin of people', as the industrialist Carl Duisberg rather cynically called it – the ultimate solution to the German labour problem.[21] The fact that Belgium appeared in this light midway through the war shows how the war had inflected German labour policies: before 1914, Belgian workers had barely figured in German industry and agriculture. Most foreign labourers in imperial Germany, employed mainly on eastern estates or in West German factories and mines, had come from Russian Poland; a smaller percentage came from Italy or the Netherlands.[22] Before the war, there had been few Belgian workers in Germany, some 8000 of them in 1910–1914. The emerging West German glass and mirror industries had been especially keen to hire them. But attempts to recruit Flemish seasonal workers for German agriculture had failed.[23]

In spite of scattered elements of coercion, and a wide-ranging system of restrictions imposed on the seasonal workers from Russian Poland, there was not, strictly speaking, a system of forced labour in place before 1914. But this changed as soon as the war started. A newly established system of forced labour was inflicted on prisoners of war and approximately 300,000 Russian–Polish seasonal workers who were in Germany to bring in the harvest as the war broke out. They were forbidden to return and to change workplaces or residences.[24] Moreover, they suffered from dismal work and living conditions and discriminatory rules.[25] Business interests and the government put pressure on the relevant military authorities to gradually eliminate existing limitations on recruitment of foreign workers. Before long, the army itself became active. In March 1915, the Prussian War Ministry approached the Governor-General in Brussels, Moritz von Bissing, with demands to recruit voluntary workers in Belgium. Weeks earlier, that same ministry had been able to prevent Rhenish–Westphalian industrialists from attempting to recruit workers in Belgium on their own initiative. However, those recruitment efforts had failed for other reasons as well: the region-wide infrastructure needed for such a systematic hiring drive was lacking. In order to recruit workers in Belgium more efficiently, several industrialists pursued a closer cooperation with the Governor-General and his civilian administration. And so, by 19 June 1915, at a joint meeting in Brussels between the Governor-General's economic department and the 'German economic board for Belgium', which was dominated by Rhenish–Westphalian industrialists, the recruitment of labour was the main subject of discussion. Representatives of the most important German businesses, the main decision makers in the Government-General and top administrators in the imperial government all agreed that many more workers had to be recruited from Belgium. All agreed, too, that such recruitment, as yet, had to proceed along voluntary lines; open means of coercion were explicitly rejected.[26] One of the meeting's outcomes was the assignment of a more central role to the 'German Industrial Office' in Brussels (*Deutsches Industriebüro*, or DIB), a lobby and recruitment agency created by the northwestern branch of the 'Association of German Iron and Steel Industrialists'. The DIB recruited German workers, albeit initially for the Rhenish–Westphalian heavy industry only. A private institution, it cooperated closely if not always smoothly with the civilian administration in Brussels. After the June 1915 meeting, the DIB was given the monopoly of recruitment of workers in the Government-General. However, it was barred, by and large, from recruiting in the Belgian and French operations and staging areas. In these areas, the Supreme Command and/or the general commands of the separate armies had exclusive authority over the allocation of labour. From the summer of 1915, a fine-meshed net of DIB recruitment offices covered the entire Government-General. Yet, by the fall of 1916, in spite of vast improvements in organization and the logistic support of the civilian administration, the achievements of the DIB were meagre. No more than about 500 people, on average, could be sent to Germany every week; by the end of October, only 30,000 workers had been recruited altogether.[27]

Until the fall of 1916, coercive labour measures – other than the *de facto* coercion of material misery – remained rare in Belgium, although they were mentioned: on 15 August 1915, the Governor-General issued an 'Ordnance against the Reluctance to Work' (literally, against *Arbeitsscheu*, 'work-shyness') to threaten workers with coercion if they refused certain jobs or tasks. In this manner, the German civilian administration had already established the notion of labour coercion.[28] However, actual coercive measures had remained restricted to small groups of workers, or the personnel of specific enterprises such as the railways, which were now under German military control. An all-encompassing coercive policy, then, did not exist yet in the Belgian Government-General until the fall of 1916. But such a policy had been introduced already in the northern French staging area (*Etappe*), which was under exclusive military control. At Easter in 1916, some 20,000 women and girls, especially from the industrial towns of Lille, Roubaix and Tourcoing, had been brutally assembled by German soldiers and officers, and carried off to do agricultural labour in the region.[29] These deportations to forced labour foreshadowed the region-wide deportations of the fall of 1916, which would strike almost the entire Belgian Government-General as well as the Belgian and French operations and staging areas.

3. The deportations to forced labour in Belgium and northern France, 1916–1918

The decisive impulse to forcibly deport Belgian workers en masse to Germany dates from March 1916. It came from the Prussian War Ministry, under direct pressure from Rhenish–Westphalian industrialists. The German civilian administration in Belgium at first opposed these plans. Governor-General von Bissing suggested instead to resolve the problem of the workers and unemployed by assigning Belgium a larger amount of war-economy orders; but his suggestion was hardly popular with German war businesses, which feared competition. Von Bissing's position was determined by two motives: first, his patriarchal self-definition as the 'leader' of a country entrusted to his care; second, his scheme to durably attach the occupied country to the German Empire, which meant securing German authority by treating the population as 'sensibly' as possible.

In following months, the option of coercing workers steadily gained ground. In May 1916, the Governor-General and the civilian administration were able once more to reject demands for 'forcible recruitment' of Belgian workers. However, as a concession to demands for harsher measures, von Bissing on 15 May 1916 issued a revised 'Ordnance against the Reluctance to Work', which was sharper in its formulation and goals: from now on, refusal to accept a job would be punished by 'forcible removal' to the German Empire.[30] After the takeover of Supreme Army Command by Hindenburg and Ludendorff, the champions of coercive measures in Belgium gained the upper hand for the first time. The unrealistic goals of the so-called 'Hindenburg Program', which aimed at the complete mobilization of German resources under government control, required a vastly expanded work force: women, young workers, prisoners of war and especially workers from the occupied territories in East and West. As shown, for instance, during the discussions in the *Reichstag* on 5 December 1916, when the 'Auxiliary Service Law' (*Hilfsdienstgesetz*) was passed, the army leadership was wagering especially on coercion of workers – including German civilians. The army leadership had to abandon the latter scheme in the face of opposition from German labour unions, the Social Democratic Party and the imperial government, but managed to impose its demand for forcible recruitment of 'enemy foreigners' from the occupied territories on the civilian administration in Belgium and on the imperial government. The army leadership was massively supported, even spurred on, by several influential industrialists. Carl Duisberg, Alfred Hugenberg, Hugo Stinnes and Walther Rathenau, to name only these men, considered the deportation of the approximately half a million Belgian unemployed to be a way – perhaps even the *only possible* way – to resolve the labour shortage problem in Germany for the duration of the war.[31]

On 3 October 1916, the army leadership issued ordnances generalizing coercive labour, at first in the Belgian and French operations and staging areas (*Operationsgebiet* and *Etappengebiet*, respectively) that were under its direct control. The forcibly recruited workers (both employed and unemployed) were allocated to so-called 'Civil Workers'

Batallions' (*Zivil-Arbeiter-Bataillone* [ZAB]). The workers in these batallions were formally considered to be civilian prisoners; they stood under military control, had to wear specific brassards and were, usually, housed in small camps.[32] Their working and living conditions were abysmal, as even the Flemish 'activists' who cooperated with the German authorities shamefacedly had to admit after a tour of inspection.[33] Altogether some 62,000 Belgian and northern French civilian workers were forced into the ZAB. Harsh conditions, brutal treatment, illnesses and undernourishment led to high mortality rates during deployment – one source mentions 1056 dead, another 1298, not counting those who were sent home to die.[34] In the Belgian Government-General, the deportations of workers started on the 26 October 1916. The selection of deportees was left to local military commanders. Arbitrary local decisions led to numerous encroachments even on the limits set by the ordnance: many employed men were taken as well. Workers were herded together for inspection; those selected for deportation were held under military guard for hours or days, before being transported by rail, often in unheated cattle cars, to Germany. Witnesses' descriptions of the scenes – the families left behind, the deportees' woefully inadequate food and clothing and the dismal weather – paint a picture of despair.[35] Even German witnesses were struck by the sheer brutality of the proceedings. Altogether 60,000 Belgian civilians were deported to forced labour in Germany between 26 October 1916, when the deportations started, and February 1917, when they were effectively stopped. In Germany, the deportees were initially housed in 'distribution centers' and 'industrial laborers' lodgings' – names deliberately chosen to avoid the term 'concentration camps', which by then had already acquired a pejorative connotation.[36] The hastily constructed camps were brutally run, chaotically organized, ill-equipped, unsanitary and insufficiently approvisioned. Hunger and disease were rife. As with the ZAB prisoners, mortality was high.[37] An estimated 900 Belgian labour deportees, at the very least, died in the camps or at their places of coerced work.[38] It should be noted that the mistreatment of Belgian workers was not just a result of the improvised and chaotic preparation of the deportations. There was method to the brutality. The 'basic rules' for the treatment of Belgian deportees, laid down by the Prussian War Ministry in December 1916, were revealing enough: 'Conditions in the distribution centers must compel all to sign a labor contract. (...) Stern discipline and forcible employment at the distribution center itself must compel every Belgian to consider any chance at well-paid work outside of the distribution center to be an improvement in his situation'.[39]

As mentioned at the start of this article, the 'Belgian deportations' met with vehement criticism both internationally and domestically. In Germany, both Social Democratic fractions, as well as the Catholic Centre Party (*Zentrumspartei*), raised objections. Representatives from other parties, too, criticized the measures in the Reichstag, both in the general assembly and in the Main Committee. But no clear and official protest was voiced. The 'liberal imperialist' representatives found fault with the deportations mainly because of – justified – fears of a negative impact on relations with the USA. Many in the civilian administration in the Government-General thought the deportations a mistake, though others, like the expressionist poet Gottfried Benn, who was stationed in Brussels as a military physician, applauded the measure. Among Belgians, the deportations elicited the expected storm of outrage. Cardinal Mercier, the charismatic Primate of the Catholic church in Belgium, condemned them in vehement terms. A vast array of associations, professional unions, political organizations and parties, and a great many individual citizens wrote letters of protest to the Governor-General. The Belgian government-in-exile in Le Havre (France) set up a protest campaign abroad. In Entente states and in many neutral nations, public opinion was swayed anew by sympathy with the Belgians' plight and condemnation of the new misdeeds of 'Prussian-German militarism'. The as-yet-neutral USA played a particularly important role: the 'Belgian deportations' together with unlimited submarine warfare decisively influenced a shift in US public opinion towards entering the war on the Entente side.[40]

By January 1917, it was clear that the coercive measures inflicted on Belgian workers fell short of high expectations. The German war economy still suffered a shortage of labour. Barely one out of four deportees had ended up signing a regular work contract. German businesses found their work unsatisfactory and lost interest in Belgian forced labour.[41] After renewed pleas to end the deportations from the Government-General, the Imperial Chancellor, the Foreign Ministry, the Ministry of the Interior, the Minister-President of Bavaria and several Reichstag representatives, the Prussian War Ministry and Supreme Army Command finally gave in. Following some rocky negotiations, an imperial decree of 14 March 1917 suspended the deportations from the Government-General, though not to forced labour. On 5 June 1917, the Prussian War Ministry decreed a 'complete halt' to forced labour. The 20,000–25,000 deportees still in Germany at that time were sent home in the summer.[42] (Those who had signed a work contract received the status of 'free enemy foreigners', which was legally equivalent to that of the Belgian workers recruited by the DIB.) But in the militarily ruled operations and staging areas of Belgium and France, forced labour continued until the end of the war.[43]

4. Further developments and end result

After the 'Belgian deportations' debacle, German labour policies in the Belgian Government-General reverted to recruitment – if in an intensified manner. The total number of Belgian workers recruited for the German war economy rose to 160,000 by the end of the war, as against a mere 22,000 at the start of the deportations.[44] This remarkable rise was due, on the one hand, to the fear of new coercive measures and to the systematic and deliberate crippling of large swaths of the Belgian economy, which further depleted employment; and, on the other hand, to enticements such as higher sign-up bonuses, financial and material support for workers' families and other advantages.[45]

At war's end, employment of Belgian workers in Germany ground to an immediate halt. Wartime projects for the permanent recourse to Belgian workers in peacetime went nowhere. Plans hatched by *völkisch* politicians and writers together with Flemish nationalists to channel the traditional movement of Flemish migrant workers from France to Germany were equally fruitless.[46] The vehement political, juridical and journalistic confrontations over the 'Belgian deportations' cast a long shadow over Belgian–German relations in the post-war era. Soon after the end of the war, Belgium and France demanded the extradition and punishment of those responsible. Administrators, soldiers and officers, as well as the emperor, were called to justice for the deportations and forced labour, which were declared war crimes by the Paris Peace Treaty. The prosecution, entrusted to the Imperial court in Leipzig, was a dead end. In the 1920s, Belgian courts condemned some German offenders, sometimes in absentia, in some cases to long prison sentences.[47]

Apart from the drawn-out juridical handling of the deportation issue, and the endless discussions over compensation for Belgian workers, the matter was also processed by parliamentary investigations committees in both countries. The Belgian committee defined the deportations as war crimes in a 1923 comprehensive report.[48] By contrast, the German committee, which met in 1925–1926, limited itself to discussing whether the deportations had been in accordance with international law so as to minimize all possible references to German responsibility, which would lay the Weimar Republic open to compensations claims.[49] When the Reichstag, in 1927, debated the committee's final report, its unsatisfactory achievement was sharply criticized by left-wing delegates, especially Communists. In Belgium, public opinion and the government were dismayed by what were seen as inappropriate German attempts at justification.[50]

One of the most interesting but also hardest questions about deportation and forced labour during the First World War is whether these practices served as an 'example' to measures enacted during the Second World War. Historians such as Ulrich Herbert have aptly defined the link between the two in terms such as 'learning process', 'try-out' and 'susceptibility'.[51] But to what extent the forced labour measures inflicted on Belgian and Polish workers during the First World War served as a template to the Third Reich has remained an open question, even in the newer scholarship that treats the German occupation regime in Belgium from the perspective of violence and through the lens of continuities from the colonial to the Nazi era, or from the more precise point of view of military culture.[52]

But it is clear, at the very least, that the coercive labour measures enacted in Belgium and France during the First World War constituted a crucial, unquestioned background of experience for agents of the Second World War. This is especially obvious in the case of labour policies, even if the empirical evidence is harder to find than one would think – precisely because the earlier experience was considered so self-evidently familiar. Documents show that when coercive labour was introduced in Nazi-occupied Belgium, the experiences of the preceding war were considered sufficiently known as to require no further discussion.[53] Having said this, even the scant references evince a very critical appraisal of the experiences of the First World War; especially at the start of Belgium's second occupation in 1940, they were seen as an example of how *not* to conduct German occupation policies. However, just as in the First World War, the issue soon took on a dynamic of its own that left initial objections in the dust. A ruthlessly exploitative labour policy prevailed, in Belgium as (to an immeasurably harsher extent) elsewhere: from 1942, the German occupation authorities in Belgium gradually introduced a system of coercive labour through compulsory service, forcible recruitment and deportation.[54] It was as ineffectual as its predecessor.

Notes

1. Fundamental references regarding occupied Belgium and France are De Schaepdrijver, *La Belgique*, Becker, *Oubliés*, Becker, *Les cicatrices rouges* and McPhail, *Long Silence*. Regarding deportations and forced labour, Thiel, *Menschenbassin* (with further bibliographic references).
2. See Horne and Kramer, *German Atrocities*; Lipkes, *Rehearsals*.
3. See Westerhoff's contribution to this volume.
4. Mayerhofer, *Zwischen Freund und Feind*, 257–72.
5. The subject of a recent colloquium of the 'Arbeitskreis Militärgeschichte', organized by Kerstin von Lingen and Klaus Gestwa under the title 'Zwangsarbeit als Kriegswaffe' (Forced Labor as a Weapon of War). For a review of the colloquium (the Acta are in progress), see http://hsozkult.geschichte.hu-berlin.de/tagungsberichte/id=3848. See also the graduate seminar, held at Trier University from 2003 to 2010, under the title 'Sklaverei – Knechtschaft und Frondienst – Zwangsarbeit. Unfreie Arbeits- und Lebensformen von der Antike bis um 20. Jahrhundert' (Slavery – Servitude and Conscription – Forced Labor. Unfree Work and Existence from Antiquity to the Twentieth Century). For an overview, see especially Herrmann-Otto (ed.), *Unfreie Arbeits- und Lebensverhältnisse*.
6. For a definition, see Thiel, *Menschenbassin Belgien*, 22–36.
7. An overview, a.o., in Bade, *Preußengänger*; Nichtweiß, *Saisonarbeiter*.
8. For recent discussions on colonial forced labour, see Kreienbaum, *Rolle der Zwangsarbeit*.
9. Conceptually, see Chickering, *Total War*. On the Belgian case, Jaumain a.o., *Guerre totale*.

10. Scheer, *Zwischen Front und Heimat*, 150–8. Further references in Westerhoff, *Zwangsarbeit im Ersten Weltkrieg*, 345ff.
11. Opfer, *Schatten des Krieges*, 114–29.
12. Zürcher, *Ottoman Labour Batallions*; Hovannisian, *Greek Labor Batallions*.
13. Starling and Lee, *No Labour, No Battle*. On employment of Belgian refugees, see also Amara, *Belges à l'épreuve de l'Exil*.
14. Summerskill, *China on the Western Front*; Xu, *Strangers on the Western Front*.
15. A comparative perspective in Jones, *Violence*, 121–251. For contribution of German prisoners of war in French war economy see Médard, *Prisonniers*, 53–68.
16. Sanborn, *Unsettling the Empire*, 315–20.
17. First considerations: Proctor, Civilians, 40–75.
18. Karl Bittmann: *Beiträge zur Frage: Welche Bedeutung würde die Einführung der deutschen Sozialgesetzgebung in Belgien für die Wettbewerbsfähigkeit der belgischen Industrie auf dem Weltmarkt haben? Denkschrift im Auftrage des Generalgouverneurs in Belgien, Generaloberst von Bissing*, Berlin 1916. Bundesarchiv Berlin (BAB), R 1501,119.565, Bl. 4
19. Hinz, *Gefangen*, 248–318; Rawe, *Ausländerbeschäftigung*, 69–154; Oltmer, *Unentbehrliche Arbeitskräfte*.
20. Daniel, *Arbeiterfrauen*, remains the fundamental reference.
21. *Protokoll der Verhandlungen im Kaisersaal des Kgl. Preuß. Kriegsministeriums am 16. September 1916, vormittags 11 Uhr*, Geheimes Staatsarchiv Preußischer Kulturbesitz Berlin PK (GHStA PK), I. HA, Rep. 120, BB VII, 1, Nr. 3f, Bd. 15, Bl. 183–201.
22. Before 1914, some 500,000 seasonal agricultural laborers and some 700,000 foreign industrial and mining workers were employed in Germany. For an overview, see Bade, *Deutsche im Ausland*, 295–332; Herbert: 13–127.
23. Thiel, *Belgische Arbeitskräfte für die deutsche Wirtschaft*, 200–6.
24. Elsner, *Ausländerbeschäftigung und Zwangsarbeitspolitik*; Oltmer, *Zwangsmigration und Zwangsarbeit*.
25. As did the several thousand Eastern Jewish workers who were recruited for the German war economy. See Heid, *Maloche*.
26. *Protokoll der Ersten Sitzung des Deutschen Wirtschaftsausschusses für Belgien vom 19. Juni 1915*. BAB, N 2181, 157.
27. Thiel, *Menschenbassin*, 68–79.
28. Verordnung gegen die Arbeitsscheu", 15.5.1915, *Gesetz- und Verordnungsblatt* No. 108, 22.8.1915. Reprint in: Huberich/Nicol-Speyer, *Gesetzgebung*, Vol. IV, 161ff.
29. Becker, *Life in an Occupied Zone*.
30. "Verordnung gegen die Arbeitsscheu", *Gesetz- und Verordnungsblatt* No. 213, 20.5.1916. Reprint in: Huberich/Nicol-Speyer, *Gesetzgebung*, Vol. VII, 290.
31. Thiel, *Menschenbassin*, 103–122.
32. Thiel, *Menschenbassin*, 123–32.
33. *Auszüge aus dem Bericht der Vertrauensleute des Rates von Flandern über eine Besichtigungsreise nach den nordfranzösischen Arbeiterlagern Aulnoye, Le Nouvion und Tournes zum Besuche der dort untergebrachten flämischen Zwangsarbeiter vom 4. bis 6. Oktober*. Bundesarchiv Koblenz (BAK), N 2022, 18. Reprint in: Ligue National Pour l'Unité Belge, *Archives du Conseil des Flandres*, 330–2.
34. Figures assembled by the Imperial Compensation Committee (Reichsentschädigungskommission) of the Imperial Ministry for Reconstruction, Department Belgian War Damages (Kriegsschäden Belgien), Part V, 50. BAB, R 3301 (the former R 38), Nr. 266. See also *Völkerrecht im Weltkrieg*, 375, and Passelecq, *Déportation et travail forcé*, 398ff.
35. Thiel, *Menschenbassin*, 140–7; Roolf, *Deportationen*.
36. Covering letter, instruction from the Prussian War Ministry, War Office (Kriegsamt), Nr. 893/10.16 AZ(S), November 15, 1916. Bayerisches Hauptstaatsarchiv (BayHSt), IV, MKr 14208.
37. Thiel and Westerhoff, *Zwangsarbeiterlager*.
38. The Imperial Compensation Committee calculated a total of 1250 dead; the official Belgian envoy, Fernand Passelecq, gave a total of 1316. Passelecq, *Déportation et travail forcé*, 398ff., see also *Völkerrecht im Weltkrieg*, 375.
39. *Völkerrecht im Weltkrieg*, 243.
40. On these protestations, see Thiel, *Menschenbassin*, 176–237.
41. Thiel, *Menschenbassin*, 163–8.

MILITARY OCCUPATIONS IN FIRST WORLD WAR EUROPE

42. Instruction from the Prussian War Ministry, War Office (Kriegsamt), Kriegsersatz- und Arbeiterdepartement, Nr. 54/6.17 A.Z.(S.), 5.6.1917. BAB, R 1501, 119.389. See on this Thiel, *Menschenbassin*, 156–62.
43. Thiel, *Menschenbassin*, 159ff.
44. It is impossible to precisely assess how many workers were recruited by the DIB, because the documentation is incomplete and some workers were counted more than once. Wilhelm Asmis. *Nutzbarmachung belgischer Arbeitskräfte für die deutsche Volkswirtschaft nach dem Kriege* [Memorandum], 105. BAB, R 1501, 113.718; see also the data assembled by the Imperial Compensation Committee (Reichsentschädigungskommission) of the Imperial Ministry for Reconstruction, Department Belgian War Damages (Kriegsschäden Belgien), Part V, BAB, R 3301 (the former R 38), 266.
45. Thiel, *Menschenbassin*, 239–47.
46. Thiel, *Menschenbassin*, 266–75.
47. Thiel, *Menschenbassin*, 296–302; on the Leipzig trials, see also Hankel, *Leipziger Prozesse*; Wiggenhorn, *Verliererjustiz*.
48. Commission d'Enquête, *Rapports et documents*.
49. For war guilt discussion see Heinemann, *Verdrängte Niederlage*.
50. *Völkerrecht im Weltkrieg*; Thiel, *Menschenbassin*, 311–16.
51. See esp. Herbert, *Zwangsarbeit als Lernprozeß*; Herbert, *Fremdarbeiter*, 24–35.
52. Zuckerman, *Rape of Belgium*, 142–64; Hull, *Absolute Destruction*, 233–42; Kramer, *Dynamic of Destruction*, 43–5.
53. Militärbefehlshaber Belgien/Nordfrankreich, Militärverwaltungschef, Abt. Wirtschaft. Belgiens Leistungen für die deutsche Kriegswirtschaft und Kriegsführung (Stand Januar 1942), BAB, Bestandsergänzungsfilm 10516.
54. Haupt, *Arbeitseinsatz*; Selleslagh, *Tewerkstelling*; Thiel, *Menschenbassin*, 319–28.

References

Unpublished sources

Bayerisches Hauptstaatsarchiv München. Abt. IV, Kriegsarchiv (BayHStA IV), M Kr 14208.
Bundesarchiv Berlin (BAB). R 1501, 113.718; 119.565; R 3301 (the former R 38), 266; N 2181, 157.
Bundesarchiv Koblenz (BAK). N 2022, 18.
Geheimes Staatsarchiv Preußischer Kulturbesitz Berlin PK (GHStA PK). I. HA, Rep. 120.

Published sources and literature

Amara, Michaël. *Des Belges à l'épreuve de l'Exil. Les réfugiés de la Première Guerre mondiale. France, Grande-Bretagne, Pays-Bas, 1914–1918*. Brussels: Éditions de l'Université de Bruxelles, 2008.
Bade, Klaus J. " 'Preußengänger' und 'Abwehrpolitik'. Ausländerbeschäftigung, Ausländerpolitik und Ausländerkontrolle auf dem Arbeitsmarkt in Preußen vor dem Ersten Weltkrieg." *Archiv für Sozialgeschichte* 24 (1984): 91–162.
Bade, Klaus J., ed. *Deutsche im Ausland – Fremde in Deutschland. Migration in Geschichte und Gegenwart*, 295–332. München: Beck, 1992.
Becker, Annette. "Life in an Occupied Zone. Lille, Roubaix, Tourcoing." In *Facing Armagedon: The First World War Experienced*, edited by Hugh Cecil, and Peter H. Liddle, 630–641. London: Cooper, 1996.
Becker, Annette. *Oubliés de la Grande Guerre. Humanitaire et culture de guerre 1914–1918. Populations occupies, déportés civils, prisonniers de guerre*. Paris: Hachette Littérature, 1998.
Becker, Annette. *Les cicatrices rouges. 14–18. France et Belgique occupées*. Paris: Fayard, 2010.
Chickering, Roger. "Total War: The Use and Abuse of a Concept." In *Anticipating Total War: The German and American Experiences, 1871–1914*, edited by Manfred Boemeke, Roger Chickering, and Stig Förster, 13–28. Cambridge: Cambridge University Press, 1999.
Commission d'Enquête sur les violations des régles du droit des gens, des lois et des coutumes de la guerre. *Rapports et documents d'Enquête. Deuxième volume: Rapport sur les déportations des ouvriers belges et sur le traitement infligés aux prisonniers de guerre et aux prisonniers civiles belges*. Bruxelles/Liège: de Wit, 1923.

MILITARY OCCUPATIONS IN FIRST WORLD WAR EUROPE

Daniel, Ute. *Arbeiterfrauen in der Kriegsgesellschaft. Beruf, Familie und Politik im Ersten Weltkrieg*. Göttingen: Vandenhoeck & Ruprecht, 1989.

De Schaepdrijver, Sophie. *La Belgique et la Première Guerre Mondiale*. Bern: P.I.E.-Peter Lang, 2004.

Elsner, Lothar. "Ausländerbeschäftigung und Zwangsarbeitspolitik in Deutschland während des Ersten Weltkriegs." In *Auswanderer – Wanderarbeiter – Gastarbeiter. Bevölkerung, Arbeitsmarkt und Wanderung in Deutschland seit Mitte des 19. Jahrhunderts, vol. 2*, edited by Klaus J. Bade, 527–555. Ostfildern: Scripta Mercaturae, 1984.

Hankel, Gerd. *Die Leipziger Prozesse. Deutsche Kriegsverbrechen und ihre strafrechtliche Verfolgung nach dem Ersten Weltkrieg*. Hamburg: Hamburger Edition, 2003.

Haupt, Mathias Georg. *Der 'Arbeitseinsatz' der belgischen Bevölkerung während des Zweiten Weltkrieges*. Bonn: Rheinische Friedrich-Wilhelms-Universität, 1970.

Heid, Ludger. *Maloche – nicht Mildtätigkeit. Ostjüdische Arbeiter in Deutschland 1914–1923*. Hildesheim, Zürich/New York: Olms, 1995.

Heinemann, Ulrich. *Die verdrängte Niederlage. Politische Öffentlichkeit und Kriegsschuldfrage in der Weimarer Republik*. Göttingen: Vandenhoeck & Ruprecht, 1983.

Herbert, Ulrich. "Zwangsarbeit als Lernprozeß. Zur Beschäftigung ausländischer Arbeiter in der westdeutschen Industrie im Ersten Weltkrieg." *Archiv für Sozialgeschichte* 24 (1984): 285–304.

Herbert, Ulrich. *Fremdarbeiter. Politik und Praxis des 'Ausländer-Einsatzes' in der Kriegswirtschaft des Dritten Reiches*. Bonn: Dietz, 1985.

Herbert, Ulrich. *Geschichte der Ausländerpolitik in Deutschland. Saisonarbeiter, Zwangsarbeiter, Gastarbeiter, Flüchtlinge*. München: Beck, 2001.

Herrmann-Otto, Elisabeth, ed. *Unfreie Arbeits- und Lebensverhältnisse von der Antike bis zur Gegenwart. Eine Einführung*. Hildesheim: Olms, 2005.

Hinz, Uta. *Gefangen im Großen Krieg. Kriegsgefangenschaft in Deutschland 1914–1921*. Essen: Klartext, 2006.

Horne, John, and Alan Kramer. *German Atrocities, 1914. A History of Denial*. New Haven, CT: Yale University Press, 2001.

Hovannisian, Richard. "Greek Labor Batallions in Asia Minor." In *The Armenian Genocide: Cultural and Ethical Legacies*, edited by Richard Hovannisian, 275–291. New Brunswick: Transaction, 2008.

Huberich, Charles, and Nicol-Speyer, Alexander, eds. *Deutsche Gesetzgebung für die okkupierten Gebiete Belgiens*. Bd. IV und VII Haag: Nijhoff, 1915 resp 1919.

Hull, Isabel V. *Absolute Destruction. Military Culture and the Practices of War in Imperial Germany*. Ithaca, NY/London: Cornell University Press, 2005.

Jaumain, Serge, Amara, Michaël, Majerus, Benoît, and Vrints, Antoon, eds. *Une guerre totale? La Belgique dans la Première Guerre mondiale. Nouvelles tendances de la recherché historique*. Bruxelles: AGR (Algemeen Rijksarchief), 2005.

Jones, Heather. *Violence against Prisoners of War in the First World War. Britain, France and Germany, 1914–1920*. Cambridge: Cambridge University Press, 2011.

Kramer, Alan. *Dynamic of Destruction: Culture and Mass Killing in the First World War*. Oxford: Oxford University Press, 2007.

Kreienbaum, Jonas. "Wir sind keine Sklavenhalter' – Zur Rolle der Zwangsarbeit in den Konzentrationslagern in Deutsch-Südwestafrika (1904 bis 1908)." In *Lager vor Auschwitz. Orte von Internierung, Zwang und Gewalt im 20*, edited by Christoph Jahr, and Jens Thiel, Berlin: Metropol, forthcoming.

National, Ligue, ed. *Les Archives du Conseil du Flandres (Raad van Vlaanderen). Documents pour servir à l'histoire de la Guerre en Belgique*. Bruxelles: Ligue National Pour l'Unité Belge, 1928.

Lipkes, Jeff. *Rehearsals. The German Army in Belgium, August 1914*. Leuven: Leuven University Press, 2007.

Mayerhofer, Lisa. *Zwischen Freund und Feind. Deutsche Besatzung in Rumänien 1916–1918*. München: Martin Meidenbauer, 2010.

McPhail, Helen. *The Longe Silence: Civilian Life under the German Occupation of Northern France, 1914–1918*. London/New York: I.B. Tauris, 1999.

Médard, Frédéric. *Les Prisonniers en 1914–1918. Acteurs méconnus de la Grande Guerre*, 14–18. Paris: Édition Soteca, 2010.

Nichtweiß, Johannes. *Die ausländischen Saisonarbeiter in der Landwirtschaft der östlichen und mittleren Gebiete des Deutschen Reiches (1890–1914)*. Berlin: Rütten & Loening, 1959.

MILITARY OCCUPATIONS IN FIRST WORLD WAR EUROPE

Oltmer, Jochen. "Zwangsmigration und Zwangsarbeit. Ausländische Arbeitskräfte und bäuerliche Ökonomie im Deutschland des Ersten Weltkrieges." *Tel Aviver Jahrbuch für Geschichte* 27 (1998): 135–168.

Oltmer, Jochen. "Unentbehrliche Arbeitskräfte. Kriegsgefangene in Deutschland 1914–1918." In *Kriegsgefangene im Europa des Ersten Weltkrieges*, edited by Jochen Oltmer, 67–96. Paderborn: Schöningh, 2006.

Opfer-Klinger, Björn. *Im Schatten des Krieges. Besatzung oder Anschluss – Befreiung oder Unterdrückung? Eine komparative Untersuchung über die bulgarische Herrschaft in Vardar-Makedonien 1915–1918 und 1941–1944*. Münster: Lit, 2005.

Passelecq, Fernand. *Déportation et travail forcé des ouvriers et de la population civile de la Belgique occupé, 1916–1918*. Paris/New Haven, CT: Les Presses universitaires de France, 1929.

Proctor, Tammy M. *Civilians in a World at War, 1914–1918*. New York/London: New York University Press, 2010.

Rawe, Kai. '… *wir werden sie schon zur Arbeit bringen!' Ausländerbeschäftigung und Zwangsarbeit im Ruhrkohlenbergbau während des Ersten Weltkrieges*. Essen: Klartext, 2005.

Roolf, Christoph. "Die Deportationen von belgischen Arbeitern nach Deutschland 1916/17." In *Projekte zur Geschichte des 20. Jahrhunderts. Deutschland und Europa in Düsseldorfer Magister- und Examensarbeiten*, edited by Christoph Roolf, and Simone Rauthe, 30–45. Neuried bei München: Ars Una, 2000.

Sanborn, Jonathan. "Unsettling the Empire: Violent Migration and Social Disaster in Russia during World War I." *Journal of Modern History* 77, no. 3 (2005): 290–324.

Scheer, Tamara. *Zwischen Front und Heimat. Österreich-Ungarns Militärverwaltungen im Ersten Weltkrieg*. Frankfurt am Main u. a: Peter Lang, 2009.

Selleslagh, Frans, ed. *De Tewerkstelling van Belgische Arbeidkrachten Tijdens de Bezetting 1940*. Brussels: Navorsings- en Studiecentrum voor de Geschiedenis van de Tweede Wereldoorlog, 1970.

Starling, John, and Ivor Lee. *No Labour, No Battle: Military Labour during the First World War*. Stroud: Spellmount, 2009.

Summerskill, Michael. *China on the Western Front: Britain's Chinese Work Forces in the First World War*. London: Michael Summerskill (privately published), 1982.

Thiel, Jens. *'Menschenbassin Belgien'. Anwerbung, Deportation und Zwangsarbeit im Ersten Weltkrieg*. Essen: Klartext, 2007.

Thiel, Jens. "Belgische Arbeitskräfte für die deutsche Wirtschaft. Arbeitsmarktpolitische Optionen und Interessen zwischen Kaiserreich und Weimarer Republik." In *Perspektiven in der Fremde? Arbeitsmarkt und Migration von der Frühen Neuzeit bis in die Gegenwart*, edited by Dittmar Dahlmann, and Margrit Schulte Beerbühl, 199–213. Essen: Klartext, 2011.

Thiel, Jens, and Christian Westerhoff. "Zwangsarbeiterlager im Ersten Weltkrieg. Entstehung, Funktion und Lagerregimes im Deutschen Reich und in den besetzten Gebieten." In *Lager vor Auschwitz. Orte von Internierung, Zwang und Gewalt im 20. Jahrhundert*, edited by Christoph Jahr, and Jens Thiel, Berlin: Metropol, forthcoming.

Völkerrecht im Weltkrieg. Dritte Reihe im Werk des Untersuchungsausschusses. Im Auftrage des Dritten Unterausschusses unter Mitwirkung von Dr. Eugen Fischer und Dr. Berthold Widmann hg. von Dr. Johannes Bell (Das Werk des Untersuchungsausschusses der Verfassungsgebenden Deutschen Nationalversammlung und des Deutschen Reichstages 1919–1928. Verhandlungen/ Gutachten/Urkunden, Erster Band). Berlin: Deutsche Verlagsgesellschaft für Politik und Geschichte, 1927.

Westerhoff, Christian. *Zwangsarbeit im Ersten Weltkrieg. Deutsche Arbeitskräftepolitik im besetzten Polen und Litauen 1914–1918*. Paderborn: Schöningh, 2012.

Wiggenhorn, Harald. *Verliererjustiz. Die Leipziger Kriegsverbrecherprozesse nach dem Ersten Weltkrieg*. Baden-Baden: Nomos, 2005.

Xu, Guoqi. *Strangers on the Western Front: Chinese Workers in the Great War*. Cambridge, MA, London: Harvard University Press, 2011.

Zuckerman, Larry. *The Rape of Belgium: The Untold Story of World War I*. New York/ London: New York University Press, 2004.

Zürcher, Jan Erik. "Ottoman Labour Batallions in Word War I." In *Der Völkermord an den Armeniern und die Shoah*, edited by Hans-Lukas Kieser, and Dominik J. Schaller, 187–195. Zürich: Chronos, 2003.

'A kind of Siberia': German labour and occupation policies in Poland and Lithuania during the First World War

Christian Westerhoff

Friedrich-Meinecke-Institut, Freie Universität Berlin, Berlin, Germany

Translated from the German by Sophie De Schaepdrijver

Forced labour was not a phenomenon limited to the Second World War. Already in the First World War, German labour policy in occupied Poland and Lithuania was increasingly marked by coercion. It is little known in scholarship that the militarily administered territory of the Baltic (Ober Ost), especially, had developed into a laboratory for forced labour and total war. This article examines the conditions, forms and consequences of forced labour and recruitment in occupied Poland and Lithuania between 1914 and 1918. It will contribute towards explaining the extent to which the German labour policy of 1914–1918 served as a blueprint for the Nazi forced labour system during the Second World War.

> One heard a great deal about the deportations of Belgian workers to Germany that were meant to fulfil the Hindenburg Program, but relatively little was said about the similar case in the East.[1]

> Leon Sklarz, Geschichte der Ostjudenhilfe, 1927

Recent scholarship considers the Eastern Front as the 'forgotten front' of the First World War.[2] This includes the Eastern European regions that were occupied by the German Empire from 1914 to 1918. Recently, Liulevicius[3] has called attention to the occupied Baltic, the so-called Ober Ost territory.[4] His work, however, concentrated on the German view of the East rather than on concrete occupation policy; German occupation policies in Eastern Europe during the First World War remain under-researched. This is particularly surprising, as recent scholarly interest has concentrated on the issue whether the occupation of the East in the First World War served as a blueprint for the Nazi occupiers.[5] Addressing this question necessitates a clear picture of German occupations during the Great War. In regard to Nazi forced labour, too, the question arises as to whether the First World War could have served as a model.[6] In both world wars, the recruitment and deployment of labour was part and parcel of occupation in Eastern Europe; and foreign labour was crucial to the German war economy. During the First World War, almost three million foreigners (about two million POWs and one million civilians) worked in Germany. In the Second World War, this figure reached eight million.[7] Hitherto, research on German labour policy during 1914–1918 has only concentrated on the treatment of

East European labourers in Germany. We know little of the recruitment of labour in occupied Eastern Europe. Many studies do not even mention the considerable use of forced labour there.[8] The following is an analysis of the recruitment and employment of labour in occupied Eastern Europe and of the reasons and extent of coercion in German labour policy. This analysis may shed light on the question whether the First World War experience served as a model for the coercive-labour regime of the Second World War. In what follows, I will compare the two territories at the Eastern Front that were occupied longest by German troops: Poland and Lithuania, heretofore part of the Russian Empire.[9] Regarding definition: in 1930, the International Labour Organization defined coercive

Figure 1. Occupied areas of the Russian Empire during the First World War.[11]

MILITARY OCCUPATIONS IN FIRST WORLD WAR EUROPE

labour as 'every kind of work or service demanded of a person under threat of punishment and which is not entered into freely'.[10] I will follow this oft-cited definition, with the caveat that it is not always possible to clearly distinguish between free and forced labour.

1. Labour policy in the eastern occupied territories, 1914–1916

The economic boom of the 1890s caused serious labour shortage in the German Empire, remedied by a yearly influx of hundreds of thousands of foreign labourers in agriculture and industry. Polish seasonal workers from Austria-Hungary and the Russian Empire, in particular, streamed into Germany in great numbers at the beginning of each year. In 1914, Germany, with 1.2 million immigrants, had the second largest foreign workforce in the world after the USA.[12]

As the switch to a war economy further raised demand for labour, the Prussian government in the fall of 1914 forbade the return of labourers to the Russian Empire, which had become enemy territory. Other German states followed. From then on, workers from the Russian Empire, forced to stay in Germany, and not allowed to change jobs without official permission from their employers, became *de facto* forced labourers.[13]

However, as this remained insufficient to meet the immense demand for labour, the obtainment of additional labour from the occupied territories took on a greater significance.[14] In the summer of 1915, the German and Austro-Hungarian armies conquered Russian Poland, Lithuania and parts of Latvia and Belorussia. In the northern half of Russian Poland, a German civilian administration was established, the Government-General of Warsaw, with Hans Hartwig von Beseler at the head, who was directly responsible to the Kaiser. In contrast to Poland, a military administration was established in the occupied areas of the Baltic and north-eastern Poland, subordinate to the Supreme Military Commander East, or *Oberbefehlshaber Ost* (a post occupied by Paul von Hindenburg until 1916, thereafter by Prince Leopold of Bavaria) and thus known simply as Ober Ost. Since Hindenburg was not particularly interested in administration, his Chief of Staff Erich Ludendorff gave the actual direction. Military administration in Ober Ost was designed to be a purely military affair, largely removed from the administrative, parliamentary and official controls of the German Empire.[15]

The occupied areas differed not only in their administrations but also in the economic and political priorities set by the German occupation authorities. The outbreak of the war and the start of the German occupation in Russian Poland were marked by a decline of industry, handicraft and trade, causing unemployment and deprivation. Especially affected was the Jewish population, which was heavily engaged in handicraft and trade.[16] The Government-General tried to recruit the indigenous population for the rebuilding and expansion of infrastructure, especially roads and railroads. Above all, it tried to resume the pre-war migrations by persuading as many labourers as possible to work in Germany. Governor-General Von Beseler stated on 4 September 1916 that

> Our most important task, in the interest of the Fatherland, is to support the movement of Polish workers into Germany. The best workers of the Government-General of Warsaw must submit to this goal, the interests of the occupied territory must come second.[17]

The Government-General was covered with a network of recruitment offices, mostly operated by the German Labour Agency (*Deutsche Arbeiterzentrale*, DAZ), a semi-official institution that had been recruiting foreign labourers before 1914. At first, recruitment met with great success. By March 1916, some 100,000 to 120,000 additional workers had joined the 300,000 men and women already in Germany,[18] even though, like them, these new workers were forbidden to change jobs and residence after their arrival.

Although the German authorities and the DAZ tried to hide the coercive character of work in Germany, most people in the occupied territories must soon have heard of the true conditions. The success of recruitment was, then, due to the economic crisis, which offered the population few alternatives. The German civil administration did not only exploit distress for recruitment purposes, but actively increased the economic pressure by shutting down businesses and cutting off support to the unemployed.[19]

Compared to the Government-General, the occupied regions of north-eastern Poland and the Baltic, now administered together as Ober Ost, were much more agrarian. This was a thinly populated area with only fledgling industry. Still, the events of 1914–1915 hit handicraft and trade hard, even if unemployment only grew to be a sizeable problem in the few larger cities such as Vilna or Białystok, where, as in the Government-General, the Jews were especially affected.

Migrant labour in Germany played a much less important role in Ober Ost than in the Government-General, because these areas had little tradition of labour migration to the German Empire. Moreover, the military's priority was not the procurement of labour for Germany, but rather the exploitation of the extensive agricultural and forest resources of Ober Ost for the German war effort. Furthermore, as in the Government-General, infrastructure was to be repaired and extended, which necessitated much local labour. Consequently, the military administration of Ober Ost deployed tens of thousands of workers for road and railroad work as well as for agricultural and forest labour, whereas a much smaller number was sent to the German Empire.[20]

Since labour on the open market was often in short supply,[21] the military administration soon shifted from recruiting voluntary workers to forcing people to work. This shift was facilitated by the Imperial German Army's habit of commandeering labour, and by the occupiers' attitude of contempt for the locals – an attitude expressed in numerous statements by German officials. In many places, farmers were forced to cultivate abandoned fields on estates, or help with road work. With time, such corvées multiplied to become a heavy burden on farmers. But at least they were usually allowed to return home in the evenings, allowing them to provide for themselves and not have to live in camps.[22]

In sum, labour policies in the Government-General and Ober Ost were quite different. In the Government-General, the emphasis lay on more or less voluntary labour recruitment for Germany; in Ober Ost, priority was given to the maximization of local labour. Here, local workers were coerced from the beginning. But in both occupation zones, German officials found it ever harder to recruit labour – partly because so many workers were already in Germany. The number of recruits fell far short of the enormous demands of the German war economy. Furthermore, in the occupied regions, work became less attractive since more of it had to be done in inaccessible areas. For example, workers employed on remote railroads had to be lodged in German camps, where provisioning was inadequate, as soon became common knowledge.[23]

The administrations of both occupation zones eventually concluded that pressure to accept work for Germany had to be increased. While most of the civil administrators in the Government-General advocated increased economic pressure, the military administrators in Ober Ost championed redoubled coercion. Here, workers were forced into work gangs far from their home villages, although this practice remained, at first, local and temporary.[24]

2. Forced recruitment and forced labour from the fall of 1916

In reaction to the urgent situation facing the Central Powers, Hindenburg and Ludendorff were promoted from their leadership of the military administration of Ober Ost to Supreme

Army Command in late August 1916. In the following two years, they used this position, and their aura in political and business circles and in public opinion as the Tannenberg victors and purported saviours of the Fatherland, to essentially determine politics in the German power sphere.[25]

Hindenburg and especially Ludendorff assumed their new task in the utter conviction that the war could be won only through a fierce concentration of forces. Their conviction that victory could only be won by subjecting all sectors of the economy and society to military necessities[26] was something they had brought with them from Ober Ost – a fact that has barely been mentioned in scholarship so far.[27] Other considerations, such as humanitarian or legal ones, had to yield.[28] The implications for labour policy were clear: if voluntary recruitment proved insufficient, force should be used to recruit and deploy workers. By the fall of 1916, these concepts of 'total war'[29] – as it came to be named in the interwar years – had already been tried out for a year by Ludendorff's military administration in Ober Ost.

Soon after the assumption of command, Hindenburg and Ludendorff took the first steps to establish a new labour policy in the German power sphere. In Germany, they demanded the introduction of mandatory patriotic service.[30] In the occupied territories, workers had to be forced to serve the German war economy if they did not do so voluntarily. While the 'Auxiliary Service Law' (*Hilfsdienstgesetz*), mandating service for Germans and passed in December 1916, was so watered down that it hardly corresponded to Ludendorff's vision, forced labour requisitions were soon carried out in the occupied territories, albeit in varying degrees. On 13 September and again on 3 October 1916, Ludendorff instructed the Governors-General of Warsaw and Belgium to institute forced labour, even though he did not formally have authority over them. His memorandum on this instruction blamed the unemployed in the occupied territories for 'unwillingness to work' (literally, *Arbeitsscheu*, 'work-shyness'). The unemployed had to be obligated to work and German officials must be allowed to force the populace in occupied territories to work even outside of their home areas.[31]

Already by 4 October, Governor-General Von Beseler issued an 'Ordinance against the Reluctance to Work'[32] that closely followed Ludendorff's blueprint. On 20 October 1916, a corresponding order was decreed for Ober Ost.[33] In this way, forced labour was introduced in the Government-General and in Ober Ost. The terms 'unwilling to work' and 'unemployed' were soon applied in a most arbitrary manner. Since German authorities in many places were unable to get hold of the unemployed, forced recruitment drives often ended up as wild raids that swept up destitute-looking people and random passers-by.[34] In the Government-General, forced recruitment was carried out in numerous places, but most forced labourers only worked for short periods on local projects. Only in the Łódź region, the authorities rounded up some 5000 persons, who were deported to far-away sites and forced to work for long durations. This concerned overwhelmingly Jewish men, who were brought to camps where they met representatives of the DAZ presenting them with 'voluntary' work in Germany. Refusal landed them in so-called 'Civil Workers' Batallions' (*Zivil-Arbeiter-Bataillone*, ZAB) that were stationed in Ober Ost.[35] In the ZAB, workers could be deployed for long stretches of time far from home in road and railroad building, harvest and forestry work.[36] Some scholars have suggested that forced labourers were deported to Germany.[37] This was not the case: first, those responsible for the coercive measures deemed them easier to justify in international law if the workers remained in the occupied territories[38]; second, in Ober Ost itself, there was a great demand for labour, and the work there did not require the skills needed in Germany.

In Ober Ost, at least 10,000 people were recruited for ZAB, and many more for short-term work gangs.[39] Here, the numerous forced recruitments, unlike those in the Government-General, were not limited to particular areas or groups, but affected the entire region and the general population. Still, in Ober Ost too, the Jews were over-represented in forced labour.[40] The sources fail to determine whether this was a result of anti-Semitism or of a higher rate of unemployment among Jews that made them more visible to the German authorities. But it is certain that, in both occupied zones, the German administrators held the population in general in low regard – a stance expressed in many a statement. The military administration in Ober Ost, specifically, adopted a colonial mentality and deemed the population 'work-shy', backward, dependent and dirty.[41] This contempt may well have helped to overcome reservations. The head of administration in Lithuania, Franz-Josef von Isenburg-Birstein, for one, thought that forced labour would raise Lithuanians' labour efficiency.[42]

Workers faced very harsh living and work conditions in the ZAB. For a pittance, they had to do heavy labour for nine hours daily. Lodgings, clothing, food and medicine were in very short supply. Due to these conditions and to the fact that the arbitrary raids had nabbed many elderly and sick people, illness and mortality were high. In addition, there were many reports of mistreatment. Consequently, productivity was low and out of proportion with the costs and efforts involved in overseeing and provisioning the captives. Workers could not leave the camp, and dismissal was only possible when they could no longer work or if they signed up for voluntary labour.[43] Numerous workers fled; others even mutilated themselves to be allowed to leave.[44] The German-Jewish writer Arnold Zweig, who served in the administration of Ober Ost, described the ZAB as 'a kind of Siberia'.[45]

3. Criticism, suspension and maintenance of coercion

In the Government-General, forced recruiting was suspended in December 1916 due to the objections of German-Jewish organizations, as well as the negative impact it had on voluntary recruitment for Germany – and, even more so, the negative impact on the proclamation of a new Polish state and the recruitment of a Polish army under German-Austrian leadership.[46] Moreover, the authorities had to admit to lacking the means to coerce; they often failed to get hold of people targeted for forced labour.[47] As a result, the civilian administrators in the Government-General soon redoubled their effort to recruit voluntary workers for Germany, an effort that had been continuing throughout. They made use of the economic crisis as well as of the threat of renewed coercion, and held out promises of vacations and better working conditions.[48] The effort to recruit Jewish labour, not a success hitherto, was stepped up.[49]

But the military administration in Ober Ost held on to forced recruitment and labour, despite low productivity and protests in the occupied territories, in the *Reichstag*, and on the international scene. The regime refused to be told how to handle a population it considered incapable of self-determination. Plans to proclaim an independent state and to mobilize the inhabitants into an army, as in Russian Poland, did not, at first, exist. Also, the military could not imagine opening up and exploiting the territory without forced labour.[50] Moreover, coercion in the occupied territories of Eastern Europe met with much less vigorous protests than did the deportation of Belgian workers. This made it easier for the military administration in Ober Ost to stick to coercive recruitment and labour.

Only Ludendorff's decision in the summer of 1917 to establish self-governance for the inhabitants of Ober Ost[51] generated some slight change in labour policy. On 22 September

1917, one day after elections to the Lithuanian provincial assembly, the so-called Taryba, were held, the ZAB were officially dissolved as a gesture of goodwill.[52] Their dissolution, however, did not imply the end of coercion; workers were simply transferred to other units and laboured under similar conditions. Forced recruitment in fact continued until late into 1918. Coercive labour in Ober Ost only came to a close with the end of German occupation in November 1918.[53]

4. Prospect: lessons of forced labour after 1918

After 1918, the coercive measures in the Government-General and Ober Ost were considered by many participants and by the relevant German ministries as a failure – but only from an economic, not from a moral point of view. While the inefficiency of forced recruitment and labour was clearly spelled out, these measures were never considered to be breaches in international law or ethical lapses. The only public criticisms of coercion as injustice came from the parties on the Left and from Jewish organizations. Such statements fell on deaf ears in the collective shock of defeat and the humiliation of Versailles; critics of the war were blamed for harming German interests and playing into the hands of the allies. Already during the war, the military was never tired of justifying coercion as a 'necessity of war'. Forced labour had been, it was also alleged, the only way to combat unemployment and secure food supplies in the occupied territories. These justifications of coercion became even more significant after the German defeat, as the allies demanded reparations and the extradition of responsible parties, including Hindenburg and Ludendorff.[54]

Moreover, the military and right-wing circles were gradually convinced that German conduct in the First World War had not been brutal, but rather too considerate. Well-known authors, especially Ludendorff, concluded from the lost war that a future 'total war' must entail a more complete and more ruthless mobilization of the entire labour force. The exploitation of future occupied territories in Eastern Europe was considered crucial. The experiences of the First World War confirmed the opinion in these circles that the peoples of Eastern Europe had to be treated ruthlessly – and that this was possible because world public opinion cared much more about events in Western Europe.[55] The Nazis, especially, adopted Ludendorff's 'lessons' drawn from the First World War with eagerness, if with some modifications. At his trial in 1924, Hitler declared that he had read Ludendorff's *Kriegsführung und Politik* (War and Politics) with enthusiasm.[56]

After 1933, and even more after 1939, the ideas of Ludendorff became government policy, especially with regard to the mobilization of all resources for war. Initially, this total mobilization was applied to the German population rather than to foreign workers. While Germans were practically subjected to labour service by 1939, the recruitment and employment of foreign workers was not yet characterized by coercion. Even after the outbreak of the Second World War, there was no talk of the systematic use of forced foreign labour. German authorities simply carried out a more focused and effective recruitment of labour in Poland. Many contradictions and setbacks characterized the road to a widespread coercive system.[57] For example, hundreds of thousands of Soviet war prisoners could not be used as forced labourers because the regime of neglect in the camps left them starving or too weak to work.[58]

Nazi ideology rendered occupation rule in Eastern Europe racist and brutal to an immeasurably greater and far more fundamental extent than had been the case during the First World War. In their selection of administrators, the Nazi leadership deliberately passed over the experienced personnel from the Government-General or Ober Ost and selected instead a new type of 'German Man'.[59] The Governor-General of Poland, Hans

Frank, for example, only wanted to employ 'pure, activist National-Socialist fighters'.[60] The genocide against East European Jewry represented an immense rupture with the First World War, when Jews had been exploited and discriminated against, but certainly not murdered. Genocide fundamentally altered German labour policies. It allowed for the total exploitation of East European Jews. Given terminally insufficient rations, worked to complete exhaustion and dying in extremely high numbers, the Jews selected for forced labour became 'less than slaves', to borrow Mark Spoerer's words.[61] No workers had been treated like this in the First World War.

5. Conclusion

During the First World War, German labour policy in the occupied territories of Eastern Europe was increasingly marked by coercion. Voluntary and coerced recruitment and work existed consecutively as well as side by side. Until the fall of 1916, the civilian administration in the Government-General recruited voluntary labour for Germany, using economic hardship to its advantage. Once in Germany, workers could not return home. Since most knew this, one might call their 'choice' a voluntary entry into forced labour, propelled by economic necessity. This kind of forced labour may be described as moderate in the sense that workers enjoyed some influence on their conditions of work since employers needed them.

In contrast to the civilian administration in the Government-General, the military administration in Ober Ost resorted from the beginning to forced recruitment and labour. In Ober Ost, few workers were available on the labour market and the military administration wanted to carry out a great many projects in remote regions. In addition, the military administration considered the inhabitants unwilling to work, which strengthened its conviction that the exploitation of the land required coercion. Until the fall of 1916, forced labour in Ober Ost could be considered moderate because it was of limited duration and the workers were not housed in camps. Up to the fall of 1916, then, both voluntary and 'moderate forced labour', which sometimes shaded into each other, existed in the occupied zones. However, the military administration in Ober Ost and different actors in the German Empire increasingly considered existing labour measures inadequate in procuring sufficient labour. With the assumption of the third Supreme Army Command by Hindenburg and Ludendorff in the fall of 1916, a new form of labour made its appearance, which I call 'hard coercive labour'. Forced labourers had to work far from home under far worsened conditions. Their only recourse against conditions of work in the ZAB was flight.

While forced recruitment occurred both in the Government-General and in Ober Ost, hard coercive labour was deployed only in the ZAB in Ober Ost. The military administration in Ober Ost enforced coerced recruitment to a much greater extent and held on to this labour policy longer. Overly imbued with a sense of its own mission, it put its faith in force, ignored criticism and proceeded with far less consideration towards the population.

The idea of forcibly mobilizing all labour for the war economy was developed in Ober Ost by Hindenburg and especially by Ludendorff. Once promoted to Supreme Army Command, they forced their idea on the entire German power sphere – in the occupied territories in the form of forced recruitment and the establishment of ZAB. Ober Ost was thus an important laboratory for forced labour and 'total war', a fact which scholarship must now recognize.

After the Armistice, the kind of forced labour practiced in the First World War was widely considered in Germany to have been an economic failure rather than a moral issue. This blind spot facilitated the emergence of an essentially broader and much more brutal coercive system under German rule in the Second World War. Greater efficiency in labour recruitment and statements made by important actors indicate that lessons were indeed drawn from the labour policy of the First World War. But rather than furnishing a blueprint or concrete directions, the First World War formed rather an abstract 'experiential background'. A specific analysis of how its 'lessons' were learned will be the task of future research.

Notes

1. Sklarz, *Geschichte und Organisation der Ostjudenhilfe*, 28.
2. For example, Groß, ed., *Die vergessene Front*.
3. Liulevicius, *War Land on the Eastern Front*.
4. References to Liulevicius' work in, a.o., Kramer, *Dynamics of Destruction*; Hull, *Absolute Destruction*.
5. For example, Bergien, 'Vorspiel'. Next to the First World War, recent scholarship has identified colonialism as a precursor and inspirator of Nazi rule in Eastern Europe. See especially the work of Jürgen Zimmerer, e.g. Zimmerer, 'Die Geburt des "Ostlandes"'. This particular continuity hypothesis is not generally accepted. See, for instance, Kundrus, 'Von der Peripherie ins Zentrum'; Gerwarth and Malinowski, 'Der Holocaust als "kolonialer Genozid"'.
6. Still the basic reference: Herbert, 'Zwangsarbeit als Lernprozeß'.
7. Bade, *Europa in Bewegung*, 241, 287.
8. See especially Zunkel, 'Die ausländischen Arbeiter'; Herbert, *Geschichte der Ausländerpolitik*; Elsner, *Ausländerbeschäftigung*; Oltmer, 'Zwangsmigration'.
9. See also Westerhoff, *Zwangsarbeit im Ersten Weltkrieg*.
10. 'Übereinkommen über Zwangs- und Pflichtarbeit'.
11. With thanks to Christoph Reichel (University of Osnabrück) for designing this map.
12. Bade, 'Preußengänger'; Bade, *Europa in Bewegung*, 222.
13. For example, Elsner, *Die polnischen Arbeiter*, 21–3.
14. Oltmer, 'Zwangsmigration', 138–39.
15. For example, Linde, *Deutsche Politik*, 105–9, 158–67.
16. For example, Schuster, *Zwischen allen Fronten*, 308–13.
17. Grabski, Stojanowski and Warężak, 'Rolnictwo Polski', 440.
18. Westerhoff, *Zwangsarbeit im Ersten Weltkrieg*, 113.
19. Szajkowski, *Jewish Workers*, 894.
20. Westerhoff, *Zwangsarbeit im Ersten Weltkrieg*, 121–27, 143–77.
21. Gayl, Wilhelm von: 'Mit Schwert und Feder!' Erinnerungen an Front- und Verwaltungsdienst in den Jahren 1914/1919, MS [1942], Bundesarchiv Koblenz (BAK), N 1031, Nr. 2, Bl. 146.
22. For example, Verwaltungsbericht des Kreises Kielmy für März 1916, Lietuvos Centrinis Valstybinis Istorijos Archyvas (LCVIA), F. 641, ap. 1, B. 306; Petras, *Der Werdegang*, 74, 76.
23. For example, Verwaltungsbericht Kupischki, 30.9.1916, LCVIA, F. 641, ap. 1, B. 572; Zwischenbericht der deutschen Verwaltung für Litauen, 1.10.1916–31.12.1916, Bundesarchiv-Militärarchiv (BA-MA), PHD 23, Nr. 49.
24. *Litwa*, 132; Čepėnas, *Naujųjų Laikų Lietuvos Istorija*, vol. 2, 95.
25. For example, Pyta, *Hindenburg*, 41–295, esp. 205–25.
26. For example, Ludendorff, *Kriegserinnerungen*, 324.
27. A few brief references in Liulevicius, *Kriegsland im Osten*, 73; Demm, 'Das deutsche Besatzungsregime', 71; Armeson, *Total Warfare*, 80; Mayerhofer, *Zwischen Freund und Feind*, 240; Echternkamp, 'Ein zweiter Dreißigjähriger Krieg', 278–79.
28. Supreme Army Command (OHL) to the Governments-General of Belgium and Warsaw, 13.9.1916, in Bell, Johannes, ed., *Werk des Untersuchungsausschusses*, 339.
29. The title of one of Ludendorff's works on his lessons from the First World War: Ludendorff, *Der totale Krieg*. Even when the actual concept was not used until the 1920s and 1930s, Ludendorff sought to realize two important components of 'total war' from 1916: full mobilization and total control. On the concept of total war, see especially Förster, *Das Zeitalter des totalen Krieges*, esp. 19–20.
30. See Feldman, *Army*; Armeson, *Total Warfare*.
31. Generalquartiermeister, i.V. Sauberzweig, to General-Gouvernement Warschau, Geheim, 3.10.1916, in: Hertz, *ZAB 23*, 50–1; Generalquartiermeister, Verordnung betreffend die

Einschränkung der öffentlichen Unterstützungslasten und die Beseitigung allgemeiner Notstände, 3.10.1916, Bundesarchiv Berlin (BAB), R 3001, Nr. 7764.

32. 'Verordnung über die Bekämpfung der Arbeitsscheu', in Verordnungsblatt für das General-Gouvernement Warschau, Nr. 47, 7.10.1916, 1, Nr. 150, BA-MA, PHD 23, Nr. 17.

33. Decree in Amtliche Beilage der Kownoer Zeitung, Verordnungen der Deutschen Verwaltung Litauen vom 20.11.1916, Nr. 4, Ziffer 17.

34. Motas and Motasowa, 'Zagadnienie', 11, 22–5, 35–7; Klimas, *Der Werdegang*, 74–5.

35. Vierteljahrsbericht des Verwaltungschefs bei dem GGW für die Zeit 1.10.1916–31.12.1916, Geheimes Staatsarchiv Preußischer Kulturbesitz (GStA), Rep. 84A, Nr. 6210; Verwaltungschef beim Generalgouvernement Warschau an den Staatssekretär des Innern, 13.12.1916, BAB, R 1501, Nr. 11978.

36. Generalquartiermeister, Dienstanweisung, 3.10.1916, BAB, R. 3001, Nr. 7764.

37. For example, Heid, *Maloche*, 129–31.

38. Bell, Johannes, ed., *Werk des Untersuchungsausschusses*, 348–51.

39. Westerhoff, *Zwangsarbeit im Ersten Weltkrieg*, 218–19, 223.

40. Szajkowski, 'Jewish Workers', 896, 902–3, 906.

41. For example, Besprechung über Arbeiterfragen, 17.12.1917, Latvijas Valsts vestures archivs (LVvA), Fonda 6428, Apr. 1, Arch 37; Verwaltungsbericht Wiezajcie für die Zeit vom 1.4. bis 30.9.1917, LCVIA, F. 641, ap. 1, B. 515.

42. Verwaltungsbericht Litauen, 1.7.1916–30.9.1916, GStA, Rep. 84A, Nr. 6210.

43. Berger, 'Ostjüdische Arbeiter im Kriege', 835; Generalquartiermeister, Dienstanweisung für die Aufstellung und Verwendung von Zivil-Arbeiter-Bataillonen (Z.A.B.), 3.10.1916, BAB, R. 3001, Nr. 7764, vgl. Hertz: Łódź, 194–95.

44. Klimas, *Werdegang*, 75, 78–81; Szajkowski, 'Jewish Workers', 902–4; Strazhas, *Ostpolitik*, 39, 41, 50, 208.

45. Zweig, *Das ostjüdische Antlitz*, 7.

46. Halbjahresbericht des Verwaltungschefs bei dem Generalgouvernement Warschau für die Zeit 1.4.-30.9.1917, GStA Rep 84a, Nr. 6210.

47. Oltmer, *Migration*, 326.

48. Herbert, *Ausländerpolitik*, 95–8; Zunkel, 'Die ausländischen Arbeiter', 302–10.

49. On the recruitment of Jewish labourers in the Government-General, see, for instance, Heid, *Maloche*; Oltmer, *Migration*, 221–38.

50. On this, see Besprechung über Arbeiterfragen, 17.12.1917, LVvA, Fonda 6428, Apr. 1, Arch 37; Zwischenbericht Litauen, 1.10.1916–31.12.1916, BA-MA, PHD 23, Nr. 49; Häpke, *Litauen*, 82.

51. Ludendorff, *Kriegserinnerungen*, 376.

52. Oberbefehlshaber Ost, Grundsätze und Übergangsbestimmungen für die Auflösung der Zivilarbeiterbataillone, 22.9.1917, in: Hertz, *ZAB 23*, 76.

53. Berger, 'Ostjüdische Arbeiter', 834, vgl. Klimas, *Werdegang*, 138–42; Häpke, *Litauen*, 82.

54. Hankel, *Die Leipziger Prozesse*, 380–93.

55. Ludendorff, *Kriegserinnerungen*, 275, 531; Ludendorff, *Kriegführung und Politik*, 157–58; Ludendorff, *Der totale Krieg*, 46. First steps towards a history of the reception and effects of Ludendorff's ideas in Chickering, 'Sore Loser', though without reference to labour policies.

56. Pöhlmann, 'Von Versailles nach Armageddon'; Knox, 'Erster Weltkrieg und Military Culture', 305–6; Demm, 'Das deutsche Besatzungsregime', 70–4; Thoss, *Der Ludendorff-Kreis*, 249–62. Even after Ludendorff had broken with the Nazis, Hitler continued to venerate him as a general. See, for instance, Pyta, *Hindenburg*, 584; Nebelin, *Ludendorff*, 10.

57. On forced labour during the Second World War, Herbert, *Fremdarbeiter*, remains the fundamental reference. See also Tooze, *The Wages of Destruction*.

58. Streit, *Keine Kameraden*.

59. Chiari, *Geschichte als Gewalttat*, 627.

60. Schlemmer, 'Grenzen der Integration', 687–88.

61. Spoerer/Fleischhacker, 'Forced Laborers in Nazi Germany'.

References

Unpublished sources

Bundesarchiv Berlin (BAB), R 1501, R 3001.
Bundesarchiv Koblenz (BAK), N 1031.
Bundesarchiv-Militärarchiv, Freiburg (BA-MA), PHD 23.
Geheimes Staatsarchiv Preußischer Kulturbesitz (GStA), Rep. 84A, Rep. 120.
Lietuvos Centrinis Valstybinis Istorijos Archyvas (LCVIA), F. 641.
Latvijas Valsts vestures archivs (LVvA), Fonda 6428.

Published sources and literature

Amtliche Beilage der Kownoer Zeitung. Verordnungen der Deutschen Verwaltung Litauen vom 20.11.1916, Nr. 4.
Armeson, Robert B. *Total Warfare and Compulsory Labour. A Study of the Military-Industrial Complex in Germany during World War I.* The Hague: Nijhoff, 1964.
Bade, Klaus J. "'Preußengänger' und 'Abwehrpolitik'. Ausländerbeschäftigung, Ausländerpolitik und Ausländerkontrolle auf dem Arbeitsmarkt in Preußen vor dem Ersten Weltkrieg." *Archiv für Sozialgeschichte* 24 (1984): 91–162.
Bade, Klaus J. *Europa in Bewegung. Migration vom späten 18. Jahrhundert bis zur Gegenwart.* München: Beck, 2000.
Bell, Johannes, ed. *Das Werk des Untersuchungsausschusses der Verfassungsgebenden Deutschen Nationalversammlung und des Deutschen Reichstages (WUA) 1919–1928, Reihe 3. Völkerrecht im Weltkrieg*, vol. 1. Berlin: Deutsche Verlags-Gesellschaft für Politik u. Geschichte, 1927.
Berger, Julius. "Ostjüdische Arbeiter im Kriege." *Volk und Land* 1 (1919): 865–78.
Bergien, Rüdiger. "Vorspiel des 'Vernichtungskrieges'? Die Ostfront des Ersten Weltkrieges und das Kontinuitätsproblem." In *Die vergessene Front. Der Osten 1914/15. Ereignis, Wirkung, Nachwirkung*, edited by Gerhard P. Groß, 393–408. Paderborn: Schöningh, 2006.
Čepėnas, Pranas. *Naujųjų Laikų Lietuvos Istorija*, vol. 2. Chicago, IL: Išleido Dr. Kazio Griniaus Fondas, 1977.
Chiari, Bernhard. "Geschichte als Gewalttat. Weißrußland als Kind zweier Weltkriege." In *Erster Weltkrieg, Zweiter Weltkrieg – ein Vergleich. Krieg, Kriegserlebnis, Kriegserfahrung in Deutschland*, edited by Bruno Thoß, and Hans-Erich Volkmann, 615–31. Paderborn: Schöningh, 2002.
Chickering, Roger. "Sore Loser. Ludendorff's Total War." In *The Shadows of Total War. Europe, East Asia, and the United States, 1919–1939*, edited by Roger Cickering, and Stig Förster, 151–78. Cambridge: Cambridge University Press, 2003.
Demm, Eberhard. "Das deutsche Besatzungsregime in Litauen im Ersten Weltkrieg – Generalprobe für Hitlers Ostfeldzug und Versuchslabor des totalitären Staates." *Zeitschrift für Ostmitteleuropa-Forschung* 51 (2002): 64–74.
Echternkamp, Jörg. "1914–1945: Ein zweiter Dreißigjähriger Krieg? Vom Nutzen und Nachteil eines Deutungsmusters der Zeitgeschichte." In *Das Deutsche Kaiserreich in der Kontroverse*, edited by Sven Oliver Müller, and Cornelius Torp, 265–80. Göttingen: Vandenhoeck & Ruprecht, 2009.
Elsner, Lothar. *Die polnischen Arbeiter in der deutschen Landwirtschaft während des ersten Weltkrieges.* Rostock: Universität Rostock, 1975.
Elsner, Lothar. "Ausländerbeschäftigung und Zwangsarbeitspolitik in Deutschland während des Ersten Weltkriegs." In *Auswanderer – Wanderarbeiter – Gastarbeiter. Bevölkerung, Arbeitsmarkt und Wanderung in Deutschland seit Mitte des 19. Jahrhunderts*, vol. 2, edited by Klaus J. Bade, 527–55. Ostfildern: Scripta Mercaturae Verlag, 1984.
Feldman, Gerald D. *Army Industry and Labor in Germany, 1914–1918.* Princeton, NJ: Princeton Univ. Press, 1966.
Förster, Stig. "Das Zeitalter des Totalen Krieges. Konzeptionelle Überlegungen für einen historischen Strukturvergleich." *Mittelweg* 36, no. 8 (1999): 12–29.
Gerwarth, Robert, and Stephan Malinowski. "Der Holocaust als 'kolonialer Genozid'? Europäische Kolonialgewalt und nationalsozialistischer Vernichtungskrieg." *Geschichte und Gesellschaft* 33 (2007): 439–66.
Grabski, Władysław, Józef Stojanowski, and Jan Warężak. "Rolnictwo Polski 1914–1918." In *Polska w czasie Wielkiej Wojny (1914–1918): Historja Ekonomiczna*, vol. 3, edited by Marcel

Handelsman, 225–489. Warszawa: Towarzystwo Badania Zagadnień Międzynarodowych, 1936.

Groß, Gerhard P., ed. *Die vergessene Front. Der Osten 1914/15. Ereignis, Wirkung, Nachwirkung.* Paderborn: Schöningh, 2006.

Hankel, Gerd. *Die Leipziger Prozesse. Deutsche Kriegsverbrechen und ihre strafrechtliche Verfolgung nach dem Ersten Weltkrieg.* Hamburg: Hamburger Edition, 2003.

Häpke, Rudolf. *Die deutsche Verwaltung in Litauen, 1915–1918.* Berlin: Reichsdruckerei, 1921.

Heid, Ludger. *Maloche – nicht Mildtätigkeit. Ostjüdische Arbeiter in Deutschland 1914–1923.* Hildesheim: Olms, 1995.

Herbert, Ulrich. "Zwangsarbeit als Lernprozeß. Zur Beschäftigung ausländischer Arbeiter in der westdeutschen Industrie im Ersten Weltkrieg." *Archiv für Sozialgeschichte* 24 (1984): 285–304.

Herbert, Ulrich. *Fremdarbeiter: Politik und Praxis des 'Ausländer-Einsatzes' in der Kriegswirtschaft des Dritten Reiches.* Berlin: Dietz, 1985.

Herbert, Ulrich. *Geschichte der Ausländerpolitik in Deutschland. Saisonarbeiter, Zwangsarbeiter, Gastarbeiter, Flüchtlinge.* Bonn: Bundeszentrale für Politische Bildung, 2003.

Hertz, Mieczysław. *Łódzki Bataljon Robotniczy, ZAB 23.* Łódź: Magistrat m. Łodzi, 1920.

Hertz, Mieczysław. *Łódź w czasie wielkiej wojny.* Łódź: Seipelt in Komm, 1933.

Hull, Isabel V. *Absolute Destruction. Military Culture and the Practices of War in Imperial Germany.* Ithaca, NY: Cornell University Press, 2005.

Klimas, Petras. *Der Werdegang des Litauischen Staates von 1915 bis zur Bildung der provisorischen Regierung im November 1918.* Berlin: Paß & Garleb, 1919.

Knox, MacGregor. "Erster Weltkrieg und Military Culture. Kontinuität und Wandel im deutsch-italienischen Vergleich." In *Das Deutsche Kaiserreich in der Kontroverse*, edited by Sven Oliver Müller, and Cornelius Torp, 290–307. Göttingen: Vandenhoeck & Ruprecht, 2009.

Kramer, Alan. *Dynamics of Destruction. Culture and Mass Killing in the First World War.* Oxford: Oxford University Press, 2008.

Kundrus, Birthe. "Von der Peripherie ins Zentrum. Zur Bedeutung des Kolonialismus für das Deutsche Kaiserreich." In *Das Deutsche Kaiserreich in der Kontroverse*, edited by Sven Oliver Müller, and Cornelius Torp, 359–73. Göttingen: Vandenhoeck & Ruprecht, 2009.

Linde, Gerd. *Die deutsche Politik in Litauen im Ersten Weltkrieg.* Wiesbaden: Harrassowitz, 1965.

Litwa za rządów ks. Isenburga. Kraków: Krakowskiego Oddziału Zjednoczenia Narodowego, 1919.

Liulevicius, Vejas G. *War Land on the Eastern Front. Culture, National Identity and German Occupation in World War I.* Cambridge: Cambridge University Press, 2000.

Liulevicius, Vejas G. *Kriegsland im Osten. Eroberung, Kolonialisierung und Militärherrschaft im Ersten Weltkrieg.* Hamburg: Hamburger Edition, 2002.

Liulevicius, Vejas G. "Von 'Ober Ost' nach 'Ostland'?" In *Die vergessene Front. Der Osten 1914/15. Ereignis, Wirkung, Nachwirkung*, edited by Gerhard P. Groß, 295–310. Paderborn: Schöningh, 2006.

Ludendorff, Erich. *Meine Kriegserinnerungen 1914–1918.* Berlin: Mittler, 1919.

Ludendorff, Erich. *Kriegführung und Politik.* Berlin: Mittler, 1922.

Ludendorff, Erich. *Der totale Krieg.* München: Ludendorff, 1935.

Mayerhofer, Lisa. *Zwischen Freund und Feind – deutsche Besatzung in Rumänien 1916–1918.* München: Meidenbauer, 2010.

Motas, M., and I. Motasowa. "Zagadnienie wywozu siły roboczej z Królestwa Polskiego do Niemiec w okresie pierwszej wojny światowej." *Teki Archiwalne* 4 (1955): 7–97.

Nebelin, Manfred. *Ludendorff. Diktator im Ersten Weltkrieg.* München: Siedler, 2010.

Oltmer, Jochen. "Zwangsmigration und Zwangsarbeit. Ausländische Arbeitskräfte und bäuerliche Ökonomie im Deutschland des Ersten Weltkriegs." *Tel Aviver Jahrbuch für deutsche Geschichte* 27 (1998): 135–68.

Oltmer, Jochen. *Migration und Politik in der Weimarer Republik.* Göttingen: Vandenhoeck & Ruprecht, 2005.

Pöhlmann, Markus. "Von Versailles nach Armageddon: Totalisierungserfahrung und Kriegserwartung in deutschen Militärzeitschriften." In *An der Schwelle zum Totalen Krieg. Die militärische Debatte über den Krieg der Zukunft 1919–1939*, edited by Stig Förster, 323–91. Paderborn: Schöningh, 2002.

Pyta, Wolfram. *Hindenburg. Herrschaft zwischen Hohenzollern und Hitler.* München: Siedler, 2007.

Schlemmer, Thomas. "Grenzen der Integration. Die CSU und der Umgang mit der nationalsozialistischen Vergangenheit – Der Fall Dr. Max Frauendorfer." *Vierteljahrshefte für Zeitgeschichte* 48, no. 4 (2000): 676–742.

Schuster, Frank M. *Zwischen allen Fronten. Osteuropäische Juden während des Ersten Weltkrieges (1914–1919).* Köln: Böhlau, 2004.

Simma, Bruno, ed. "Übereinkommen über Zwangs- und Pflichtarbeit der Mitglieder der Internationalen Arbeitsorganisation (ILO) vom 29. Juni 1930 (Art. 2, Abs. 1)." *Menschenrechte, ihr internationaler Schutz. Textausgabe mit ausführlichem Sachverzeichnis und einer Einführung.* 3rd ed. 122–32. München: Deutscher Taschenbuch-Verlag, 1992.

Sklarz, Leon. *Geschichte und Organisation der Ostjudenhilfe in Deutschland seit dem Jahre 1914.* Berlin: Deyhle, 1927.

Spoerer, Mark, and Jochen Fleischhacker. "Forced Laborers in Nazi Germany. Categories, Numbers, Survivors." *Journal of Interdisciplinary History* 33, no. 2 (2002): 169–204.

Strazhas, Abba. *Deutsche Ostpolitik im Ersten Weltkrieg. Der Fall Ober Ost 1915–1917.* Wiesbaden: Harrassowitz, 1993.

Streit, Christian. *Keine Kameraden: Die Wehrmacht und die sowjetischen Kriegsgefangenen 1941–1945.* Stuttgart: Deutsche Verlags-Anstalt, 1978.

Szajkowski, Zosa. "East European Jewish Workers in Germany during World War I." In *Salo Wittmayer Baron. Jubilee Volume on the Occasion of his 80th Birthday,* edited by Saul Liebermann, 887–918. Jerusalem: American Academy for Jewish Research, 1974.

Thiel, Jens. *'Menschenbassin Belgien'. Anwerbung, Deportation und Zwangsarbeit im Ersten Weltkrieg.* Essen: Klartext, 2007.

Thoss, Buno. *Der Ludendorff-Kreis 1919–1923: München als Zentrum der mitteleuropäischen Gegenrevolution zwischen Revolution und Hitler-Putsch.* München: Wölfe, 1976.

Tooze, Adam. *The Wages of Destruction. The Making and Breaking of the Nazi Economy.* London: Penguin Books, 2007.

Westerhoff, Christian. *Zwangsarbeit im Ersten Weltkrieg. Deutsche Arbeitskräftepolitik im besetzten Polen und Litauen 1914–1918.* Paderborn: Schöningh, 2011.

Zimmerer, Jürgen. "Die Geburt des 'Ostlandes' aus dem Geiste des Kolonialismus. Die nationalsozialistische Eroberungs- und Beherrschungspolitik in (post)-kolonialer Perspektive." *Sozial.Geschichte* 19, no. 1 (2004): 10–43.

Zunkel, Friedrich. "Die ausländischen Arbeiter in der deutschen Kriegswirtschaftspolitik des Ersten Weltkrieges." In *Entstehung und Wandel der modernen Gesellschaft. Festschrift für Hans Rosenberg zum 65. Geburtstag,* edited by Gerhard A. Ritter, 280–311. Berlin: de Gruyter, 1970.

Zweig, Arnold. *Das ostjüdische Antlitz.* Berlin: Welt-Verlag, 1920.

Warsaw University under German occupation: state building and nation *Bildung* in Poland during the Great War

Jesse Kauffman

Department of History and Philosophy, Eastern Michigan University, Ypsilanti, MI, USA

The German occupation of Russia's Polish territories from 1915 to 1918 remains one of the least-explored chapters in the history of the Great War. This article examines the policies pursued by the occupation authorities in wartime Poland with a particular focus on the Polish university opened by the Germans in 1915. An analysis of the Germans' ambitions for the university, as well as how the occupiers and the university's students and faculty interacted during the occupation, reveals a great deal about the sources and nature of the ambitious state-building plan that developed under the German Governor-General, Hans Hartwig von Beseler, during the war. In turn, this provides new perspectives on the relationship between occupier and occupied in the Great War, German-Polish relations, the history of sovereignty and nationalism, and the continuities of German history in the era of total war. This article draws on both Polish and German published and archival sources.

Introduction

Neither Germany nor Austria-Hungary ever intended to raise the Polish Question: the fortunes of war raised it. Now it is with us and awaits a solution.

—Theobald von Bethmann Hollweg, 5 April 1916[1]

On 2 May 1915, Austro-German forces under the command of August von Mackensen launched what would become one of the greatest battlefield victories of the First World War. The attack began with an assault on Russian lines to the south-east of Kraków. By mid-May, the Russians had been driven back 80 miles; by June, Mackensen's troops had pushed them entirely out of Galicia. Subsequent summer attacks all along the Eastern Front brought further victories. In stark contrast to the nearly static slaughters that marked the fighting in the west, the eastern offensives of mid-1915 rolled steadily forward, claiming hundreds of miles of Russian territory and ultimately ejecting the forces of the Tsar from Central Europe. By the time the attacks ground to a halt in September, the Central Powers were in command of a vast front that stretched from the Baltic to the Carpathians.[2] The victory brought a sense of exhilaration after the bloody frustrations of the western slaughterhouse. One German soldier who fought in the eastern campaigns later recalled 'the enormous lift' the triumph 'gave to German spirits'.[3]

For all the euphoria they inspired, these battlefield victories were tactical, not strategic. Russia, while battered and humiliated, had not been knocked out of the war. In addition, Germany now had to secure and occupy vast stretches of formerly Imperial Russian territory, an undertaking for which it had not planned, and for which it could spare little manpower. The demands of occupation were exacerbated by the shattered state of the lands that passed under Austro-German control, the result not only of months of combat, but also of the nature of the Russian retreat, which had been accompanied by the deliberate destruction of infrastructure and the brutal deportation of thousands of Russians, Germans and Jews.[4] Nor were the Central Powers able to exercise their authority through existing state institutions, since the Russians had evacuated their government as their troops fled east. Finally, Central Europe seethed with a great variety of political movements – nationalist, Zionist, and Bolshevik, among others – that were energized by the war and the Russian defeat. Even if the occupiers had wished to remain aloof from the political struggles with which the region seethed, it is difficult to see how they could have avoided entanglement in them. Whatever fantasies of imperial conquest may have been inflamed in Germany by the eastern victories, more perceptive observers realized that the occupation of these devastated, fractious territories was going to present the occupying powers with considerable challenges.

This was particularly the case with the Polish territories wrested from Russia's control. In the wake of the Napoleonic Wars, Russia had annexed most of the lands of the former Polish Commonwealth; these territories became known as 'Congress Poland' or the 'Congress Kingdom' after the Congress of Vienna. As a result of the 1915 offensives, this 'Kingdom' had now passed under German and Austrian control, with the Germans assuming control of the bulk of the territory. This was a decidedly mixed blessing. Germany, too, had annexed Polish territories after the defeat of Napoleon. The result was a large Polish Prussian minority that, in the decades before the outbreak of the Great War, was locked in a bitter nationality struggle with its German rulers who, for their part, deeply distrusted their Polish subjects. Whatever policy the Germans decided to pursue in occupied Poland, they would have to constantly consider the potential ramifications on domestic German *Polenpolitik*. Finally, Austria, too, had its own Polish minority; thus the occupiers not only had to be mindful of the links between their domestic policies and those pursued in their zones of occupation, but the already-strained relations between the allies would also be complicated by the Polish connection as well.

Control over occupied Congress Poland was divided unequally between the Powers. The Germans established control over the bulk of Central European Poland, with the Austrians controlling a smaller sector to the south. To administer their territory, the Germans established a mixed civil–military administrative apparatus, the Imperial Government-General of Warsaw, which operated independently of the German occupation regime established to the north, the so-called territory of 'Ober Ost'. The Government-General was commanded by a veteran Prussian officer, Hans Hartwig von Beseler, who was answerable only to the Emperor. Over the course of his tenure, Beseler became convinced that Germany's interests would be best served by creating a Polish satellite state in Central Europe. While the military and foreign policy of this state would be subordinate to the Reich, it was to enjoy broad autonomy in matters of domestic politics and cultural life. By the fall of 1916, the leadership of the Reich had decided, for a variety of reasons, to support Beseler's ambitions.[5] On 5 November 1916, the governments of Germany and Austria-Hungary publicly announced their intention to sponsor the restoration of a Polish kingdom in Central Europe.

The attempt to realize this nation-building project in occupied Poland remains one of the great unexplored episodes of the First World War.[6] The phenomenon of occupations

MILITARY OCCUPATIONS IN FIRST WORLD WAR EUROPE

during the Great War has only recently begun to receive scholarly attention, most of which has continued the long-standing historiographical focus on the Western Front.[7] The work that has been done on the occupied East has mostly been limited to the policies of the Ober Ost regime.[8] The occupation of Poland has remained a 'forgotten occupation' embedded within an 'unknown war'.[9] Yet an exploration of the Imperial Government-General and its policies can pay rich dividends for our understanding of both the Great War and the vexed relationship between Germany and Poland, as a closer look at the Polish university opened by the occupiers in Warsaw illustrates. The Germans established a number of institutions, such as a Polish army and elected city governments, to further their ambitions. Warsaw University, however, was to play a special role in creating Germany's post-war Polish satellite state, by moulding the Polish bureaucrats and administrators who would run this state's affairs into competent and politically reliable subordinates. More broadly, Warsaw University's wartime rebirth illustrates several key aspects of the German occupation. First, it shows in a microcosm the cluster of attitudes, beliefs and interests that informed the German state-building project in Poland, which cannot be reduced to either a classic case of nineteenth-century colonialism or a kind of trial run for Nazi brutality. In addition, the relationship between the University and the occupation government reveals the Germans' continuing attempts to calibrate the balance between consent and coercion in occupied Poland, adding a layer of complexity to our understanding of the mechanics of occupation during the Great War. Finally, a closer look at the University suggests that the institutions of occupation, far from being simple instruments of German control, actually served to bind the regime to native tensions. Acknowledging this is a remedy for an enduringly deep-seated flaw in much of the scholarship on Germany's relationship with Eastern Europe: the tendency to ascribe to the Germans a degree of power that they did not have. Some German nationalists may have conceived of the East as an empty *Raum* waiting to be filled and dominated by Germany, but it (obviously) was not. To overlook the role played by native forces in shaping events in the German-ruled East is to continue, however unwittingly, to perpetrate a view of the region that is derived mainly from propagandists and ideologues.[10]

The Polish background and initial German steps

Warsaw had not had a Polish university since the late 1860s. As part of the harsh Russian reprisals that followed in the wake of the Polish uprising of January 1863, the Szkoła Główna the Congress Kingdom's Polish university, had gradually been transformed into an instrument of Russification. In the lecture halls and classrooms of the Imperial University of Warsaw – its name after 1869 – Russian professors taught Russian subjects in Russian to an increasingly Russian student body. The Polish historian, Tadeusz Manteuffel described the Imperial University as 'foreign' and 'filled with lecturers ... hostile to all things Polish'.[11] This may smack of hyperbole, but a resolution passed by its faculty in 1897, celebrating the establishment of a monument to 'a great statesman of Russia, M. Muravev, who saved the North-West region from Polish-Catholic slavery', suggests that Manteuffel's characterization was not wide of the mark.[12] Polish scholarly life nonetheless endured in Warsaw, where it was kept alive – along with the dream that one day Polish education would return to the erstwhile Polish capital – primarily by academic societies and organizations.

That day seemed to arrive with the outbreak of the Great War. When hostilities began, the Russian Government began issuing promises to restore to Poland the cultural and political freedoms it had once enjoyed. This spurred the Polish elite into a frenzy of activity, including planning for the re-establishment of a Polish university in the capital. While the Russians never followed through on their promises, the evacuation precipitated by the German invasion presented the Polish educational activists with a golden opportunity: the Imperial University, along with most of its personnel, equipment and books, was moved to the city of Rostov-on-the-Don.[13] A void at the centre of the city's educational life was thereby created, a void that the local intellectuals were eager to fill. By the time the Imperial Government-General was established in August 1915, local plans for the establishment of a new university were well advanced. On 25 September 1915, at a meeting of senior occupation officials in Warsaw, the head of the civilian branch of the occupation government, Wolfgang von Kries, informed Beseler of the locals' desire to re-establish both a Polish university and a technical college in the city. Kries endorsed the idea, arguing that it would keep young people out of trouble and provide the Germans with good publicity. With little comment, Beseler granted permission for the institutions to open.[14]

It is difficult to say why Beseler agreed, since he had not yet arrived at his ambitious plans for creating a Polish satellite state. At this early date, he still believed that his primary duty was maintaining security and order in the land under his control. His November 1915 report to the Emperor explaining his decision to allow the schools to open was in keeping with this vision of his duties: the institutions, he argued, would give young people something to do, thereby preventing them from engaging in 'sterile political agitation'.[15] It is possible that Beseler was also influenced by his family background. His father, Georg, was a professor of law in Berlin, and the Governor-General had been brought up steeped in the values and the society of Berlin's *Bildungsbürgertum*. The list of visitors to the Beseler household during the general's youth and adolescence reads like a roster of the nineteenth-century northern German intellectual elite – Mommsen, Treitschke, Ranke and Sybel.[16] While it is difficult to say what role such august company played in Beseler's intellectual development, he was no stranger to the world of *Geist*.

Whatever motives led Beseler initially to approve the opening of the schools, by the following year the University (and, to a lesser extent, the technical college) had come to assume a central role in Beseler's vastly expanded ambitions for the territory under his control. By 1916, Beseler had concluded that the war had already destroyed the Central European political arrangements made by the Powers at the Congress of Vienna. Whatever would take its place would, he believed, have to take account of Polish wishes for self-determination.[17] Beseler recognized that the varieties of Polish nationalism often harboured conflicting visions of Poland's future. He also knew that it was not necessarily a sentiment important to the *Volk* as a whole, noting, for example, that the peasantry despised 'their' nobles and remained loyal to the Tsar. Yet his time in Poland convinced him that, despite its many internal contradictions, Polish nationalism was widespread enough, and potent enough a political force, to make ignoring it impossible. Policies of repression would merely breed more instability of the sort that had characterized Poland for much of the nineteenth century.

Beseler drew the conclusion that Germany's best move would be to patronize the establishment of a Central European Polish satellite kingdom under German control. This kingdom would have autonomy in its domestic affairs, but its foreign and military policy would be controlled by Germany. Beseler believed that this would provide the Germans with several advantages. First, it would give them control over an army that stood between them and Russia. Second, and just as important, it would prevent the Austrians from setting up their own client state in Congress Poland. Beseler was in many respects a typical nineteenth-century northern German of the educated Protestant middle class: he loved

Bismarck and the army, and loathed junkers, capitalists, Catholics and the Austrians. His distrust of the Austrians was deep-seated ('As individuals they are quite nice, but their state, their army and their system are horrible', Beseler wrote to his wife Clara in November 1916[18]). Beseler believed that future tensions and even another war with Austria were a possibility. If the Austrians controlled a Polish dependency on Germany's eastern frontier, this would give them a major strategic advantage: not only would they be able to launch attacks into German territory from Poland, but they would also be able to use their policies in Poland to stoke irredentism among Prussia's Polish subjects, creating a situation resembling the pre-war conflict between Austria and Serbia.[19] Beseler recognized that his own project created the potential for the same tensions, but he predicted that a sort of voluntary ethnic cleansing of Germany's eastern provinces would take place once the Polish state was created. Those Prussian Poles who wished to live as Poles in a Polish Kingdom would leave Prussia and settle there.[20]

While Beseler was prepared to make concessions to Polish demands for autonomy, he did not believe that self-government could be entrusted to the Poles of the Congress Kingdom immediately. A key element in his view of the Polish people, and one that would play a major role in shaping his occupation policy, was his belief that they were 'immature'. It is a word that appears in his public and private correspondence time and again, usually when he felt exasperated.[21] The implication was that the Poles needed a firm yet sympathetic hand to guide them to the 'adulthood' of autonomy. While crass and condescending, this chauvinistic paternalism should not be confused with the racism of later German occupiers. Unlike them, Beseler did not believe Poles to be biologically incapable (or unworthy) of governing themselves; rather, he reasoned that decades of Russian oppression meant that no native political class with governing experience existed in Poland. A combination of intense Polish nationalism and political inexperience was bound to produce a disaster: 'If they were left to their own devices', Beseler wrote to Clara in October 1915, 'they would soon be biting each other's heads off'.[22]

As Beseler's ambitions for Poland expanded and crystallized, so did his thoughts on what role the University – and, to a lesser extent, the technical college – was to play in realizing his nation-building strategy. No longer a mere holding pen meant to keep youths out of trouble, by 1916 Warsaw University had become the key to creating the sort of post-war Polish state he had conjured up in his imagination. In its classrooms and lecture halls, the 'immature' Polish students who would one day become the bureaucrats, intellectuals and lawyers of Germany's Polish satellite would be moulded by their teachers into nationally conscious, but wholly apolitical subjects of an autonomous, but non-sovereign kingdom. While this seems like an unrealistic idea, Beseler's belief that it was possible owes much to nineteenth-century German ideas about politics and education. The ideal of a German university was that of an apolitical institution, where professors and their charges dwelt in the higher, transcendent realm of *Geist*.[23] German bureaucrats were also traditionally supposed to be apolitical. Finally, the German idea of *Bildung* – of education as total character formation – lent itself very well to Beseler's imperial ambitions in Poland. Given that the Polish students were 'unreif', they could be carefully moulded into the kind of Polish elite that Beseler wanted to create: thoroughly Polish culturally, willing and able to run a complicated state administration, but ultimately content to leave affairs such as foreign policy and war in the hands of others.

The importance of the University to the Germans' plans was crystallized in a statement made by Kries at the 25 September 1915 meeting. 'Germany does not intend', he announced:

to keep this land forever, but rather wishes to bind it permanently to itself. It must be well-administered, it must have good civil servants, jurists, physicians, engineers, architects, technicians, indeed even philosophers. It is important that the Poles, when they one day assume the administration of the state [*Landesverwaltung*], have the necessary specialists.[24]

It is difficult to say why Kries said this at the September meeting. It did not yet reflect Beseler's – or Berlin's – intentions for Poland at the time. Nonetheless, it provides a perfect summary of how Beseler eventually came to view the role that higher education was to play in German-dominated Poland. In the Governor-General's official mid-1916 report to Berlin, he noted that the University and technical school were both doing a fine job of producing the professional elite needed for the 'country's future administration', which Beseler now termed as the institutions' 'essential task'.[25]

This increased importance was more publicly announced in the new statutes granted to the University by the Germans in 1916. The preamble to these statutes illustrates the role that *Bildung* was to play in shaping the new Polish elite: the faculty were rather sternly informed that it was their responsibility to shape the character of their students and ensure that they became responsible, respectable citizens. Towards this end, faculty were to ensure that the University became a kind of political sterile zone, quarantined off from the upheavals taking place outside its lecture halls. In a similar vein, the statutes celebrated the power of 'pure scholarship' to draw peoples together in the common pursuit of knowledge, while simultaneously assuring that the University's curriculum would be built 'on the foundation [of the] national language and culture'.[26] The flaws at the heart of the Germans' plans for Poland were encapsulated in a microcosm in these statutes. While these tensions remained latent for the time being, as the occupation dragged on they would become increasingly difficult to conceal.

These troubles still lay in the future when the University was opened in the fall of 1915. After the 25 September meeting, a joint Polish–German commission of scholars and administrators convened to work out the necessary details. The committee worked remarkably quickly, given the difficulty of the task and the pressures under which each side laboured, and several disagreements were worked out over the course of the early fall. The politically loaded question of where the professors would come from, for example, was solved with remarkable rapidity. The Polish side hoped to draw some of its faculty from Galicia, where the universities of Kraków and Lemberg nurtured Polish intellectual life. Beseler, anxious to minimize Austrian influence in his zone of occupation, resisted the appointment of Galician Poles. In the end, the two sides managed to settle upon a list of mutually acceptable faculty candidates.[27] Owing to the speed with which these officials worked, the University and the technical school were ready to open formally in November 1915. Józef Brudziński, a physician, was named rector. Bogdan Graf von Hutten-Czapski, a conservative Prussian-Polish nobleman attached to Beseler's staff, became curator, the occupation government's official representative to the institutions.

The University was opened to a great fanfare on 15 November 1915. The day began with a mass at St John's Cathedral, where excited crowds gathered to watch the dignitaries assemble. The occupation government was represented by Hutten-Czapski, Beseler having expressly forbidden a more conspicuous German presence. Within the church, a place of honour had been accorded to the rectors of the University and the technical school.[28] The formal opening of the University took place afterwards in its main lecture hall, where the Germans were better represented. Beseler was in attendance (the choir assembled for the event sang *Veni Creator* as he made his entrance, almost certainly a coincidence), as was Kries. The Germans took care not to offend Polish sensibilities; security, for example, was provided by firefighters rather than soldiers or policemen.

MILITARY OCCUPATIONS IN FIRST WORLD WAR EUROPE

Excited young students greeted the guests as they assembled, addressing Poles and Germans in their respective native tongues. Brudziński gave a speech in which he quoted the romantic writer Zygmunt Krasiński's declaration that 'we have great memories, thus may we also harbor great hopes'. Beseler then pronounced the University open.[29] One German attendee, who disparaged the event in his post-war memoirs, nonetheless grudgingly admitted that 'one went away in the end conscious of having taken part in an academic celebration beyond national discord'.[30]

The decision to open the University was received favourably in the occupied territory.[31] Over 1000 students enrolled for the first semester; the most popular courses of study were medicine and law, followed by humanities.[32] Not everyone was so pleased, though. In a letter written to his wife, shortly after the University opened, Beseler noted that he would probably be criticized by 'Balt[ic] Germans and Pan-Germanists'.[33] He was right. *Die Ostmark*, the newspaper of the German Marches Association, a group of German nationalists who considered themselves Germany's front-line soldiers in the nationality struggle going in Prussia's Polish provinces, offered Germany's educational policy in occupied Poland as 'splendid evidence of the cultural sensibilities of the German people', but also darkly warned that 'nations are usually ungrateful'.[34] The Russian press, meanwhile, erupted into a chorus of outrage.[35] There were also critics of the University within Polish Europe itself. The Galician writer Adolf Nowaczyński apparently did not think the faculty was quite 'Polish' enough, judging by the following lyrics he wrote for a 1916 puppet show, the *Szopka Warszawska* (Handelsman and Kleiner were both faculty members):

> In the Warsaw 'Alma Mater'
> Handelsman lectures on Polish history, and
> Kleiner drills romanticism into students' heads.
> Let's hope that even
> The new faculty of theology
> Will soon become circumcised and Jewified.[36]

Deceptive stability, 1915–1917

Such criticism aside, the promise of peaceful accommodation made at the opening ceremonies seemed to be realized during the first year and a half of the University's existence. Student enrolments increased from 1039 to 1621.[37] The ranks of the academic staff increased as well, from 36 lecturers in 1915–1916 to 50 in 1916–1917.[38] The occupation authorities exercised formal control over the curriculum, but this seems to have had little impact on the courses offered. The University's students could choose from a rich variety of courses that were unmistakeably geared towards the production of a new, thoroughly Polish, elite. The satellite kingdom's future bureaucrats, for example, studied in the Department of Law and Administrative Sciences. There they could take courses taught by Józef Siemieński, a nationalist and scholar who had studied at the Imperial University of Warsaw, where he had submitted a thesis in Polish, in violation of the university's rules. Siemieński instructed the kingdom's future administrators in topics such as Polish law, the 'history of the Polish system' and the Polish Constitution of 3 May 1791.[39] Other departments offered Polish-language coursework in subjects ranging from classical philosophy to Polish literature and history. German *Kultur* found its due representation in the Department of Philology, where a German scholar, Wilhelm Paszkowski of Berlin University, lectured on Faust.[40]

Students could seek further intellectual stimulation and the fellowship of their peers in one of the University's many clubs and organizations. When the University had first opened,

71

tight German restrictions on where and when students could associate limited such opportunities. In its first year, Warsaw University had only two official student organizations: a club for medical students and the mutual-aid society 'Bratnia Pomoc' (Fraternal Aid).[41] As the University increased in importance in German eyes, however, they began to ease these restrictions, which led to a flowering of associational life. Students could now opt, for example, to join the Lelewel Society (Towarszystwo im. Lelewala), which was led by history professor Marceli Handelsman. The Society was named after the nineteenth-century historian Joachim Lelewel, a republican and staunch partisan of Polish independence. According to the Society's German-approved statutes, it had been established to conduct 'research on native [Polish] civilization and culture and [prepare its] members in this manner for ... civic employment'. Bratnia Pomoc, meanwhile, expanded the scope of its activities, organizing events such as a boating excursion on the Vistula.[42]

The University also began to assume a prominent role in the cultural life of the city, which, despite extreme privations suffered by its citizens during the war, was remarkably vibrant, owing to the abolition of decades of Russian restrictions. In May 1916, for example, Warsaw staged a parade to celebrate the anniversary of the 1791 Constitution, a celebration that had been forbidden by the Russians. Before the parade, the curator, Hutten-Czapski, representatives of the city's academic elite – drawn from the University, the technical college, and scholarly societies and organizations – as well as students with their institutions' flags gathered for a quiet ceremony in the Botanical Garden where Brudziński solemnly unveiled a special commemorative plaque.[43] Rector Brudziński had also been a member of the committee that had organized the parade that took place later that day.[44] The students marched in that parade with their flags, a sight that became a common feature of many of the city's most important cultural and political events, such as the public proclamation on 5 November 1916 of the Central Powers' intent to restore Poland to statehood after the war. When Beseler delivered the proclamation in Warsaw, he did so flanked by students from the University and technical college bearing their flags. Rector Brudziński gave the official Polish reply to the announcement.[45]

By early 1917, it seemed that Beseler had been right to risk the opening of the University; it had not caused a great deal of trouble and was popular with the native population. But the seemingly orderly and amicable relations between the occupiers and the University community were deceptive. Beneath the surface, a combustible mixture of political and economic resentments was brewing. These resentments would finally erupt into a massive student strike in 1917, an event less important in itself than in the way the occupiers responded to it. The combination of pleading, half-hearted threats, and stern but empty admonitions with which the Germans met the students' blatant challenge to their authority revealed their reluctance to rely solely – or even primarily – on coercion in their pursuit of their Polish satellite kingdom.

The student strike and German response

A number of factors eventually led to trouble with the University's students. As a whole, they were highly politicized. While political movements of every variety flourished at the University, the predominant political orientation was that of the left-wing nationalism of the sort represented by Józef Piłsudski and the nationalist wing of the Polish Socialist Party (PPS).[46] While the nationalists of this camp believed that the sovereign independence of Poland was a goal which was not open to compromise, they were willing to work with the Germans in the initial phase of the occupation, since they believed Russia to be the primary enemy of Polish aspirations. The February Revolution in Russia, therefore,

MILITARY OCCUPATIONS IN FIRST WORLD WAR EUROPE

resulted in a major political shift within occupied Poland. With the Tsar gone and promises of a new era of Polish–Russian cooperation issuing from St Petersburg, the main enemy of the PPS' aspirations now seemed to be the occupying powers. The student body could not have remained immune from this general political shift. Resentment at the occupiers' economic policy also fed student hostility. The occupiers were ruthless in their plunder of whatever Polish resources could be put in the service of the German war effort. In economic terms, life in occupied Poland was difficult for all and wretched for many. The students, of course, shared in this general state of privation. Not surprisingly, the civilian arm of the German occupation government noted in 1917 that, far from being apolitical, the various student clubs and organizations were becoming hotbeds of hostility to the occupiers. Finally, tensions within the student body itself were also festering throughout 1916–1917, with Jewish students being subjected to hostility by some of their peers. Fraternal Aid was singled out by the Germans as an organization that was both anti-German and unfriendly to Jews (who, the authorities noted, were the only students who could be relied on to show up for courses and lectures offered by German professors).[47] Given the large number of Jewish students – the percentage fluctuated, but usually fell between 40% and 50% – tensions between Polish Gentiles and Polish Jews within the student population had the potential to become a very serious source of instability.[48]

The students had indeed proved themselves troublesome before the 1917 strike. An altercation between authorities and the students had occurred in November 1915 during a celebration of the November Uprising. A January celebration of that month's uprising likewise led to a clash, with German troops actually entering University grounds.[49] A noteworthy display of defiance by the students occurred in January 1917. In that month, in the course of his 'Peace Without Victory' speech, Woodrow Wilson proclaimed that 'statesmen everywhere are agreed that there should be a united, independent, and autonomous Poland'.[50] In response, a crowd of cheering students gathered outside the residence of the US' consul in Warsaw, who later paid a return call to the University.[51]

In May 1917, these festering tensions erupted into a student strike. The spark was provided by a clash between the authorities and students at a celebration of the 3 May Constitution. The celebrations became rowdy, leading to the arrest of two students, one of whom was led away in handcuffs. The enraged students immediately called a strike to protest the 'violence and impudence' of the authorities. The immediate release of both the students was demanded.[52] One of them was in fact released by the Germans. The students, however, were not mollified and the strike continued. Students armed with 'sticks and riding whips' took the streets, where they brawled with the authorities.[53]

In May, the Germans shut down the technical college, whose students were also on strike. Hoping to avert a similar fate, the faculty at the University fruitlessly pleaded with the students to return to their classes. The students escalated their demands: they would return to their classes only if the University and technical school were granted full autonomy. Hutten-Czapski let the students know that such plans to do just that were, in fact, currently being made.[54] The students were not mollified, and, though they started to return to their classes, they now refused to pay their fees and forbade their fellows from having any further dealings with Hutten-Czapski. The unfortunate Paszkowski, the professor from Berlin, reported in June that the door of the German Seminar had been repeatedly vandalized with 'filthy inscriptions'.[55]

Beseler finally moved to end the strike by convening a meeting attended by the rectors of the University and technical college, senior German officials and representatives of the city's private colleges. In a lengthy harangue, an angry Beseler accused the Poles of neglecting their responsibility to maintain order at the University. The students, he added, had betrayed their responsibility to be apolitical. Beseler delivered a warning, which sought to convince the Poles that they were acting against their own interests. 'Gentlemen', he told the rectors, 'I not infrequently have the feeling, [that] I would like to leave this land today rather than tomorrow'. But, he warned, if Germany simply handed over full authority to the natives, Poland would 'descend into chaos'.[56]

Hutten-Czapski was offended by the speech, though he realized that Beseler was probably venting not merely his frustration with the University, but also a gnawing unease about the wisdom of these policies in Poland. The rectors of the schools were also angered by the speech, a sentiment they made known to Hutten-Czapski.[57] The rectors themselves made their grievances known directly to Beseler as well as sending him a response to his accusations in which blame for the disturbances was assigned to the occupiers and their policies.[58]

The crisis reached its peak in June, when the University was closed by the Germans. Brudziński had tried to avoid this fate by pleading with the students to pay their fees and end their boycott. He assured them that the University was on the verge of being transferred to the Polish authorities.[59] The Germans likewise assured the students that autonomy for the University was on its way, but the students demanded a written guarantee that this was so. Hoping to avert a showdown, the Germans extended the enrolment deadline while simultaneously promising that those who did not meet it would be expelled. The deadline passed with only a handful of students at the University and technical college registering for classes. On 23 June, the institutions were decreed closed by the Germans. Beseler ordered that all those who had not enrolled be expelled.[60]

The closure of the schools was followed not by mass imprisonment or exemplary executions, but by the promised transfer of control over the University to Polish authorities in the fall. The occupiers, who still considered themselves the ultimate sovereign authority over the occupied territory and, therefore, over its educational institutions, reserved the right to block faculty appointments. Otherwise, control over the University was handed over in the fall to a Polish Department of Religion and Education, which set itself to the task of creating new rules and statutes for the University. A reopening ceremony was held in early November 1917, where the Polish head of educational affairs, Józef Mikułowski-Pomorski, celebrated the opening of schools that were under full Polish control 'for the first time'. Shortly thereafter, the faculty elected Antoni Kostanecki, an economist, as their new rector (Brudziński was ill and died in December.)[61] Over 2000 students enrolled for the 1917–1918 school year.[62] Beseler, explaining himself to Berlin, blamed the troubles with the students on a small number of rabble-rousers and the electrifying effects of the upheavals in Russia. He also, however, wondered if the undertaking had not been flawed from the outset. 'It was an unusual enterprise', he wrote, 'to ... cultivate as a foreign power this branch of national life, which must spring from the innermost essence of a people'. He did not believe the entire affair to be a waste of effort, however. After the war, he argued, the University would remind the Poles of the great blessings that German occupation had brought them.[63] Whether Beseler really believed this is hard to say, though in a moment of despair he may have been able to convince himself that it was possible.

Certainly the University did nothing to assuage the bitterness that marked German–Polish relations in the years after 1918. The occupation regime lasted until the end of the war, when its soldiers mutinied, forming councils that claimed to be the legitimate representatives of the German troops in Poland. At the same time the occupation army was dissolving, Polish insurgents linked with the PPS launched a coup. The German soldiers were disarmed virtually without resistance. Amidst the chaos, Beseler fled Warsaw, an act that was to tarnish his reputation in post-war Germany. The soldiers themselves followed

MILITARY OCCUPATIONS IN FIRST WORLD WAR EUROPE

later, having worked out a deal with the new Polish government whereby they turned over their remaining weapons in exchange for safe passage to Germany, a bargain that caused outrage in the Reich. 'It is deeply regrettable', Matthias Erzberger announced to the National Assembly in March 1919 'that 16,000 German soldiers and officers [ran] away from Warsaw because 800 poorly armed Poles [formed] a mob'.[64]

The collapse of the occupation government added fuel to the fiery hatred for Poland that was kindled in Germany at the end of the war. The Polish uprising in Prussian Poland was another source of anti-Polish hostility after 1918. Most anger was generated by the terms of the Versailles treaty, which awarded portions of pre-war German territory to the new Polish state. This was a particularly bitter pill to swallow for many Germans; their armies had, after all, been victorious in the East; the Polish state to which its land had been awarded had not existed in 1914; and, finally, the territories awarded to Poland had a significant German minority, whose members now became Polish citizens. The suspicion that this minority was being ill-treated by Poland provided further grounds for German animosity towards Poland in the years after the signing of the Versailles treaty. Gerhard Weinberg has noted that a widely shared, bitter hatred of Poland was a key characteristic of Weimar political culture.[65] While pre-war hostilities to the Prussian Poles certainly fed into these hatreds, one important difference should be pointed out: the Ostmarkenverein was founded, in part, to combat supposed German indifference towards the Polish Question. The war, occupation and peace treaty all accomplished what the Verein's schoolteachers and pastors could not – the transformation of this general indifference into generalized hostility.

The return

While the precise connections have yet to be documented, some of this hatred must be responsible for the actions of the German soldiers and administrators who returned to Poland in 1939, inflicting a hellish occupation on that country. Population expulsions, the closing of cultural institutions and wanton, unrestrained violence were all part of a brutal policy of exterminating Poland culturally, and, perhaps, physically. This policy bears faint resemblance to that pursued by Imperial Germany during the Great War. A brief look at the University serves to highlight how different the occupations were. The University that Beseler helped established was still functioning when the Germans arrived in 1939. It was closed by the Nazis and university-level study was strictly forbidden on pain of death. Some of the very same people who had gotten faculty jobs at the 1915 University were still in Warsaw when this new German army arrived. Siemieński, for example, who had taught the satellite kingdom's 'apolitical' bureaucrats, went on to become the director of Warsaw's Main Archive. Siemieński joined the resistance when the Nazis invaded and was later arrested by the Gestapo while attending a clandestine meeting at a Warsaw museum. He died in Auschwitz. Marceli Handelsman, the history professor who led the Lelewel Society, also perished in the second occupation. An established scholar by the time the Nazis came to Poland, he taught in secret under an assumed name. In 1944 he was arrested by the Gestapo, his identity and location being passed on to them by right-wing Poles. He died in a Nazi concentration camp.

The differences between the two occupations were, as the example of higher education shows, enormous. Nor were the differences merely the result of the greater restraint shown by the officials of Imperial Germany. The occupations were, rather, animated by fundamentally different political imaginations. Beseler's concerns were not particularly extreme: how to neutralize the threat to Germany still posed (in his mind) by Austria, how to successfully defend Germany from a Russian invasion, and how to contain the disruptions and tensions caused by nationalist movements that spread across the borders of

75

MILITARY OCCUPATIONS IN FIRST WORLD WAR EUROPE

existing states. Thoughts of a master race engaged in a struggle for space had nothing to do with Imperial Germany's occupation policies in the Great War. This should not trivialize the extreme hardships inflicted on the occupied population, but it does suggest that the supposed continuities between the two eras, established by historians mainly on the basis of Imperial Germany's unrealized plans to create an ethnically cleansed 'border strip', have been a little cheaply bought.[66] Nonetheless, links between the occupations exist. Perhaps the most important link between them is the subtle way the war brutalized the post-war political imagination. A 1917 letter from Beseler to his wife illustrates the ideological gulf that separates the Imperial occupation from that of the Nazis:

> I would ... prefer it if there were *Germans* living here, but there are Poles here, and you can't chase them all away or kill them all, so you've got to find a way to live with them somehow.[67]

The subsequent occupiers would be bound by no such scruples or limits – either in their ambitions for the East, or the means used to pursue them.

Notes

1. Reichstag, *Verhandlungen des Reichstags*, vol. 307, 852.
2. Tucker, *Great War*, 75–7.
3. Ritter, *Sword and the Scepter*, 67.
4. Lohr, *Nationalizing the Russian Empire*.
5. Conze's *Polnische Nation* is still an indispensable guide to the vicissitudes of Germany's Polish policy during the war.
6. Conze, *Polnische Nation* is the standard work; my 2008 dissertation (Kauffman, 'Sovereignty and the Search for Order'), currently being revised into a manuscript entitled *The Elusive Alliance: War, State-Building, and the Search for Order in German-Occupied Poland, 1915–1918*, also addresses the occupation of Poland. Other recent work includes Stempin's, '"Das vergessene Generalgouvernement"' and Hofmann's article, 'Die vergessene Okkupation'. Zilch's *Okkupation und Währung im Ersten Weltkrieg* is excellent on Poland.
7. See Becker, *Les cicatrices rouges*; de Schaepdrijver, *La Belgique*; de Schaepdrijver, '*Belgium*'; McPhail, *Long Silence*.
8. Liulevicius, *War Land on the Eastern Front*.
9. The phrase 'unknown war' is Winston Churchill's.
10. See Zahra, 'Looking East'. At times, Liulevicius' *War Land on the Eastern Front* comes uncomfortably close to this view.
11. Manteuffel, *Uniwersytet Warszawski*, 1.
12. Quoted in Porter, *When Nationalism Began to Hate*, 81.
13. Handelsman, *Polska w czasie wielkiej wojny*, vol. 1, 109.
14. Hutten-Czapski, *Sechzig Jahre*, 253–4.
15. Beseler to Emperor, 3 November 1915. BAB-L/R1501/119699/5–6.
16. Conze, *Polnische Nation*, 107.
17. See Conze, *Polnische Nation*, 178–80.
18. 28 November 1916. BA MA/N 30/54/p. 78.
19. Beseler to Chancellor, 12 November 1917. BAB-L/N2126/426/2–6.
20. Conze, *Polnische Nation*, 179–80.
21. See, for example, Beseler's letter to Clara, 30 July 1917. BA-MA/N30/55/p. 82.
22. Quoted in Conze, *Polnische Nation*, 115.
23. Nipperdey, *Deutsche Geschichte*, 590–1.
24. Hutten-Czapski, *Sechzig Jahre*, 253–4.
25. Bericht des Generalgouverneurs über die Verwaltung des Generalgouvernements Warschau. Zeitraum: 1. Juli bis 30 September 1916. BAB-L/R1501/119760/42/p. 13.
26. Ginschel, *Handbuch für das Generalgouvernement*, 325–6.
27. Warschauer, *Deutsche Kulturarbeit*, 277; Hutten-Czapski, *Sechzig Jahre*, 254–6; Manteuffel, *Uniwersytet Warszawski*, 5–8.
28. Muszkowski, *Kalendarz Uniwersytecki: Semestr Letni*, 22–3; Hutten-Czapski, *Sechzig Jahre*, 256–7.
29. *Otwarcie Uniwersytetu i Politechniki*.

30. Warschauer, *Deutsche Kulturarbeit*, 278.
31. Bericht des Generalgouverneurs über die Verwaltung des Generalgouvernements Warschau. Zeitraum: 1.10.1915 bis 31.12.1915. BAB-L/R1501/119759/130.
32. Kries, 'Deutsche Staatsverwaltung', 144.
33. Quoted in Conze, *Polnsiche Nation*, 119–20.
34. *Die Ostmark*, October–December 1915.
35. Bericht des Generalgouverneurs über die Verwaltung des Generalgouvernements Warschau. Zeitraum: 1.1.1916 bis 31.3.1916. BAB-L/R1501/119760/3/p. 13.
36. Quoted in Segel, 'Culture in Poland', 80.
37. Manteuffel, *Uniwersytet Warszawski*, 273–5.
38. Garlicki, *Dzieje Uniwersytetu*, 314.
39. For courses, see Muszkowski, *Kalendarz Uniwersytecki: Semestr Zimowy*, 66.
40. Muszkowski, *Kalendarz Uniwersytecki: Semestr Letni*, 91–9.
41. Muszkowski, *Kalendarz Uniwersytecki: Semestr Letni*, 130–41.
42. Muszkowski, *Kalendarz Uniwersytecki: Semestr Zimowy*, 105–9.
43. Hutten-Czapski, *Sechzig Jahre*, 270.
44. Archiwum Polskiej Akademii Nauk/TNW/70/993.
45. Hutten-Czapski, *Sechzig Jahre*, 299–301.
46. Dunin-Węsowicz, *Warszawa w czasie pierwszej*, 201.
47. Kries to Beseler, 19 June 1917. BAB-L/R1501/119700/42–43, 45–46.
48. Garlicki, *Dzieje Uniwersytetu*, 55.
49. Manteuffel, *Uniwersytet Warszawski*, 16.
50. Wilson, 'Address to the Senate'.
51. Bericht des Generalgouverneurs über die Verwaltung des Generalgouvernements Warschau. Zeitraum: 1 Oktober 1916 bis 31 März 1917. BAB-L/R1501/119761/4/p. 31.
52. BAB-L/R1501/119700/70.
53. Kries to Beseler, 19 June 1917. BAB-L/R1501/119700/52.
54. Hutten-Czapski, *Sechzig Jahre*, 361.
55. BAB-L/R1501/119760/112.
56. Ansprache des Herrn Generalgouverneurs an die Rektoren der Warschauer Hochschulen am 25.5.1917. HIA/WWC/Box 2/Folder: German Authorities in Occupation of Poland, 1916–1917/p. 3.
57. Hutten-Czapski, *Sechzig Jahre*, 358–61.
58. HIA/WWC/Box 2/Folder: German Authorities in Occupation of Poland, 1916–1917.
59. Aufruf des Rektors, 16 June 1917. BAB-L/R1501/119700/121–122.
60. BAB-L/R1501/119700/126.
61. Manteuffel, *Uniwersytet Warszawski*, 22–5, quote on page no. 24.
62. Manteuffel, *Uniwersytet Warszawski*, 277.
63. Bericht des Generalgouverneurs über die Verwaltung des Generalgouvernements Warschau. Zeitraum: 1. April bis 30 September 1917. BAB-L R1501/119761/46/p. 28.
64. Reichstag, *Stenographische Berichte über die Verhandlungen der Deutschen Nationalversammlung*, vol. 326, 509.
65. Weinberg, *Germany, Hitler, and World War II*, 42.
66. Geiss, *Der Polnische Grenzstreifen*.
67. 16 December 1917. BAMA N30 55, p. 153.

References

Archival sources

Archiwum Polskiej Akademii Nauk (APAN)

- Towarzystwo Naukowe Warszawskie (TNW)

Bundesarchiv Berlin-Lichterfelde (BAB-L)

- N2126 Nachlass Bogdan Graf von Hutten-Czapski
- R1501 Reichsamt des Innern

Bundesarchiv-Militärarchiv, Freiburg-im-Breisgau (BA-MA)

- N 30 Nachlass Hans Hartwig von Beseler

Hoover Institution Archives (HIA)

- Włodzimierz Wiskowski Collection (WWC)

Published primary sources

Die Ostmark., Ginschel, E., ed. *Handbuch für das Generalgouvernement Warschau*, vol. 1. Warsaw: Deutscher Verlag, 1917.

Hutten-Czapski, Bogdan Graf von. *Sechzig Jahre Politik und Gesellschaft*, vol. 2. Berlin: E.S. Mittler, 1936.

Muszkowski, Jan, ed. *Kalendarz Uniwersytecki: Semestr Letni 1915/16*. Warsaw: F. Hoesicka, 1916.

Muszkowski, Jan. *Kalendarz Uniwersytecki: Semestr Zimowy 1916/17*. Warsaw: F. Hoesicka, 1917.

Otwarcie Uniwersytetu i Politechniki w Warszawie, 1915. Warsaw: Deutsche Staatsdruckerei, n.d., ca, 1915.

Reichstag. *Verhandlungen des Reichstags*, vols. 307–311. Berlin: Druck und Verlag der Norddeutschen Buchdruckerei und Verlags-Anstalt, 1916–1920.

Reichstag. *Stenographische Berichte über die Verhandlungen der Deutschen Nationalversammlung*, vols. 326–328. Berlin: Druck und Verlag der Norddeutschen Buchdruckerei und Verlags-Anstalt, 1920.

Warschauer, Adolf. *Deutsche Kulturarbeit in der Ostmark*. Berlin: R. Hobbing, 1926.

Wilson, Woodrow. "Address to the Senate on Peace Without Victory." Washington, DC, 22 January 1917. http://www.mtholyoke.edu/acad/intrel/ww15.htm (accessed 26 January 2012).

Published secondary sources

Becker, Annette. *Les cicatrices rouges 14–18: France et Belgique occupées*. Paris: Fayard, 2010.

Conze, Werner. *Polnische Nation und deutsche Politik im Ersten Weltkrieg*. Köln: Böhlau, 1958.

de Schaepdrijver, Sophie. *La Belgique et la Première Guerre Mondiale*. Bern: PIE-Peter Lang, 2004.

de Schaepdrijver, Sophie. "Belgium." In *A Companion to World War I*, edited by John Horne, 386–402. London: Wiley-Blackwell, 2010.

Dunin-Węsowicz, Krzysztof. *Warszawa w czasie pierwszej wojny światowej*. Warsaw: Państwowy Instytut Wydawniczy, 1974.

Garlicki, Andrzej, ed. *Dzieje Uniwersytetu Warszawskiego 1915–1939*. Warsaw: Państwowe Wydawnictwo Naukowe, 1982.

Geiss, Imanuel. *Der polnische Grenzstreifen, 1914—1918: Ein Beitrag zur deutschen Kriegszielpolitik im Ersten Weltkrieg*. Lübeck: Matthiesen, 1960.

Handelsman, Marceli, ed. *Polska w czasie wielkiej wojny, 1914–1918*, vol. 4. Carnegie Endowment for International Peace Paris: Les Presses Universitaires de France, 1933; Warsaw: Towarzystwo Badania Zagadnień Międzynarodowych, 1932–1939.

Hofmann, Andreas. "Die vergessene Okkupation: Lodz im Ersten Weltkrieg." In *Deutsche, Juden, Polen: Geschichte einer Wechselvollen Beziehung im 20. Jahrhundert*, edited by Andrea Löw, Kerstin Robusch, and Stefanie Walter, 59–77. Frankfurt: Campus, 2004.

Kauffman, Jesse. "Sovereignty and the Search for Order in German-Occupied Poland, 1915–1918." PhD diss., Stanford University, 2008.

Kries, Wolfgang von. "Deutsche Staatsverwaltung in Russisch-Polen." *Preußische Jahrbücher* 233 (1933): 130–58.

Liulevicius, Vejas. *War Land on the Eastern Front: Culture, National Identity and German Occupation in World War I*. Cambridge: Cambridge University Press, 2000.

Lohr, Eric. *Nationalizing the Russian Empire: The Campaign Against Enemy Aliens During World War I*. Cambridge, MA: Harvard University Press, 2003.

Manteuffel, Tadeusz. *Uniwersytet Warszawski w latach 1915/1916–1934/35: Kronika*. Warsaw: Józef Piłsudski University, 1936.

McPhail, Helen. *The Long Silence: Civilian Life Under the German Occupation of Northern France, 1914–1918*. London: IB Tauris, 1999.

Nipperdey, Thomas. *Deutsche Geschichte, 1866–1918, Vol. 1: Arbeitswelt und Bürgergeist.* Munich: C.H. Beck, 1990.

Porter, Brian. *When Nationalism Began to Hate: Imagining Modern Politics in Nineteenth-Century Poland.* Oxford: Oxford University Press, 2000.

Ritter, Gerhard. *The Sword and the Scepter: The Problem of Militarism in Germany.* Trans. Heinz Norden, vol. 4. Coral Gables, FL: University of Miami Press, 1969–1973.

Segel, HaroldB. "Culture in Poland During World War I." In *European Culture in the Great War,* edited by Aviel Roshwald, and Richard Stites, 58–88. Cambridge: Cambridge University Press, 1999.

Stempin, Arkadiusz. "'Das vergessene Generalgouvernment'. Deutsche Besatzungspolitik in Kongresspolen während des Ersten Weltkrieges. Kultur-, Bildungs- und Kirchenpolitik." Habilitationsschrift, Albert-Ludwigs-Universität Freiburg, 2008.

Tucker, Spencer. *The Great War, 1914–1918.* Bloomington: Indiana University Press, 1998.

Weinberg, Gerhard. *Germany, Hitler, and World War II.* Cambridge: Cambridge University Press, 1995.

Zahra, Tara. "Looking East: East Central European Borderlands in German History and Historiography." *History Compass* 3 (2005): 1–25.

Zilch, Reinhold. *Okkupation und Währung im Ersten Weltkrieg: Die deutsche Besatzungspolitik in Belgien und Russisch-Polen, 1914–1918.* Goldbach: Keip, 1994.

The fruits of occupation: food and Germany's occupation of Romania in the First World War

David Hamlin

Department of History, Fordham University, New York, USA

This article explores the multiple fashions in which food and the pursuit of food structured the policy and experience of occupation in Romania during the First World War. It compares the occupation regime to systems of grain acquisition before the war and during the period of Romanian neutrality to emphasize the depth of state intervention in the economy during occupation. It also emphasizes the impact of this regime on the behaviour of German and Habsburg soldiers and the costs for Romanian civilians.

Food, particularly wheat, played an unusually large role in shaping the occupation of Romania in the First World War. Imperial ambitions, modernizing self-images and orientalist assumptions all played significant roles in constructing both occupation policy and the experience of occupation. Food, however, was the most urgent driver. Food was at the forefront of concerns articulated by the political elite in Berlin. It structured the incentives shaping the decisions of the occupying military authority, and mediated interactions between German and Austro-Hungarian soldiers and Romanian civilians.[1]

Romania's decision to abandon its pre-war alliance with Austria-Hungary and Germany and to invade Transylvania in late August 1916 came at a time of crisis for Germany. Aside from the battering the Army sustained at Verdun and the Somme, there was waxing concern about the ability of Germany to maintain the basics of organized social and political life. Georg Michaelis recalled that experts had suggested that the population required a minimum of 450 g of grain daily. Throughout 1914 and 1915, a maximum of 200 g was possible.[2] The daily flour ration in Freiburg had fallen to 185 g by May 1916.[3] In the lengthy breadlines, the legitimacy of the existing order was gradually eroding.[4] The grumbling, even riots, looked to become even more ominous given the early and wet autumn of 1916. That prospect sent anxious memoranda criss-crossing Berlin in October[5] even as German arms fought their way through the Carpathians towards the plains of Wallachia. The two phenomena were hardly unrelated. Indeed, Romania had already loomed large in the food calculations of Germany. General Wilhelm Groener, then Chief of Military Railroads, observed in his memoirs that by late 1915, 'it became impossible not to see the growing threat to the subsistence of the population and army ... Our harvest was in no way sufficient to cover the shortages of others, and large stockpiles were collected nowhere. Since almost every external source was blocked by the English blockade, we turned to the only great European granary that was not yet among our enemies: Romania.'[6]

Before the war, Romania had emerged as the fourth largest wheat exporter in the world.[7] In a mediocre year like 1913, for example, Romania had exported more than 1.1 million tons of wheat.[8] The wheat was largely grown on the latifundia of the Romanian elite. Once harvested, that portion intended for export was purchased by a largely indigenous merchant class and dispatched by rail, generally to the shores of the Danube, where it would be transferred to barges for transport to Braila and Galatz on the mouths of the Danube. There the grain would be sold to international grain dealers who sent the grain through the Dardanelles into the Mediterranean. Usually the destination for the ship would not be fixed until it arrived at Gibraltar, where a telegram would indicate the final purchaser as negotiated on one of the grain exchanges in Belgium or Britain.[9]

That system had come to a screeching halt when the war closed the Dardanelles. Romanian wheat could not be sent to its usual markets in Western Europe. The ensuing struggle to control Romanian grain need not be explored in detail. Both the British and the Germans bought substantial quantities of wheat, but the British were unable to transport it home, while the Germans were largely forbidden to. That changed in late 1915 as the armies of the Central Powers pushed back the Russians and occupied Serbia. Alone in a sea of German and Austro-Hungarian troops, Romania swiftly made arrangements to sell and ship 2.5 million tons of much-needed grain to the Central Powers. This was the grain to which Groener was referring. By way of comparison, Reichstag member Hans Peter Hannsen recalled being told that Germany had a total of 1.88 million tons of grain to see it through March–August 1915.[10] Purchasing and shipping so much grain was a massive undertaking. The Central Purchasing Agency (ZEG), the German body charged with purchasing material from abroad, required 3000 employees, 250 of whom would be in Bucharest, others scattered around 450 rail stations, to take possession of the grain. Many of these were apparently Romanian grain merchants hired by the Germans to purchase grain from the market and deliver it to river ports. Along the Danube, 22 grain elevators were purchased or leased and a fleet of 312 ships and barges was pressed into service. These sent the grain not downstream as before the war, but rather upstream. Eventually, the grain would be transferred to rails for the trip to Germany. The ZEG expected to handle approximately 1000 train wagons daily bringing grain out of Romania.[11] The trains were code named 'Ceres'.

When Romania entered the war, then, German decision makers were well conditioned to see it as a crucial source of food supplies. In fact, Germany had developed a sizeable organization, incorporating indigenous expertise, and deployed throughout Romania, to acquire and ship grain to Germany and Austria-Hungary. Romania's entry into the war put this at substantial risk. It comes as little surprise then that the conjunction between a rapidly deepening food crisis (that winter would be the dreaded 'Turnip Winter') and the incipient invasion of Romania spurred serious discussions in Berlin about the organization and ultimate political control over the occupation of Romania. The supplies of oil, but especially food, were central to the continuing war effort.[12]

Planning

Planning for the occupation began in October 1916, before the occupation began. Initial discussions between the Habsburgs and Germans at German General Headquarters led to a series of meetings in Berlin on 28 and 29 October that established the basic outlines of the administrative structure and the primacy of economic exploitation. Financial details were also discussed.[13] Unlike in Belgium, Poland and OberOst, the structures and policies of the occupation of Romania would be hammered out beforehand, smoothing the transition to exploitation of the occupation economy for the war effort.

The October meetings in Berlin gave the flavour of the occupation. There were representatives from Austria-Hungary, Bulgaria and Turkey as well as from the Prussian War Ministry, and the German Supreme Command (OHL). The representative for the nascent occupation, Major Kessler, explained that the military government 'has the obligation to use all its powers to ensure that what can be gotten out of the land is gotten out'. The crucial materials to be 'gotten out' were to be 'oil, food, animal feed, war-critical raw materials generally, wood, machines, labor, and, under conditions, also horses'. This process of extraction would be organized by an economic staff staffed on a parity basis by Germans and Austro-Hungarians.

The Berlin meeting reflected a learning process about the relationship between military occupation and economic exploitation. Pre-war international law and military planning had assumed short wars and emphasized issues such as paying for and feeding armies of occupation. The evolution into an extended war of industrial attrition had introduced novel strains into the economic systems of the Central Powers. The initial efforts to squeeze resources out of occupied peoples in Poland and Lithuania for an industrial economy accustomed to international sources of supply, had emphasized force and requisitions, occasionally purchase in the case of Belgium.[14] In the words of Major Kessler, acquisition by requisition quickly 'exhausted the well'. That is to say, requisitions discouraged the production of materials and encouraged wide-scale evasion. Better to use money to encourage the continuing production and easy acquisition of products like grain. The problem with such a system was that the use of Germany's or Austria's own currency would have inflationary consequences at home. The costs of acquiring grain for Germany and Austria-Hungary had to be shifted onto the shoulders of Romanians without explicitly using force. The solution the policymakers hit on was, to simplify the rather complex accounting, to vastly inflate the Romanian currency.[15] This was on top of the usual financial obligations that would be levied on the population to pay for the upkeep of the occupying army.

The clear implication of the planning process was that the projected occupation of Romania was to be centrally concerned with extracting raw materials for the benefit of the Central Powers. This object was at the heart of not only the military planning for the occupation but also the roughly contemporaneous exchanges between Chancellor Bethmann Hollweg and General Ludendorff on the matter.[16] Concern for the economic exploitation of Romania also clearly informed Ludendorff's approach to the Foreign Ministry in late October for advice on individuals who would be appropriate for the 'administration and economic exploitation of occupied Romania'.[17] Moreover, this was to be undertaken at minimal cost to the Germans and Habsburgs. As much as possible, the costs of extracting material from Romania were to be transferred to Romanians. Before the occupation even began, pressure was mounting from Berlin to maximize the economic utility of Romania, particularly in the extraction of food and petroleum.

Organization

Continuing the push for swift incorporation of Romanian resources into their war effort, an embryonic Economic Staff was deployed to the Danube town of Turnu Severin on 5 December, just before the fall of Bucharest, to begin organizing the local acquisition and trans-shipment of food products back to the homelands.[18] By the end of the month, elements of the expanding Economic Staff would begin transferring their operations to Bucharest as they prepared to bring the whole of Wallachia under their control. To emphasize the significance of the activities of the Economic Staff for the whole of the occupying armies, the first issue of the *Verordnungsblatt der Militär-Verwaltung in*

Rumänien on 29 December 1916 published an Order of the Day, which emphasized that 'the economic exploitation of the conquered Romanian lands is of extraordinarily significance for our own homeland and our allies. Every officer and man must be infused by the idea the Fatherland must be helped in this fashion'.[19]

The Economic Staff was initially divided into 10, later 17 divisions, such as Agriculture, Petroleum, Finances, Labour, Machinery and Wood.[20] The territory of occupied Romania was then divided into districts. District Officers were dispersed across Wallachia, charged with organizing the planting and harvest. District Officers were assigned wide powers to ensure that both came off successfully, controlling the distribution of oxen, seed grain, etc. As the apparatus expanded, the District would be further divided into Regions (*Bezirke*) and Subregions (*Unterbezirke*). The District Agriculture Officer was expected to travel the district twice monthly, and the Local Agriculture Officer would travel weekly.[21]

The staffing, however, was initially quite limited. As of 20 March 1917, the Agriculture Division could count 18 Habsburg and German officers (mostly Habsburg) as well as approximately 100 Habsburg non-commissioned officers and enlisted troops. The Germans added a handful of enlisted men. This obviously inadequate staff was supplemented by recruiting Romanian grain traders into the occupation apparatus.[22] Romanian grain traders were often utilized in the countryside, purchasing and arranging transport for grain as before the war.[23] Farmers were obligated to sell their grain, aside from a subsistence minimum, to these traders at prices fixed by the occupation authorities.[24] Grain would be laboriously transported to railheads in vehicles ranging from ungainly ox carts, to horse-drawn wagons, to trucks. The railroads would sometimes ship the grain through the Carpathian passes directly to the Central Powers; more commonly, however, they would send their grain to the Danube. There a gathering fleet of steamers and barges would haul the grain upstream to Turnu Severin for trans-shipment around the Iron Gates.[25]

The devastation and disruption of the war created substantial challenges to the efficient acquisition of resources. In some limited respects, combat operations were actually a boon. Most obviously, the British government had purchased enormous quantities of grain and simply stored them in Romania. These massive depots of grain fell like ripe fruit into the hands of the Central Powers. Indeed the first great organizational task of the Economic Staff was the swift transport of captured grain from Romania.[26]

For the most part, however, the violence and disruption of war created immense and sometimes enduring difficulties for the occupation regime. Most clearly, the mobilization of military-age men into the Romanian Army had created a vast shortage of agricultural labour. That shortage was compounded by the flight of many peasants who preferred to take their chances as refugees rather than await the violence of the contending armies. That violence had also done a great deal to destroy the Romanian transportation network, particularly the rail systems. The retreating Romanians and Russians had taken many of the locomotives and much of the rail system and associated buildings, bridges and storage facilities had taken substantial damage. As Gerhard Velburg observed, 'The great grain bins at the train stations smoke (*qualmen*) still; the Russians have ensured as they retreated that as little as possible falls into our hands. Here and there, dead horses lay next to the rails, here and there broken wagons have been left behind'.[27] The retreat of the Romanian state and much of the elite had also undermined the financial system that had greased the wheels for rents, taxes and spring plantings. Thus, the war had undermined the established systems of agricultural production by sweeping away a large part of the labour force, destroying the network for transporting grain from farms to distant markets, and by reducing the financial system to a shambles.[28] The resolution of each of these problems will be addressed in turn, and it will be clear that in answering these problems, the occupation inserted itself ever further and more aggressively into Romanian life.

As General Ludendorff explained to Foreign Minister Arthur Zimmermann, 'the greater part of Romania offers a portrait of a land badly damaged by a war of movement. The population, particularly the rural population was partly driven from their homes, partly fled. Oxen driven off by friend and foe. The flat land is therefore almost entirely denuded of labor'.[29] Indeed, the Economic Staff estimated that the population of the occupied territories had dropped from 4,243,222 in 1914 to 3,438,002 in March 1917.[30] Obviously the spring planting was in danger if the problem of labour could not be settled quickly. The first point was encouraging refugees to return home. Thus, freedom of travel on foot or by wagon was quickly reinstated – notably in contrast to the situation in OberOst, where the military's efforts to control and direct indigenous society produced a series of limits on movement. Civilian use of the rail system was limited because of the demands made on a damaged system for the war effort.[31] That was a useful first step, but returning refugees ultimately could not make up for the larger problem of Romanian peasants called into the Romanian army.

A crucial means of addressing the persistent labour shortage was to enlist Prisoners of Wars (POWs). First, the occupation authorities furloughed over 11,000 Romanian POWs so that they might return to work on their own farms. A further 22,000 largely Romanian POWs were used at the discretion of the occupation to supplement the labour force. This number did not include slightly over 3000 'colored' Muslim POWs, largely from the French Army who were initially brought to help overcome the labour shortage but were largely limited to isolated farms and construction projects in deference to the feelings of the conservative Romanians who were collaborating with the occupation.[32] The POWs were divided into Work Details (Arbeiter-Abteilungen) and assigned varying tasks. Thus, for example, POW Work Detail 906, with 164 men, was assigned in June 1917 to load grain in Vida. It was hoped that POW Work Detail 907 would be able to be similarly transferred to agricultural labour once they completed work on the road from Bucharest to Giurgiu.[33] So important did POW labour become for the functioning of the occupation in Romania that it appears that POWs were kept as prisoners and labourers well after the conclusion of peace.[34]

An additional 18,000 workers were recruited from the northern hill districts and sent to the grain-producing flat lands to the south.[35] The occupation army would also routinely make transport assets available for the harvest.[36] Finally, civilians were also made, in principle, liable for forced labour in a system reminiscent of the Auxiliary Service law in Germany. Nonetheless, the Economic Staff estimated in June 1917 that it would need to find an additional 40,000 workers for the harvest.[37] It is unclear to what extent this power was utilized, particularly since the problem was less idle or inefficiently utilized labour so much as missing labour. To ensure that the maximum was realized from the deployment of this labour, it was forbidden to rest on Sundays or holidays during harvest periods[38] (it should be noted that wheat, in particular, has a comparatively narrow window for harvest before the top-heavy plant is knocked to the ground and the seeds begin to sprout). Mayors and local officials were also made legally responsible for ensuring that all available labour power was employed in the fields.[39] To ensure that this burgeoning demand for labour did not drive wages too high (thereby putting pressure on the prices that the Military Administration itself paid for grain), the occupation also set up wage limits.[40] Conveniently, POWs required no wages.

The transportation system posed very substantial difficulties as well. The disappearance of locomotives required the Central Powers to send their own machines. The problems tended to increase in the summer periods when combat operations claimed additional locomotives even as the harvest increased demand in Romania.[41] More intractable was the collapse of the Romanian rail and road system. Laboriously built up over decades, largely financed through international loans organized by the Disconto-Gesellschaft, the transport system had once distinguished Romania from its neighbours. Now it lay in ruins. Stations had to be rebuilt and expanded. Bridges needed to be replaced, grain elevators constructed in new places. Aside from agricultural work, gangs of POWs were put to work in rebuilding Romanian infrastructure. POW Work Detail 812, for example, was detailed to rebuild a bridge in Tindarai, while Detail 907 worked on the road to Giurgiu and Detail 813 did roadwork in the oil-producing regions. In addition, the occupation authorities laid a number of temporary 'field railroads', thereby expanding the network of rail connections.[42] A number of riverside grain elevators were also hurriedly thrown up.

The war disrupted the usual flow of capital through the countryside. Rural access to capital was an issue even before the war, but the Romanian state's decision to close the banks coupled with the flight of many bankers, not to mention the removal of the National Bank's gold reserves, had only made the problem greater.[43] To ensure that peasants had access to capital, the occupation regime used its powers as temporary administrators of the National Bank to create a network of rural lending institutions (*Darlehenskassen*). These were intended to finance sowing by letting peasants borrow against their expected harvest.[44] Advances could be made in either cash or seed grain. The amount would be determined by the regional Economic Office, with general guidance from the Economic Staff.[45] The Military Administration made the Romanian government assume a guarantee for the repayment of all advances through the *Darlehenskassen*.[46] And while the private banks remained closed, the volume of purchases made by the occupation coupled with the rudimentary *Darlehenskassen* was easing the flow of money by May 1917.[47] Indeed, there would soon be, if anything, too much money flowing through occupied Romania.[48]

In all three areas, the occupation authorities found themselves assuming a central, directing role in the Romanian economy. The occupation state found itself marshalling labour, fixing wages, constructing infrastructure and establishing banks in a bid to ensure that the production and transportation system did not collapse under the damage caused by the war. Distrust of the Romanians coupled with the lingering consequences of the war combined to convince the Military Administration that Romanian agriculture would collapse, to the detriment of tens of millions, without active Austro-German guidance. The high modernist cast to the occupation is clear.[49]

Occupier and occupied

Over and above occupation policy, food suffused the experience of German and Austro-Hungarian soldiers in Romania. This is, in part, due to the blunt fact that humans must eat. Yet, the soldiers occupying Romania also found themselves entering into a social relationship with the local food producers, one marked by multiple, cross-cutting pressures and implications.

One common experience recalled by soldiers was gifts of food spontaneously offered by Romanian civilians. Landser Gerhard Velburg, for example, recalls that he was repeatedly given food and invited to meals in his months of occupation duty in rural Romania. On his first day in the country, a farmer and priest apparently spontaneously made separate presents of eggs, animal fats and tobacco to his unit. Once his unit settled in occupation duty around Fetesti, such gifts, coupled with invitations to meals became regular features in his diary. Erwin Rommel reported that his unit was feted with 300 loaves of bread, several heads of cattle and casks of wine in one Romanian village.[50]

One can read these accounts in several manners. Taken at face value, one can suggest that the gifts of food re-established a moral community between soldier and civilian. The terror that Philip Aschauer described at his arrival in a village, with women and children crouching and wailing,[51] was ultimately the terror that the usual sense of mutuality that prohibits open murder and larceny had disappeared. The Romanians sensed that the Germans could do anything. The bestowal of gifts was more than a simple bribe – though it could be that as well. It was a means of constructing some limited sense of community and obligation, in such a way that it would no longer be morally possible to overstep boundaries. Once Germans received the gifts, and acknowledged them as something other than a bribe or requisition, they had entered into a fuller relationship with their new subjects; a relationship in which they came to have something akin to responsibilities. The other side of this same coin was the avoidance of acts of symbolic resistance. Many of the usual 'weapons of the weak'[52] were, at least temporarily, abandoned. The feast prepared for Rommel, for example, carefully effaced any hint that the German presence might be illegitimate or undesirable. Rather it mimicked a feast of welcome. The apparent acceptance of German authority implicit in the gift removed important potential sources of conflict.

One could also read this relationship rather more cynically. Our knowledge hinges on how Germans – armed foreigners – chose to remember or portray the exchange. There is considerable evidence that, in fact, soldiers were engaged in wide-scale plundering. The Order of the Day published in December 1916 that announced the significance of the economic exploitation of Romania for the Fatherland moved on to condemn the 'often senseless and excessive manner in which returning refugees were robbed of their goods'. In March 1917, Austrian officers were sternly reminded that 'every personal requisition as well as appropriation of enemy property is forbidden and perpetrators will be subject to the harshest judicial punishment ... We Austro-Hungarian soldiers are honorable warriors'.[53] Likewise, the German Foreign Ministry was receiving reports from 'absolutely reliable' sources that 'theft and plunder by German and Austro-Hungarian troops allegedly occur often'.[54] Later, in October, Austrian officers were reminded that the acceptance of gifts was in contradiction of 'the spirit and word of their oath and service regulations'.[55] By 1918, the Romanians were all but begging the Germans not to requisition supplies explicitly labelled for civilian use.[56] It is not difficult to imagine that fond German memories of gifts of food misrepresented a more extortionate relationship. Indeed, it may well have been the unregulated, illegal appropriation of Romanian food that led Romanian peasants to hide their stores of grain. David Mitrany, for example, tells of Romanian peasants holding elaborate funerals for caskets filled with grain, an evil the Military Administration felt compelled to specifically outlaw.[57]

Whatever the precise form of the relationship that was constructed with Romanian peasants around food, it may have taken on a particular significance for Germans. German soldiers were permitted to send 10 kg of food home through the mail and to take 50 kg of food home when they went on leave.[58] Given the growing food crisis that was driving German state policy, this created a powerful incentive to use private initiative in order to expropriate Romanian food. Certainly, Gerhard Velburg could not help comparing the food around him in Romania to the deprivation at home. Indeed, he was ordered to do so before inspecting Romanian homes for hidden food, when Leutnant Vieweg 'instructed us before the search of the first house that we wanted a very strict implementation of our orders, since our families in Germany had to starve for a while now, now the enemy has to starve'.[59] Should unit commanders fail to emphasize it, the *Bukarester Tagblatt*, the German language Bucharest newspaper, helpfully reminded them.[60] Velburg recalled reading about privation in letters from home before going on home leave with five crates, a sack of flour and two bags of bread. In fact, none of the soldiers going on leave with Velburg were able to carry all their bags. All required assistance to get on the train.[61]

The conscious connections drawn between deprivation at home and the acquisition of food in Romania clearly informed the attitude of Lt. Vieweg towards his official duties. The influence of official pressure as well as the invitation to assume an antagonism between Romanian and German bellies manifested itself in multiple ways. One striking example involved two Besserabian gendarmes, Leopold Suck and Wilhelm Hubich. Assigned to run a large estate in Cernatesti in western Wallachia, Suck and Hubich were credibly accused in late May 1917 of selling food in the black market and with maintaining intimate relations with 'women of bad reputation'. A Habsburg military policemen, Major Kuczinsky, acted on those accusations, ordering Suck and Hubich to report to Turnu-Severin. The two suspects instead went to Craiova to meet with his superior Local Agricultural Officer von Blücher, and on the way Suck encountered the head of the regional Economic Office (*Wirtschaftsstelle*), Rittmeister Manteuffel. Manteuffel, after hearing of Kuczinsky's orders, allegedly crumpled up those orders and told him 'under no circumstance to leave Cernatesti'. Continuing to Craiova, Suck met with von Blücher who stated that he would intervene on his behalf. Von Blücher then sought out Kuczinsky and asked that action be deferred since the two were 'very useful'. Kuczinsky refused to relent, offering only to permit them to remain until 4 June. On 3 June, Suck and Hubich appeared in Craiova with orders from Manteuffel dated the same day instructing the two of them to remain in Cernatesti. Kuczinsky ordered Suck and Hubich to ignore Manteuffel's order and to report to Turnu-Severin the next day. Then, Kuczinsky complained to Lt. Colonel Lösch about the behaviour of the German officers. At that point, Kuczinsky learned that the German Adjutant (Lt. Col. von Damnitz) had called Lösch and threatened to have Kuczinsky arrested, which Lösch deplored. The next day, German Major General Krahmer ordered both Suck and Hubich be released and returned to Cernatesti.[62]

Ultimately, what was at issue in this confrontation between the Habsburg Gendarmerie and the German economic officers was a conflict between duties. Kuczinsky did have specific and credible grounds for suspecting Suck and Hubich of systematic corruption, an issue we will return to below. Indeed, there were unsubstantiated accusations of corrupting German officers. But the German officers repeatedly returned to the overriding significance of ensuring the smooth operation of the estate. The two men, fluent in both Romanian and German, were highly valued and the highest levels of the German occupation authorities expressed their belief that the investigation 'made bringing in the harvest more difficult'.[63] German officers never dedicated much effort to disputing the charges levelled by Major Kuczinsky, focusing instead on the utility of Suck and Hubich. It would appear that, in this case, the District Economic Office was prepared to tolerate corruption in the larger interests of maximizing agricultural production. The vehemence of their response – overriding lawful orders, obstructing a criminal investigation and threatening to arrest an officer of an allied army who was exercising the lawful rights of his position – betrayed the substantial pressure placed on the administration as a whole to produce food.

Romanian consumption

Of course, production and acquisition were only a part of the formula that would determine how much grain could be sent back to Vienna and Berlin. There was also the question of consumption in Romania. The Economic Staff sought to reduce the consumption of food inside Romania 'in order to increase exports … for the provision of the homeland'.[64]

The administrative control over the domestic grain market enabled the Germans to progressively reduce Romanian food consumption to enable increased exports of grain back to Germany.[65]

The most obvious means of controlling consumption was to decree daily maximums. Rationing in a land of plentiful food represented another deep intervention in the lives of Romanians, this time into the basic details of subsistence. Rationing will also provide an opportunity to compare the impact of war and occupation in different geographic regions.

Rationing was established with levels that varied between urban and rural populations, as well as for POWs.[66] The rations introduced for the urban population in January 1917 authorized 225 g of wheat flour and 150 g of corn meal per person daily. Those engaged in heavy labour 'namely those laboring in our interests' could be granted an additional 300 g of flour daily. The weekly meat ration was 150 g.[67] The rural population has been permitted 750 g of corn meal daily. In September, this was reduced to 500 g as a result of the 'rapid decline in stocks of old corn as a result of the shipments to the homeland'.[68] In the summer of 1918, civilian rations were cut once more to 125 g of wheat flour and 125 g of corn flout for urbanites, while rural peasants would be permitted 400 g of corn meal.[69]

POWs employed in heavy labour were permitted up to 600 g of bread, as well as 40 g of butter every 15 days and 100 g of sausage fats, as well as 100 g of meat every 5 days. POWs engaged in light duty were limited to at most 400 g of bread.[70] The rations for POWs were reduced, however, in April 1917. At that point, POWs doing heavy labour were reduced to 400 g daily while those engaged in less strenuous activity had their bread ration reduced to 330 g, or 175 g of Zweiback biscuits. Romanian and Italian POWs were reduced further to 230 g of bread and 150 g of corn meal. Fortunately, this was raised after the harvest back to the levels mandated in January.[71]

These figures are rather abstract; contextualization in several directions might be useful. They can be compared to the daily rations of German soldiers serving in the midst of the Romanians. These were set at 500 g of bread, 200 g of fresh or salted meat, various vegetables, 65 g of butter or 125 g of fruit.[72] Perhaps more useful would be a comparison to civilians elsewhere. Roger Chickering, for example, tells us that daily flour rations in 1916 fell from 200 g in February to 185 g in May. This would appear to confirm Michaelis' claims that Germany had sufficient supplies in 1914 to permit a ration of 200 g daily.[73] Viewed in that way, the rations for Romanians were reasonably generous. This impression grows substantially when compared to the rations in comparable zones of occupation. For example, on 1 April 1917, the flour ration for the General-government Warsaw was reduced to 120 g daily.[74] Even that could not hold out long, as rations were reduced further in the period 1 April 1918 to 1 August 1918 to 70 g of flour. The landless peasants in the country were denied any flour ration. The occupation authorities in Warsaw hoped that the 1918 harvest would permit them to maintain a daily flour ration of 120 g.[75] In November 1917, Major Hecker informed Berlin that OberOst needed an additional 70,000 tons of grain to maintain its daily flour rations at 225 g. To make up the shortfall, OberOst proposed to eliminate the ration for all locations aside from Riga and Vilnius.[76]

Compared to other regions, particularly hard-hit Poland and OberOst, the occupation rations in Romania appear almost generous. Indeed, when the Navy's liaison officer in Bucharest, Schulz, compared Romania's peacetime export statistics to the deliveries made to the Central Powers in 1917, he concluded that 'the labor of the Military Administration and to a certain extent the Economic Staff benefits much too much the indigenous population and the occupiers, while the homeland and the front does not enjoy in full the advantages to which they are entitled'. He thought daily rations for Romanians were much too high and should be reduced.[77]

We must keep very much in mind, however, that those relatively generous daily rations that bothered Schulz were effectively reduced in often unplanned and catastrophic fashions by occupation soldiers. The 'gifts' of food discussed earlier were from the limited supplies permitted to Romanians. In such cases, the peasants themselves had some control over the volume of food turned over to the occupiers. Significantly more problematic were the illegal requisitions of food. These were intrinsically outside the control of the peasants and were limited only by what the soldiers wanted to take and the extent of food that they could uncover. Such situations could easily result in the loss of crucial reserves of food. Indeed the vulnerability of peasants in such situations made them subject to blackmail by occupation soldiers.[78]

Clearly, then, daily rations were not the last word in controlling domestic food consumption. Gifts and illegal requisitions formed one unofficial means of distributing food. There were other ways. Even where there were genuine food shortages, as in Germany, Austria, even Great Britain, there was a powerful black market. Romania, by contrast, had ample food available. The Military Administration's determination to reduce domestic consumption below 'natural' levels so that it could expand exports opened substantial opportunities for profiting through redirecting the surplus. To prevent this, the occupation regime sought to further extend its control over the Romanian economy by narrowing the realm of legitimate distribution.

It was made illegal, for example, to sell or purchase grain except from bakeries authorized by the occupation.[79] As a direct consequence, 19-year-old Nicolae Scaripa was imprisoned for 15 days for illegally selling bread on the streets of Ploiesti.[80] Similarly, the sale or slaughter of meat without authorization was forbidden.[81] Transporting food without authorization was forbidden. As a result, the pages of the *Bukarester Tagblatt* were littered with individuals fined for transporting or receiving illegal food. Thus, for example, the butcher Janku Dangiulescu was fined in February 1917, 300 Lei for unauthorized trade in beef and in May, a milkmaid was fined 200 Lei for illegally transporting meat.[82] The occupation regime clearly hoped to narrow the possible beds through which food might flow so as to better control and limit food consumption in Romania.

As the penalties levied might suggest, the ability of the occupation state to effectively control the domestic Romanian market for food was continually contested. Occupiers and occupied alike exploited the controlled market for food to profit through the black market. The flow of material and money through illegal channels came from multiple sources. For example, the gendarmes Suck and Hubich were suspected of illegally appropriating and selling on their own account chickens, lambs, eggs, pork, ham as well as wheat. In one instance, Suck was alleged to have sold 52 bags of wheat to Jon Radu Kuku and Ifram Dan for 639 Lei and 80 Bani.[83] That volume of wheat strongly suggests sales not for individual consumption but rather for resale in the black market. In another case, Gerhard Velburg explored the illegal money exchange maintained on the Piata de Florii in Bucharest that Germans and Romanians alike made use of. According to Velburg, the daily wage of a German soldier would not cover the cost of a cup of coffee, forcing them onto the black market to sell Marks and to buy ordinary luxuries like a razor of a bottle of wine.[84] What was most interesting in Velburg's description of the black money market was the appetite of Romanian and Jewish currency traders for German money. There were no imports from Germany and it was illegal to buy in Marks inside Romania. It strongly suggests the accumulation of Marks with which to buy products from individuals inside the occupying army. Indeed, by October 1917, the Military Administration felt moved to formally clarify the punishments for black marketing (prison up to a year and a fine of up to 10,000 Lei).[85] The fact that the administration felt compelled to do so slightly more than 10 months after the occupation began strongly suggests that it was responding to rather than anticipating a problem.

The efforts of the occupation state in Romania to exercise maximum control over the supply of food inside Romania was thus continually undermined, in part by Romanians but more often by its own servants. The imperatives that the occupation state created, imperatives that in turn responded to the needs of civilians on their home fronts, shaped how personnel understood their official duties. This could easily lead to an excess of zeal, or a willingness to overlook smaller infractions. Perhaps more importantly, soldiers might react to the same imperatives on a more individual level, supplementing their own limited supplies as well as those of family members at home by either stealing additional food from Romanian civilians or by engaging in black marketeering.

Ultimately, the costs for occupation food policy were borne by the Romanians. The resulting squeeze on the resources of Romanian peasants, particularly given the uncooperative weather in 1917 and 1918, had tangible effects. One measure of the cost on peasants would be the increasing unwillingness, perhaps inability, to labour in the fields in 1918. The villages of Kaioasa, Odaia and Dorobantul were fined thousands of Lei each for repeatedly refusing orders to take in the harvest. Maldaeni, Scriostea and Papa were fined 500 Lei each for refusing demands to take in the harvest, despite 'extensive instruction'.[86]

It also seems likely that the susceptibility of Romanian civilians to disease increased greatly as a result of inadequate nutrition. The German Army reported a typhus epidemic in 1917 and expressed considerable anxiety that troops movements in 1918 would result in increased contact between combat troops and the 'epidemically infected civil population'.[87] Captain Kosch recalled of his time in Romania that typhoid and dysentery had become disturbingly common, while earlier the military administration had warned that the civil population suffered enormously from typhus and sleeping sickness.[88] By July 1918, small pox was on the rise in the civil population.[89] The figures for fatalities are vague and disputed, but according to the most commonly sited figure, the war and occupation killed an estimated 400,000 Romanian civilians from starvation and disease (out of a pre-war population of 7.5 million).[90] This was clearly influenced heavily by infectious diseases, the breakdown of public sanitation and an overstretched medical system, but the politically induced malnutrition must also had played a substantial role. Against this could be counted the 1,920,305 tons of grain that had been extracted from Romania, as of 31 May 1918 (before the 1918 harvest was brought in), of which Germany received 788,179 tons.[91]

Food played an enormously important role in the occupation of Romania. It deeply influenced how policy makers at the highest levels in the German state viewed Romania as German troops began to enter. It shaped the policies of the occupation government and the formal structure of the occupation. Alternative approaches to securing Romania and its grain were ultimately rejected in favour of a more rigorous, intrusive regime – in part as a response to the problems created by the war and the retreat of the Romanian state. Food also created a contested object that powerfully structured social relations between Romanians on the one side and Germans and Austro-Hungarians on the other.

Notes

1. The subject of this essay is admittedly ambiguous. Both Germany and Austria-Hungary participated in a joint occupation of Romania. Policy, however, was largely guided by the German Army – a fact that provoked considerable bitter comment by the Habsburgs. As a consequence, while source material is used for both occupiers, German policy and German experience are privileged.
2. Michaelis, *Für Staat und Volk*, 270–3; Hannsen, *Diary of a Dying Empire*, 98–9.
3. Chickering, *Great War and Urban Life in Germany*, 170.
4. See Davis, *Home Fires Burning*; Healy, *Vienna and the Fall of the Habsburg Empire*.
5. Feldman, *Army, Industry and Labor in Germany 1914–1918*, 114–5, 283.

MILITARY OCCUPATIONS IN FIRST WORLD WAR EUROPE

6. Groener, *Lebenserinnerungen. Jugend – Generalstab – Weltkrieg*, 329.
7. Berend, *History Derailed*, 167.
8. Südhof, *Die rumanische Getreideproduktion*, 20–2.
9. See Bundesarchiv (BA) Lichterfelde R 901/1662 bl 103–6 Deutsche Konsulat Galatz to Reichskanzler BH, 21 Sept 1909; also Morgan, *Merchants of Grain*.
10. Hannsen, *Diary*, 98.
11. Bundesarchiv Militärische Abteilung (BA/MA) PHD 7/174, Die Zentraleinkaufsgesellschaft. Dr. Lübbert, Kriegspresseamt, Berlin, 1917; BA-Lichterfelde R5/1594 Niederschrift über die Sitzung bet. Erörterung von Verkehrfragen wegen Einführung von Getreide und Futtermitteln aus Rumänien, am Freitag, den 7 January 1916.
12. For discussion about political control of occupied Romania, see R3101/883 Bl. 3–5 Reichskanzler an den Generalquartiermeister, Berlin 31 October 1916; Generalquartiermeister to Reichkanzler, 6 November 1916.
13. *Oesterreichisch-Ungarischer Tätigkeitsbericht des Wirtschaftsstabes der Militaerverwaltung in Rumanien. Vom Beginn bis 30 November 1917*. (Wien: K.k. Hof – und Staatsdrukerei, 1918), 5.
14. Hull, *Absolute Destruction*. See also Kries, 'Die wirtschaftliche Ausnutzung des General-gouvernements Warschau', 235, no. 3; Zilch, *Okkupation und Währung im Ersten Weltkrieg*.
15. BA Lichterfelde, R901/3919 Bl. 138–146 Niederschrift uber die Besprechungen in Berlin am den 28. Oktober 1916 und den 29 Oktober 1916. Betrifft: Militarische Verwaltung in Rumanien. A fuller treatment of the financial complications in David, '*Dummes Geld. Money and Grain and the Occupation of Romania in World War I'*, *Central European History*, 451–71. See also Zilch, *Okkupation und Währung*.
16. BA-Lichterfelde R3101/883 Bl. 3–5 Reichskanzler an den Generalquartiermeister, Berlin 31 October 1916; Generalquartiermeister to Reichkanzler 6 November 1916.
17. National Archives and Records Administration (NARA) T 136 Reel 95 AA Verwaltung besetzter Gebiet Rumaniens, Generalquartiermeister to AA, 24 October 1916.
18. *A-H Tätigkeitsbericht des Wirtschaftsstabes. Beginn bis 30.11.17*, 6.
19. BA Lichterfelde R1501/119869 R.I. bl. 36 Verordnungsblatt der Militar-Verwaltung in Rumanien, Nr. 1 29 December 1916, 2.
20. *A-H Tätigkeitsbericht des Wirtschaftsstabes. Beginn bis 30.11.17*, 6, 36–42.
21. *A-H Tätigkeitsbericht des Wirtschaftsstabes. Beginn bis 30.11.17*, 82.
22. *A-H Tätigkeitsbericht des Wirtschaftsstabes. Beginn bis 30.11.17*, 48–9.
23. Velburg, p.
24. BA Lichterfelde R1501/119869 R.I., bl. 186, Verordnungsblatt der Militar-Verwaltung in Rumanien, Nr. 24 18 May 1917, 191, 'Festsetzung der Getreidepreise der neuen Ernte ab Bahn- oder Schiffstation und Festsetzung von Pramien'.
25. Österreichisches Kriegsarchiv (OKA) NFA 1774 MGG Rumänien 1917 20.5-18.6 Etappenstationkommando Galicea/Mare to Sendler, 2.6.17; Velbug, p.
26. BA/MA PH 5-I/74 p. 61 Bericht des Wirtschaftsstabes 1.7. – 31.12.1917. For an examination of utilization of Hungarian ports to move captured grain from January to March 1917, see BA Lichterfelde R 3101/3181 bl. 12–14 ZEG Berichtigungabzug 20.7.17.
27. Velburg. *Rumaenische Etappe*, 39.
28. A useful overview of the problems confronting the occupation regime in BA Lichterfelde R901/3919 Bl. 125–131 Reise Bericht des Ministerialdirektors und Hauptmann D.L. Dr. Graf von Keyserlingk uber die Wirtschaftliche Lage in Rumanien.
29. BA Lichterflede R 901/3919 Bl. 105–107 Ludendorff to state Secretary of AA, Zimmermann, 10 March 1917.
30. OKA NFA 1772 MGG Rum 1917 1.4-22.4 Halbmonatsbericht No. 2 des Wirtschaftsstabes (11.3.17 to 25.3.17)
31. NARA T 136 Reel 95 AA Verwaltung besetzter Gebiet Rumaniens, Wirtschaftsstab response to Mirbach report, 25.2.17. On OberOst's *Verkehrspolitik*, see Liulevicius, *War Land on the Eastern Front*.
32. BA/MA PH 5-I/74 p 11 Halbjahresbericht des Oberquartiermeisterstabes 1.7.17–31.12.17; on 'colored' POWs, see also T 136 Reel 95 AA Verwaltung besetzter Gebiet Rumaniens, Legationssekretar Lersner, to AA, 7.2.17; Wirtschaftsstab response to Mirbach report, 25.2.17.
33. OKA NFA 1774 MGG Rumänien 1917 20.5-18.6 Oberquartiermeisterstab to AH Bevoll. MVR, 14.6.17.
34. BA/MA N 127/15 89th Infantry Divisions-Tagesbefehle 11 July 1918.

MILITARY OCCUPATIONS IN FIRST WORLD WAR EUROPE

35. *A-H Tätigkeitsbericht des Wirtschaftsstabes. Beginn bis 30.11.17*, p. 190.
36. OKA NFA 1769 MGG Rumänien 1917 21.10–22.11 Kommandantur Landwirtschaft to MVR Wirtschaftsstab, 5.11.17; OKA NFA 1772 MGG Rum 1917 1.4–22.4 Militär-Gouverneur to all Distrikts-Kommandanten, 5.4.17.
37. OKA NFA 1774 MGG Rum. 1917 20.5-18.6 Chief of Wirtschaftsstabes to Sendler, 9.6.17.
38. BA Lichterfelde R1501/119869 R.I., bl.245 Verordnungsblatt der Militar-Verwaltung in Rumanien, Nr. 33 20 July 1917, 255.
39. BA Lichterfelde R1501/119869 bl. 57 Verordnungsblatt der Militar-Verwaltung in Rumanien, Nr. 7 31 Jan 1917, 43.
40. BA Lichterfelde R1501/119869 R.I., bl. 218–219 Verordnungsblatt der Militar-Verwaltung in Rumanien, Nr. 29 22 June 1917, 224–5.
41. BA/MA PH 5-I/74 p. 61, 63 Bericht des Wirtschaftsstabes 1.7. – 31.12.1917. See also PH 3/102 'Denkschrift über die kriegswirtschaftlichen Leistungen der Eisenbahnen' 1916–1917.
42. See, OKA NFA 1774 MGG Rumänien 1917 20.5-18.6 Etappenstationskommando Galicea-Mare to Sendler, 2.6.17.
43. BA Lichterflde R901/3919 Bl. 125–131 Reise Bericht des Ministerialdirektors und Hauptmann D.L. Dr. Graf von Keyserlingk uber die Wirtschaftliche Lage in Rumanien 6 April 1917.
44. BA Lichterfelde R1501/119868 RI, bl 162 Verordnungsblat der Militar-Verwaltung in Rumanien, Nr. 19 13 April 1917, p. 144; OKA NFA 1772 MGG Rum 1917 1.4–22.4 Militär-Gouverneur to all Distrikts-Kommandanten, 5.4.17.
45. BA Lichterfelde R1501/119869 R.I., bl. 105 Verordnungsblatt der Militar-Verwaltung in Rumanien, Nr. 14 11 March 1917, p. 101 'Bevorschussung der Ernte 1917'.
46. BA Lichterfelde R1501/119868 RI, bl 162 Verordnungsblat der Militar-Verwaltung in Rumanien, Nr. 19 13 April 1917, 144 'Verordnung uber die Einrichtung einer landwirtschaftlichen Darlehnstelle'.
47. BA Lichterfelde R901/3919 Bl. 185 Zweite Reise Bericht des Wirtschaftberaters beim Generalquartiermeister, Ministrialdirektors und Hauptmanns d.L. Graf von Keyserlingk uber die wirtschaftliche Verhaltnisse in Rumanien, 18 May 1917.
48. See Hamlin, *'Dummes Geld'*, Central European History.
49. Scott, *Seeing Like A State*.
50. Rommel, *Infantry Attacks*, 107.
51. Anschauer,. *Auf Schicksalswegen gen Osten.*, 66.
52. Scott, *Weapons of the Weak*.
53. OKA NFA 1786 MGG Rum 19.9–21.10 Officer Reservatbefehl from K.k. Bevoll bei MVR and Oberquartiermeister in Rum, 25.3.17.
54. NARA T 136 Reel 95 AA Verwaltung besetzter Gebiet Rumaniens Aufzeichnung, 2 May 1917, Lübitz.
55. OKA NFA 1786 MGG Rum 19.9–21.10 K.u.k. Kriegsministerium, 12.10.17.
56. BA/MA N 127/15 Division-Tagesbefehle 14 June 1918.
57. Mitrany, *The Effect of the War*150; BA Lichterfelde R1501/119869 R.I., bl. 338, Verordnungsblatt der Militär-Verwaltung in Rumänien, Nr. 46 12 Oct 1917, Vergrabenes Getreide.
58. OKA NFA 1764 MGG Rum 1917 1.4–13.5 AOK QAbt. Attachment to 24 March report. Habsburg troops were permitted to send 5 kg home but allegedly these rarely arrived at the indicated address.
59. Velburg, *Rumanische Etappe*, 24, 57–58. Vieweg on p. 62–3.
60. 'Die Lebensmittelfrage gesichert', *Bukarester Tagblatt*, 16 May 1917, 3.
61. Velburg, *Rumanische Etappe*, 197–8.
62. OKA NFA 1766 MGG Rum 1917 4.7–6.8 Kuczinsky to Gendarmiekommando Rittmeister Jaskiewsz, 14.6.17; Strafanzeige gegen Leopold Suck und Wilhelm Hubich.
63. OKA NFA 1766 MGG Rum 1917 4.7–6.8 Chief of the General Staff, Oberst Hentsch to Generalmajor v. Sendler, 16 July 1917.
64. BA MA PH 5-I/74 p. 61, Bericht des Wirtschaftsstabes, 1.7. – 31.12.1917; see also *A-H Tätigkeitsbericht des Wirtschaftsstabes. Beginn bis 30.11.17*, 56.
65. *A-H Tätigkeitsbericht des Wirtschaftsstabes. Beginn bis 30.11.17*, 56.
66. BA Lichterflde R1501/119869 R.I. Verordnung der Militar-Verwaltung 16.1.17, 29, Bl. 50; R1501/119869 R.I., bl.428 Verordnungsblatt der Militar-Verwaltung in Rumanien, Nr. 58 4

MILITARY OCCUPATIONS IN FIRST WORLD WAR EUROPE

Jan 1918; R1501/119869 R.I. bl. 48 Verordnungsblatt der Militar-Verwaltung in Rumanien, Nr. 5 21 Jan 1917; R1501/119869 R.I., bl. 156, Verordnungsblatt der Militar-Verwaltung in Rumanien, Nr. 21 27 April 1917; BA MA PH 5-I/74, p. 57, 59 Bericht des Verpflegungsoffiziers für die Zivilbevölkerung 1.7 - 31.12.1917; N 127/15 Divisions-Tagesbefahle (89th Div.) 11 June 1918.

67. BA Lichterfelde R1501/119869 Bl. 50 Verordnung der Militar-Verwaltung 16.1.17, 29.
68. *A-H Tätigkeitsbericht des Wirtschaftsstabes. Beginn bis 30.11.17*, 56.
69. BA/MA N 127/15 Division-Tagesbefehle 14 June 1918.
70. BA Lichterfelde R1501/119869 bl. 48 Verordnungsblatt der Militar-Verwaltung in Rumanien, Nr. 5 21 Jan 1917, 26.
71. BA Lichterfelde R1501/119869 bl. 156 Verordnungsblatt der Militar-Verwaltung in Rumanien, Nr. 21 27 April 1917, 161; Verordnungsblatt der Militar-Verwaltung in Rumanien, Nr. 44 28 Sept 1917, 356.
72. OKA NFA 1773 MGG Rumänien 1917 23.4–20.5 Deutsche Feldkost- und Rationssätze.
73. Chickering, 170; Michaelis, *Für Staat und Volk*, 273.
74. BA/MA PH 30 II/15 Halbjahresbericht des Verwaltungchefs bie dem General-gorvernement Warchau 1 October 1916–31 March 1917, 49–50.
75. BA/MA PH 30 II/18 Halbjahresbericht des Verwaltungschefs bei dem General-Gouvernement Warschau 1 April–30 Sept 1918, 55–7.
76. BA/MA PH 30 II/33, bl. 13–21 Niederschrift über die Besprechung der Ernährungslage der Ausfuhr der besetzten Gebiete von 16. November 1917. Unter Vorsitz des Herrn Staatssekretär des Kriegsernährungsamt.
77. BA/MA RM 5/4128 bl. 24–31 Kriegstagebuch Adm.Staboffizier OKM 3 Nov 1917.
78. OKA NFA 1764 MGG Rum 1917 1.4–13.5 K.u.k. Gendarmiekommando Rittmeister Jaskiewicz to Gendarmiekommdo, Etappenpost 346, 1.4.17.
79. BA/MA PHD 23/54 Verordungsblatt für die Stadt Ploesti, No. 1, 6.3.17.
80. BA/MA PHD 23/54 Verordnungsblatt für die Stadt Ploesti, No. 624.3.17.
81. 'Viehhandelsverbot', *Bukarester Tagblatt*, 13 Feb 1917, 4.
82. A sample: 'Strafen wegen Nichtbefolgung von Verordnungen.', *Bukarester Tagblatt*, 15 Feb 1917, p. 3; 'Unbefugter Viehhandel', *Bukarester Tagblatt*, 25 Feb 1917, 3; 'Bestrafungen', *Bukarester Tagblatt*, 6 April 1917, 6; 'Bestrafungen', *Bukarester Tagblatt*, 17 May 1917, 3; 'Warnung', *Bukarester Tagblatt*, 4 July 1917, 5; 'Bestrafungen' *Bukarester Tagblatt*, 27 July 1917, 3.
83. OKA NFA 1766 MGG Rum 1917 4.7–6.8 File on the Case of Gendarmeriewachtmeistern Suck and Hubich, June and July 1917.
84. Velburg, *Rumanische Etappe*, 270–3.
85. BA Lichterfelde R1501/119869 R.I., bl. 331 Verordnungsblatt der Militar-Verwaltung in Rumanien, Nr. 45 5 Oct 1917 1917, 359.
86. BA/MA R1501/119872 bl. 36 Verordnungsblatt des Oberkommandos. Nr. 8 22.7.18; R1501/119872 bl. 38 Verordnungsblatt des Oberkommandos. Nr. 9 29.7.18.
87. Weindling, *Epidemics and Genocide*, 99–100; BA/MA PH 5-I/135 bl. 128 Wochenbericht 17.3–23.3.18.
88. BA/MA Nachlaß General Kosch N 754/9, 10 'Erlebnisse während des Weltkrieges. Band IX. Okt, 1917-März 1918'; PH 5-I/134 bl. 23 Heeres-Tagesbefehl Nr. 166 12.2.17 OKM.
89. BA/MA N 127/15 Divisions-Tagesbefehle 5 July 1918.
90. Hersch, 'La mortalite causee par la guerre mondiale', 7 76–80. Hersch's estimates are echoed by the leading English language historian of Romania, Keith Hitchens. Hitchens put military casualties at 'approximately 300,000' and, when these were added to civilian deaths, Romania 'is estimated to have lost one-tenth of her pre-war population', which would suggest a civilian death toll between 400,000 and 450,000. Hitchins, *Rumania. 1866–1947*, 291.
91. R3101/884 bl. 292–304, Export Statistics up to 31 May 1918. After May 1918, the statistics become more spotty and apparently unreliable.

Archival Sources

Bundesarchiv Lichterfelde.
Bundesarchiv, Militärische Abteilung.

National Archive and Records Administration.
Politische Archiv des Auswärtigen Amtes.

Published Official Documents

Oesterreichisch-Ungarischer Tätigkeitsbericht des Wirtschaftsstabes der Militaerverwaltung in Rumanien. Vom Beginn bis 30. November 1917. Wien: K.k. Hof – und Staatsdrukerei, 1918.

Published Primary Sources

Anschauer, Phillip. *Auf Schicksalswegen gen Osten. Kriegserlebnisse eines deutsche Jägerregiments in Rumänien, auf der Krim und im Kaukasus.* Münster: Helois-Verlag GmbH, 1931.
Groener, Wilhelm. *Lebenserinnerungen. Jugend – Generalstab – Weltkrieg.* Göttingen: Vandenhoeck & Ruprecht, 1957.
Hannsen, HansPeter. *Diary of a Dying Empire.* Bloomington, IL: Indiana University Press, 1955.
Hertling, Georg Graf von, Hugo Graf von und zu Lerchenfeld. *Briefwechsel Hertling-Lerchenfeld, 1912–1917. Dienstliche Privatkorrespondenz zwischen dem bayerischen Ministerpräsidenten Georg Graf von Hertling und dem bayerischen Gesandten in Berlin Hugo Graf von und zu Lerchenfeld. Band II*, ed. Ernst Deurlein. Boppard am Rhein: Harald Boldt Verlag, 1973.
Köster, Adolf Dr. *Die sturmschar Falkenhayns. Kriegsberichte aus Siebenburgen und Rumänien.* München: Albert Langen, 1917.
Kries, Wolfgangvon. "Die wirtschaftliche Ausnutzung des Generalgouvernements Warschau." *Preussische Jahrbücher* 235 (1934): 221–48.
Michaelis, Georg. *Für Staat und Volk.* Berlin: Furche Verlag, 1922.
Rommel, Erwin. *Infantry Attacks.* London: Greenhill Books, 1990.
Velburg, Gerhard. *Rumaenische Etappe. Der Weltkrieg, wie ich ihn sah.* Minden–Berlin–Leipzig: Druck und Verlag von Wilhelm Koehler, 1930.

Secondary Sources

Berend, Ivan. *History Derailed.* Berkeley, CA: University of California Press, 2003.
Chickering, Roger. *The Great War and Urban Life in Germany: Freiburg, 1914–1918.* New York: Cambridge University Press, 2007.
Davis, Belinda. *Home Fires Burning. Food Politics and Everyday Life in World War I Berlin.* Chapel Hill, NC: University of North Carolina Press, 2000.
Eidelberg, PhilipGabriel. "Causes of the Great Rumanian Peasant Revolt of 1907." PhD diss., Columbia, 1970.
Feldman, Gerald. *Army, Industry and Labor in Germany 1914–1918.* Princeton, NJ: Princeton University Press, 1966.
Hamlin, David. ""Dummes Geld": Money Grain and the Occupation of Romania in World War I." *Central European History* 42 (2009): 451–71.
Healy, Maureen. *Vienna and the Fall of the Habsburg Empire. Total War and Everyday Life in World War I.* New York: Cambridge University Press, 2004.
Hersch, Liebmann. "La Mortalite causee par la Guerre Mondiale." *Metron* 7 (1925).
Hitchins, Keith. *Rumania. 1866–1947.* New York: Clarendon Press, 1994.
Hull, Isabel. *Absolute Destruction: Military Culture and the Practices of War in Imperial Germany.* Ithaca, NY: Cornell University Press, 2006.
Liulevicius, Vejas. *War Land on the Eastern Front. Culture, National Identity, and German Occupation in World War I.* New York: Cambridge University Press, 2000.
Mitrany, David. *The Land and the Peasant in Rumania. The War and Agrarian Reform (1917–1921).* London: Oxford University Press, 1930.
Scott, James. *Weapons of the Weak; Everyday Forms of Peasant Resistance.* New Haven, CT: Yale University Press, 1985.
Scott, James. *Seeing Like A State: How Certain Schemes to Improve the Human Condition Have Failed.* New Haven, CT: Yale University Press, 1998.
Weindling, Paul. *Epidemics and Genocide in Eastern Europe 1890–1945.* New York: Oxford University Press, 2000.
Zilch, Reinhold. *Okkupation und Währung im Ersten Weltkrieg. Die deutsche Besatzunspolitik in Belgien und Russisch-Polen 1914–1918.* Goldbach: Keip Verlag, 1994.

Norms of war and the Austro-Hungarian encounter with Serbia, 1914–1918

Jonathan E. Gumz

Department of History, University of Birmingham, Birmingham, UK

This essay first explores European assumptions regarding occupation and war in the late nineteenth and early twentieth centuries. These assumptions found their way into international law, but are best understood as a series of international norms. The article then goes on to examine how these norms changed over the course of the war, paying attention to the Austro-Hungarian occupation of Serbia from 1916 to 1918. The European approach to war within Europe attempted to contain the expansion of conflict and created a strict divide between civilian and military realms. Occupiers were to maintain the sovereignty of the departed government until the conclusion of a peace treaty, while the occupied population owed obedience to the occupier. Austria-Hungary's war against Serbia and subsequent occupation two years later placed heavy pressure on these pre-war norms. In some cases, such as the use of military law in occupied Serbia, Austria-Hungary departed entirely from these norms. As the war progressed, however, a growing realization that such norms of contained conflict also buttressed Austria-Hungary's place in the international system led Austria-Hungary to restrain its occupation of Serbia. While Austria-Hungary attempted to resituate itself and its occupation of Serbia back within these norms from mid-1917 forward, this attempt went largely unrecognized. Broadly seen, such international norms fell under severe pressure in Eastern Europe with the implosion of imperial sovereignties in this region, most notably that of Tsarist Russia.

For the seminal event of the twentieth century, the First World War had strangely local roots in a conflict between Serbia and Austria-Hungary. Yet, the intensely local nature of this conflict could not restrain the reverberations that rippled slowly outward, but with increasing power, from Sarajevo after 28 June 1914. The conflict between Imperial Russia and Austria-Hungary over influence in the Balkans, the showdown between multinational and national states in European politics since the mid-nineteenth century and Imperial Germany's combustible sense of weakness and strength in the years after 1905 made this local event into something momentous for European and world history. Yet, how this conflict between Austro-Hungarians and Serbs was eventually resolved and how it played out over the course of the war also offer important insights for European and world history. That resolution centres on the crucial issue of military occupation. Through the Austro-Hungarian occupation of Serbia, we can sharpen our understanding of how Europe constructed war in the early twentieth century and how that particular construction of war began to degenerate in the First World War.

MILITARY OCCUPATIONS IN FIRST WORLD WAR EUROPE

Occupation as an international norm played a key role in that pre-1914 construction of war. Into that norm went not only an assemblage of international legal codes but also armies' expectations regarding the limits within which states would pursue military conflict, as well as cultural assumptions about what constituted the 'law and order' that occupation governments had to secure.[1] Occupation was not only the product of policies internal in origin but also an external, international institution that functioned within a larger system of international norms governing war and conflict. The containment of conflict formed what could be considered the *Grundnorm* that linked this assemblage of individual norms together whether they concerned occupation, international law, the strict division between soldiers and civilians or sovereignty. Many historians have pointed out over the last 10 years that this commitment to the containment of conflict was also something geographically limited to Europe.[2] These norms were the creation of a particular system of sovereign states as well as international legal thinkers in Europe in the late nineteenth century.[3] When it comes to norms, as Sarah Percy explains, it is important not to conflate international law and international norms. The law, to the extent that it exists, derives from the norm, not the other way around. In addition, the law does not capture the entirety of the norm. Finally, norms tend to be more robust than international law and can persist in the face of repeated violations. Only when the fundamental assumptions of the norm are thrown away by various international actors do they begin to buckle.[4]

This focus on norms provides an externalist perspective on occupation that comes into relief when examining Austria-Hungary's occupation of Serbia during the First World War. More than other states, Austria-Hungary was highly invested in the post-Napoleonic international system and partially relied on its status as a great power for its legitimacy.[5] Austria-Hungary's own confidence in the rescuing power of international norms extended both to occupation and to its own survival in 1917. In the case of its occupation of Serbia, this externalist perspective on occupation helps provide another lens through which to understand not only the actions of Austria-Hungary but also the way in which the First World War changed the European construction of war and occupation. In fact, occupation and Austro-Hungarian survival crossed paths during the war only to find that the pre-1914 structures of international norms would neither support Austro-Hungarian survival nor continue to bolster occupations in places like Serbia.

The Austro-Hungarian occupation of Serbia officially began on 1 January 1916. Subject to three Austrian invasion attempts since August 1914, Serbia fell to a combined German, Bulgarian, Austro-Hungarian invasion that commenced in November 1915. Bulgarian aid came with a price, however, and Bulgaria garnered a sizeable occupation zone for itself extending from far southern Serbia into Macedonia. The defeated Serb Army did not surrender, but chose to embark on a winter trek across the mountains, many civilians in tow, to the Albanian coast where the Italian Navy belatedly picked it up and transported it to Salonika. The Serb Army spent the rest of the war fighting against the Bulgarian Army, which, with German help, defended the Salonika front. Given Austria-Hungary's military weakness, occupied Serbia contained only a small number of occupation units, reaching a maximum of 50,000 soldiers. Some units were in Serbia for only a short span, refitted there and redeployed to more active fronts. In addition, the occupation's soldiers were older and in many cases had been deemed militarily unfit. This skeleton occupation ruled over approximately 1.4 million Serbs. The occupation of Serbia was an emphatically Army-run show. Bureaucratically, the occupation was subordinated to the Armeeoberkommando (Army High Command – AOK), under Franz Conrad von Hoetzendorff and later Arz von Straussenberg. The occupation divided its occupation zone

MILITARY OCCUPATIONS IN FIRST WORLD WAR EUROPE

in 13 provinces, with another layer of Habsburg administration below this, but did not have the capacity to directly rule in every small hamlet in Serbia. From the perspective of the AOK as well as the occupation government itself, this occupation became a shining example of the effectiveness of Habsburg methods of rule. It exemplified a bureaucratic-absolutist tendency in the Austro-Hungarian state that was most developed within the Army. It brooked little opposition in Serbia, pushed the rest of the Habsburg state aside in Serbia and sought to administer little Serbia in as 'apolitical' a manner as possible. Of course, such a programme was deeply political given the context of imperial politics, but the occupation government and the Army hardly saw it this way. This occupation lasted until late October 1918 when the Bulgarian withdrawal from the war in late September 1918 finally opened up the Salonika front. This exposed the weak military power of the occupation of Serbia to the entente and with it a frail and collapsing Habsburg Empire to threat from the south.[6]

The Austro-Hungarian Army considered its occupation of Serbia a shining success compared to what the Army viewed as the civilian government's mismanagement of the internal war effort, especially within the Austrian half of the Empire. Yet, when we place the Austro-Hungarian occupation of Serbia during the First World War within an externalist frame, one that considers it in light of the established norm of occupation in Europe, the picture changes. First, we see how even for states most firmly situated within the system of norms governing European war, such as Austria-Hungary, these norms came under stress almost as quickly as the war began. That pressure came in part from the war's chaotic start in Serbia, which helped to further entrench a sense of superiority within the Austro-Hungarian Army vis-à-vis Serbia. This sense of superiority, stemming in part from a perception of how Serbia had organized for war, led the Austro-Hungarian Army to believe that it dealt with a semi-criminal state. But Austria-Hungary found it difficult to break completely free of international norms in its treatment of Serbia. Those norms continued to retain relevance among policy-makers in the Empire even if they were at times dismissed. They had to be argued around, pushed to the side and dealt with, even if some considered them an unnecessary burden. As the war wore on, situating the occupation of Serbia within European norms of occupation actually rose in importance for many within the Army as well as other parts of the imperial government. From this point, we can peer through the occupation of Serbia into the crisis of European norms of war and imperial sovereignty in the war's final years and to Austria-Hungary's attempts to extract itself from this crisis.

Austria-Hungary's occupation of Serbia did not take place in a vacuum confined to the interaction between Austria-Hungary, its institutions, the remnants of the defeated government in Serbia and the remaining populace of the defeated country. As an international norm, occupation was externally constituted among European states in the late nineteenth and early twentieth centuries. It was, as I mentioned earlier, part of a broader complex of norms directed towards containing conflict and ensuring that states, at least within Europe, did not lose control of wars.[7] Occupation sought to protect European state sovereignty through treating the occupying power as a 'trustee' for the departed sovereign government. The Brussels Declaration of 1874 used the term 'usufructuary' to describe the role of the occupier. The occupier was bound to respect existing laws as long as they did not interfere with 'military necessity' and to, as much as possible, avoid transforming the country it occupied. Local officials were to remain at their posts and obey the occupying authorities so as to ensure as little disruption as possible in the lives of the occupied.[8] In turn, this meant that defeated countries had an incentive to accept defeat and hope for a more amenable deal at the peace table instead of choosing to continue what

99

might be an ever more destructive conflict. Those who resisted an established occupation did not receive the protection of belligerent status, and attempts to explicitly recognize resistance to occupation were rejected at the Hague Conference of 1899.[9] Needless to say, this was the subject of much wrangling among European states, but a careful reading of the Hague discussions reveals that if any country at the conference wanted to depart from contained war in Europe, it was Belgium, not Germany. Certainly, internally within the German Army, as Isabel Hull has argued, voices maintained that war could no longer be contained by norms but was simply the playing out of unrestrained force.[10] But it was the Belgian delegate who rued the fact that the Hague Convention would separate civilians from conflict and de-legitimize a patriotic resistance against an established occupation.[11] Prior to the war, the acceptance of occupation was such that presenting an occupation as being in conformity with the norm tended to reinforce the norm, even if the occupier violated it at times. Russia, for instance, felt compelled to present its occupations during the Russo-Turkish War of 1877–1878 as having been in conformity with the standards of occupation worked out in the Brussels Declaration of 1874.[12] Yet, intentional and continual disregard for the norm of occupation could have the effect of undermining the norm. The First World War would provide a test for the norm of occupation along just such lines, especially with regard to Austria-Hungary in Serbia.

Austria-Hungary confidently believed it was the 'just' actor with regard to Serbia. Serb military intelligence's ties to Franz Ferdinand's assassination provided Austria-Hungary with a basis for the use of force. Austria-Hungary's position as a European great power led it to assume that it had the right to use or at least threaten force when it felt that its 'honour' was aggrieved. Whether this was an advisable line of policy to pursue given the constellation of European powers and Russia's own assumptions about its perceived humiliation during the Bosnian Annexation Crisis was an entirely different question. Nonetheless, policy-makers' conviction that criminality and lawlessness marked the Serbian government's pre-war behaviour primed them to accept that Serb prosecution of war also contained such intentional lawlessness. If the Austro-Hungarian Army's failed invasion attempts of Serbia in 1914 convinced it of anything, it was that the Serb state embarked on a war that deliberately crossed the nineteenth century's norm on the boundary between soldiers and civilians. In turn, this made adhering to the norm of occupation once Austria-Hungary occupied Serbia in 1916 more difficult given that this norm rested on the occupier acting as the trustee for the departed sovereign state. Could one be a trustee for a state that so blatantly disregarded European norms of war?

Even in those hectic days of July 1914, elements of the Army became convinced that the Serb government wanted to 'insurgentize' Serb communities in Bosnia that owed allegiance to the Empire.[13] This violated norms of war that viewed insurgencies as highly problematic because they undermined consensus on contained conflict and the divide between soldier and civilian. Conrad, the Army chief of staff, noted that 'revolutionary actions directed against the Monarchy took place with the knowledge and patronage of the Serbian government'.[14] Such convictions deepened during the August 1914 invasion of Serbia. Serious confusion plagued the invading Austro-Hungarian armies, and unsurprisingly for the early part of the war the invasion plans outpaced the capacities of the Army. In this case, the invasion called for one part of the Austro-Hungarian attack to come from the west of Serbia over very mountainous terrain. In the sweltering August heat, units became detached from one another, lost orientation and found themselves facing what they thought to be a mass of armed Serb civilians. While they did not entirely face that, what they did face was the Serb third levy, which the Serb government could not give adequate uniforms. The third levy occupied defensive positions in north-western

Serbia precisely because Serb Army leaders believed the Austrians would not choose this invasion route due to the difficult terrain.[15] For Habsburg Army officers, this encounter with the Serb third levy quickly became a narrative of a government that again transgressed the norms governing the soldier–civilian divide in war. Atrocity stories abounded within the Army as soldiers were told of the hideous treatment that befell soldiers upon capture by Serb guerrillas or Komitadjis. Habsburg Army units also saw Serb civilians as potential combatants as word swept through the invading army that Serb civilians participated in combat. Of course, the veracity of such rumours was hardly tested and officers moved such accusations across the Army's communication systems. Circulars sped through the various units, condemning 'atrocious actions' on the part of Serbs who wore civilian clothing on the battlefield and thus violated 'international law'.[16]

Word that part of the Serb Army had no uniforms did not lead to a rethinking of how to deal with an un-uniformed enemy. Serbs suspected of fighting without uniforms would be treated as criminals and executed. Army units invading Serbia gave very little reflection to the finer points of the Hague Conventions on this issue. The Hague Conventions allowed for civilians to spontaneously defend their country prior to the establishment of a military occupation provided that their behaviour was in accord with the 'laws and customs of war'.[17] This was where atrocity stories played a key role. Atrocities helped place the perceived participation of Serb civilians and Komitadjis in the invasion outside the 'laws and customs of war'. Already in July 1914, the Army reached the conclusion that Serb guerrillas, or 'Komitadjis' as the Army frequently called them, were 'outside international law'. They were to be 'completely wiped out'.[18] Habsburg officers repeatedly stressed that the Serb state and army intentionally violated international law. General Liborius Frank declared that 'the brutal, deceitful actions of the Serb military and Serb population against our troops... violated every norm of war and all laws of humanity'.[19] This only further entrenched the Army's sense of 'moral superiority' vis-à-vis Serbia.[20] Small, but routine, gestures of respect between the two armies were called into question. General Michael von Appel, for example, refused to treat captured Serb officers as officers and instead ordered them to be handled as enlisted men.[21]

The experience of the 1914 invasion created an image of the Serb state for the Army that made the pre-1914 trustee element of the norm of occupation almost impossible for it to implement. How could the Army entrust governance to a state that had violated international norms from the assassination of Franz Ferdinand forward? The answer rested in a turn to apolitical 'administration'. This was something to which the Army was already inclined, given its perception that only this could save Austria-Hungary as a whole. Politics in Serbia would come to an end. Those with connections to the Serb political class, especially those connected to the nationalist Liberal Party, were subject to a wide variety of surveillance. The occupation government tracked their movements and if necessary interned those who in its words 'agitated' in the Empire. Of course, this was an imprecise tool and often swept up people who had little to do with political agitation, but who ran afoul of Austro-Hungarian occupation officials. Such a de-politicization of the country, especially when it envisioned a broader de-politicization of the population through fundamentally reworking the school curriculum to eliminate national histories or attempting to replace Serb teachers with Habsburg soldiers, went well beyond the 'trustee' concept of sovereignty embodied in the norm of occupation. Moreover, such policies seemed to point far more in the direction of annexation of Serbia, something that Army leaders like Conrad and the Minister-President of the Austrian half of the Empire, Karl Graf von Stürgkh, advocated.[22]

But to the extent that such annexation desires existed, they remained future questions and required more than the overheated demands of Conrad, whose credibility was

MILITARY OCCUPATIONS IN FIRST WORLD WAR EUROPE

declining in conjunction with military disasters on other fronts. Conrad's annexationist desires aside, however, the moment the occupation most egregiously transgressed the norm of occupation came in its administration of justice in Serbia. Already in the Hague Conference in 1899, there was no sense that the military law of the occupiers would displace large portions of the domestic law of the occupied country.[23] The trustee concept embedded in the norm of occupation meant that the justice system of the occupied country would continue to function during the occupation. Yet, this was absolutely not the case during the first year and a half of the occupation of Serbia. The Serb justice system, according to General Hugo Kerchnawe, the occupation's chief of staff, was hopelessly corrupt, filled with politically inclined officials, and incapable of impartial justice.[24] It was the precise opposite of the apolitical administration of justice that the Army favoured. Moreover, the Habsburg Army was in the midst of an extensive campaign since the war's start to extend military law across the Empire in the belief that this draconian form of law, supposedly equitably enforced by apolitical officers, would keep unruly civilians in line. While the Army engaged in a relentless battle with politicians and the bureaucracy at home over applying military law to civilians, the occupation administration faced no opponent in Serbia and thus military law struck with full force. Military courts even tried Serbians for the crime of *Majestätsbeleidigung* [insulting the Emperor or his family], which was certainly a stretch to apply to Serbia. In addition, the crisis produced by Italy's approaching entry into the conflict, the disastrous Carpathian mountain offensive that began in January 1915 and the looming fall of Przemysl led the Army to dramatically escalate the penalties associated with military law through the extensive application of *Standrecht* in Army operational zones. *Standrecht*, which only allowed an acquittal or a death sentence, was an emergency system of law hardly applicable to an occupied country. Nonetheless, *Standrecht* even applied to crimes such as *Majestätsbeleidigung*, causing mere verbal attacks on Franz Josef occasionally to lead to a death sentence.[25]

These measures pushed the Austro-Hungarian occupation of Serbia well beyond the norm of occupation established before 1914. It was all the more ironic that it was precisely the Austro-Hungarian Army's belief that Serbia had abandoned such norms that justified its departure from the norm of occupation. Yet, here we should be careful not to link the Empire's broader position vis-à-vis international norms too tightly to its evolution with regard to the norm of occupation. First, Habsburg decision-makers, including the most radical elements of the Army, never moved to decouple their state entirely from international norms governing war (even if some voices called for this). Despite his outrage at what he thought were Serb violations of the norms of war in August 1914, General Liborius Frank ruled out a 'competition' with the Serbs when it came to violence, because Austria-Hungary belonged to 'European culture' and its people were 'civilized'. Such language reflected how Austria-Hungary's continued link to nineteenth-century norms of war could act to restrain violence.[26] Later in the fall, Oskar Potiorek warned soldiers to refrain from a campaign of devastation against the Serb countryside whatever their beliefs as to Serb transgressions of 'international law'. 'Such an advance', Potiorek asserted, 'is unworthy of an army of a great power'.[27] The Empire's conception of itself as a great power meant it had rights that others did not have, such as to go to war over questions of honour and a natural, privileged position over other smaller states. But it also meant responsibilities. The moment the Empire began to operate as if it lived in a norm-free world when it came to war, it undercut its claims to great power status.

Such concerns also extended to the occupation's initial stages. After the final invasion of Serbia in November 1915, the Austro-Hungarian Army encountered a country on the brink of starvation. After nearly four years of constant war, multiple invasion attempts and a massive mobilization effort, Serbian agriculture reached a standstill. This was a moment when the more visibly anti-Serb elements of the Austro-Hungarian Army, Conrad in particular, toyed with the idea of wilfully neglecting Serbia's precarious situation. Serbia had, in Conrad's eyes, brought this on itself. Yet, voices within the government, in particular in the Foreign Ministry, but even Conrad himself, quickly understood the implications of such a position. The norm of occupation demanded that the occupier provide for law and order in the occupied area and ensure adequate provisioning for the occupied population. Moreover, the picture of Austria-Hungary ruling over an occupied territory whose population lacked even the most basic provisions was simply too much for the Foreign Minister István Burián and Foreign Ministry representatives at the AOK. One diplomat demanded that Austria-Hungary start 'as soon as possible' transporting foodstuffs to Serbia. Even Conrad acknowledged a few weeks later that 'one could only disregard what the population needs to live within certain boundaries'.[28] The point here is not that the provisioning of Serbia was a smooth functioning, humanitarian gesture. Nothing about Austria-Hungary's handling of food supply issues during the First World War suggests that it fully understood the issues at play concerning food supply and distribution.[29] But norms relating to war and occupation remained relevant within the government and Army. They could not be dismissed out of hand even when policy-makers argued for their irrelevance. Characteristically, the flighty Conrad found himself on both sides of this issue.

Nonetheless, we should not discount the impact of the Empire's and other powers' transgression of such norms by the time we reach late 1916. Taken as a whole, these transgressions began to subvert the fundamental norm of war containment, not just in word but in deed, and did so in Europe, at the heart of this system of norms, not in some far-off colonial territory. When it came to occupation, the overall relevance of this norm within the international system began to weaken. The war began with incredible violence, not all of it consciously directed from the top, some driven by standard military practices, perceptions of a dangerous 'other', confusion on the part of officers and soldiers whose experience of war was limited at best, a breakdown of military supply systems or a toxic combination of all of the above. Whether we turn to Belgium and northern France during the German invasion of 1914, Russian Poland, East Prussia, Galicia or Serbia, nineteenth-century norms of war came under pressure from the very beginning.[30] That pressure was most intense when it came to norms of occupation and various armies' understanding of the dividing line between civilians and war. Moreover, the way in which various foreign ministries worked to individually document their opponents' violations of norms of war had the aggregate effect of creating further doubt as to the applicability of nineteenth-century norms of war to the conflict. It should be clear that Austria-Hungary was as much a player in helping to destabilize the norms of war, including the norm of occupation, as any other belligerent, whether or not some of these policies came in response to perceived Serb violations of such norms. Yet, Austria-Hungary always retained an attachment to such norms as shown by their continued relevance even when it came to Serbia. This was what distinguished Austria-Hungary from Imperial Germany where, as Jost Dülffer argues, army officers and diplomats perceived international norms of war as instruments designed to constrain German power.[31]

For Austria-Hungary, this perilous foothold within the norms of war and occupation with regard to Serbia became one of the places from which it attempted, in 1917, a broader return to the world of the pre-1914 international system with its emphasis on contained conflict. The occupation government began to dismantle the system of military law in Serbia, encountered greater restraints from military and civilian authorities in Vienna anxious about the departures from the pre-1914 international norms and faced policy-makers who decided against simply annexing Serbia as a trophy of war. All of this took place in spite of images of Serbs as brutal and criminal people. The Vienna *Kriegsausstellung* [war exhibition] of 1917, for example, came complete with a special exhibit on guerrilla war in Serbia. Viennese learned about how police units in Serbia tracked Komitadjis to their various lairs as they gazed at a model of a Komitadji hideout.[32]

What the Viennese public did not see at the exhibition was the atmosphere of restraint that began to settle over Serbia. At one point, the occupation attempted to compel labour from Serbs on large agricultural domains, run by the occupation government, where the labour had largely been done by Army units rotating through parts of the country. Given dwindling availability of troops, the occupation government believed it found the perfect solution. It would resurrect an old Serb law from the 1880s, the Kuluk law, which required that Serbs labour for a small number of days for the state. The occupation government emphasized to the AOK that this was a Serbian law and thus did not constitute a violation of the Hague Convention which required occupations adhere as much as possible to existing national laws. Yet, the AOK rejected this, noting that this law was relatively antiquated and had its roots in the Turkish period of rule. Moreover, old laws could not be resurrected to suit the needs of the occupiers. The AOK's legal officer noted, 'In the occupation administration, international law must be upheld'.[33] On another occasion, the occupation government was kept from instituting a so-called Hajduk law to deal with guerrilla unrest in the far south of occupied Serbia. This would have allowed the occupation to designate certain guerrillas as beyond the law, essentially making it legal for anyone to kill them. Again, the occupation government noted that the law had been on the books in parts of Serbia, newly annexed in the aftermath of the Balkan Wars. Thus, argued the Governor-General, Adolf Rhemen von Barensfeld, this was compliant with the Hague Conventions. For the AOK, this hardly sufficed for a legal justification. Such laws, maintained the legal officer at the AOK, did not conform to the 'spirit of modern criminal justice'. Even more problematic, once word escaped that the occupation was using Hajduk law in Serbia, it would 'damage the Monarchy's prestige as a *Kulturstaat*'.[34] Again, here we see how the norm of occupation was embedded in a broader set of international norms governing war and how the Monarchy's own self-perception was integrated into this set of norms. Culture and civilization were bounded by norms of law and restraint. Occupation had to be a part of that.

As these examples reveal, this return to the norm of occupation was not simply a matter of flipping a switch, which compelled the entire Habsburg Army, policy-makers and the occupation government to strictly adhere to the norm of occupation in Serbia. Rather, it was a movement marked by fits and starts and the same hesitance that marked the Empire's early moves out of the norm of occupation. But the direction of the Empire's movements was unequivocal. There was a new determination to ensure that the Army 'abide strictly by the law' as the legal officer at the AOK later maintained.[35] Above all, that movement back to within the norm came from the most fundamental question of all: What would be the final disposition of Austrian-occupied Serbia? If we look to discussions in 1915 and early 1916, there was little doubt where occupied Serbia would end up. Conrad steadily beat the drum for the immediate annexation of the country. He was supported by the Austrian Minister-President, Karl Graf von Stürgkh, who hoped that Serbia would provide foodstuffs for the struggling Austrian half of the Monarchy. An annexation would have undoubtedly contravened the norm of occupation which sought above all to protect the sovereignty of an occupied country until its status was finally settled in a peace treaty ending the conflict. Moreover, from an internal political point of view, the Minister-President of Hungary, István Tisza, looked askance at annexation since he feared this foreshadowed a 'trialist' solution for Austria-Hungary, would create a south Slav state in the Empire and undermine Hungarian influence. Still, it was not until mid-1917 that leading policy circles in the Empire, in particular the new Emperor, Karl, and his Foreign Minister, Count Ottakar von Czernin, realized that the wartime annexation of Serbia was definitively off the table as it became clear that continuing the war brought the Empire's very survival into question. Serbia would be offered up in attempt to secure an exit from the war.[36]

The growing restraints on the occupation and the turn away from wartime annexation were parts of a broader effort to resituate Austria-Hungary within the pre-1914 norms governing war and occupation. It is impossible to understand Austria-Hungary's gradual de-escalation in occupied Serbia without linking it to this broader retrenchment on Austria-Hungary's part internally and externally. A peace of annexations had to go. Violations with regard to norms of war and occupation in places such as Serbia had to be scaled back. Internal legal norms associated with the pre-war Austrian *Rechtsstaat*, in particular, had to return as Karl prominently signalled in his speech to the newly reconvened Austrian *Reichsrat*.[37] The Army's internal crackdown on perceived civilian insubordination, linked closely to its demands for the expansion of military courts across the Empire, including Serbia, had to be reined in. Thus, Karl issued a general amnesty for crimes such as *Majestätsbeleidigung* that stood before military courts, even in Serbia. Karl's turn against military law within the Empire also meant that it was drawn back everywhere else. By the fall of 1917, Standrecht had largely been abandoned in Serbia, which meant that the truly extreme aspects of Austro-Hungarian military justice in Serbia disappeared. From this new position, more in line with international and internal norms, plays for peace abroad could be made. In short, Austria-Hungary, its leaders despairing of a hopeless supply situation, increasing unrest in urban areas and looking to what they viewed as the evolving disaster in Russia, threw itself on the international system in an attempt to save the Empire. This entailed moving occupied Serbia back in the direction of international norms.

As is well known, the Habsburg peace effort of 1917 failed for a variety of reasons. The first was internal political rage at the Army's heavy-handed efforts to control civilian society through the use of military law and an identification of politics with treason in the Austrian half of the Empire. The second was Austria-Hungary's acceptance, under heavy pressure, of the grandiose war aims of Hindenburg and Ludendorff. Perhaps less noticed amidst the reasons for the failure was that pre-1914 norms of war, including occupation, had been critically undermined. The Empire itself had contributed to this through its behaviour vis-à-vis Serbia. Thus, these were attempts to return to norms of contained conflict that, by then, were in tatters. In this respect, Britain's response to Austro-Hungarian indications of restraint was telling. Britain was the power most invested in defending the values of 1914 and had essentially gone to war over the violation of an international norm in the German invasion of neutral Belgium.[38] But by 1917, even though British policy-makers and David Lloyd George, in particular, wanted to encourage an Austro-Hungarian defection from the Central Powers, they only viewed the Habsburg moves towards peace within a purely wartime strategic calculus, not as part of a broader signal – however unrealistic – to return to contained conflict.[39] In other words, even Britain, even when it showed the most interest in the Empire's search for peace, instrumentalized peace with Austria-Hungary within the broader pursuit of war.

Conclusion

If the Habsburg search for a return to contained conflict and the attempt to resituate the Empire back within the norm regarding occupation in Serbia came to naught, should we just dismiss this as evidence of an out of touch imperial leadership oblivious to the realities of the First World War? Or should we instead take this as a sign of a moment when the norms of war associated with the nineteenth century, with it the norm of occupation, were increasingly less applicable, foreshadowing a tectonic shift in how war and occupation would be constituted? If we concentrate on the latter question, we can begin to bring the occupations of the First World War into closer relation with one another and begin to lay the groundwork for links to occupations in wars to come.

In the end, occupation was an international norm embedded within a larger set of norms governing the conduct of war in Europe from the nineteenth century, directed towards the containment of conflict, undergirded by a commitment to sovereignty and a stark divide between soldiers and civilians. This externalist approach to occupation adds another dimension to the standard historical approaches to occupation. While historians are keenly attuned to the internal elements of occupation such as the ideological policies of the occupiers or everyday life under occupation, they have paid less attention to occupation as part of an international system embedded in a larger system of norms governing war among European states.[40] On those rare occasions when historians turn to the external construction of occupation, they often adopt a highly legalistic perspective, laying out legal transgressions committed by occupation governments as if international law was a set of hard and fast rules whose mere violation indicates its irrelevance and a particular actor's wholesale dismissal of it.[41] We should be careful, however, not to equate violations of international law with operating in a norm-free realm. They are not the same thing. Norms and the assumptions that undergird them can be very robust. Citing violations of the law does not suffice to show that actors no longer consider the law and the norms that support it valid. This short examination of the Austro-Hungarian occupation of Serbia shows how pre-1914 norms came under pressure, how they eked out relevance for Austria-Hungary in the face of violation and how Austria-Hungary attempted to return to them in 1917. The attempt to return to these norms, however, revealed how the international system had begun to abandon them. By the fall of 1917, indifference towards Austria-Hungary turned into an attempt to undermine it as Austria-Hungary was increasingly viewed as a client state of Germany. Britain began to look for ways to undermine Austria-Hungary internally through sponsoring events such as the Congress of Oppressed Nationalities in Rome. Power politics and winning the war, not nineteenth-century norms of great power preservation, now stepped to the fore.

As we turn this externalist lens to other occupations during the First World War, the question becomes whether these occupation governments detached themselves from the international norms of the nineteenth century. How did they move beyond the transgression of international norms to dismissing the relevance of such norms altogether? A recognition on the part of various occupation governments that the norms had disappeared, that they were no longer operable, could lead to radically new forms of occupation. It is this sense of possibility, this freedom from old restraints that animated the German occupation of the Baltics in Ober Ost, as Vejas Liulevicius detailed.[42] If we move to the Ukraine from March 1918 forward, what is notable here was that the German and Austrian presence there was not even conceived of as an occupation, but rather as an intervention on behalf of a friendly government in the Ukrainian Rada.[43] The norms of occupation began to diminish in importance because this was no longer acknowledged as an occupation.

Intervention became possible because the norms of occupation no longer applied. This recognition of normlessness is what distinguished these occupations from the Austro-Hungarian occupation of Serbia. It is important to view such normlessness as proceeding not only from ruthless strategic calculations on the occupiers' parts, a military culture, or an ideological or racialized fear of the inhabitants of the occupied territory. While all of these were important to various occupations, the absence of norms governing occupation was also produced by a fundamental instability in the condition of imperial sovereignties in Eastern Europe as the war progressed. Because imperial sovereignty and the nineteenth-century norm of occupation were closely linked, when the former began to buckle, the latter could not hold. While national sovereignty was reinforced as a result of the war, imperial sovereignties in Eastern Europe collapsed. In this respect, we might look to the rolling implosion of imperial Russian sovereignty from the Great Retreat forward as helping to create conditions that fundamentally undermined the nineteenth-century norm of occupation. In this sense, we could read the way in which violence persisted and actually expanded in Eastern Europe well after the First World War had supposedly concluded as the product not of occupation, but of the inability to re-establish the norms of occupation, linked in turn to this crisis of imperial sovereignty.[44] This crisis paved the way for the Paris system, as Eric Weitz calls it, with its emphasis on populations as opposed to state sovereignties to firmly take hold in Eastern Europe.[45] In that crisis, Germany was more prepared to accept the international normlessness that came with it and to consciously operate from this assumption than was Austria-Hungary. One road led to Ober Ost, the other led to a hesitant but noticeable retrenchment in occupied Serbia.

Notes

1. On the treatments of legal developments in the nineteenth century, see Best, *Humanity in Warfare*; Benvenisti, *International Law of Occupation*, 7–31.
2. The pioneering historical work on this issue is Hull, *Absolute Destruction*. Most recently, see Baranowski, *Nazi Empire*. An older literature already made much of the division between Europe and the colonial world in the international system. See Schmitt, *Nomos of the Earth*. On the links between colonialism and genocide in Europe, see Arendt, *Origins of Totalitarianism*.
3. On the rise of the international legal profession in the late nineteenth century, see Koskenniemi, *Gentle Civilizer of Nations*, 3.
4. Percy, *Mercenaries*, 14–32.
5. On the problems the Habsburg Empire had in attempting to get the USA to understand 'great power' culture during the war, see Phelps, 'Sovereignty, Citizenship, and the New Liberal Order', 132–59.
6. Gumz, *Resurrection and Collapse of Empire*; Scheer, *Zwischen Front und Heimat*; Mitrović, *Serbia's Great War*; Knezevic, 'Austro-Hungarian Occupation of Belgrade'.
7. Schroeder, *Transformation of European Politics*, 575–82.
8. See Declaration Concerning the Laws and Customs of War, Brussels, 27 August 1874, http://www.icrc.org/ihl.nsf/FULL/135?OpenDocument
9. This was the clear implication of explicitly granting belligerent status to civilians that rose to defend their country against invasion but carried themselves in accordance with the laws and customs of war as Article 2 of the Hague Convention of 1899 did. See Article 1, Chapter 1, Article 2, Annex to the Convention (II) with Respect to the Laws and Customs of War on Land, The Hague, 29 July 1899, at http://www.icrc.org/ihl.nsf/FULL/150?OpenDocument
10. Hull, *Absolute Destruction*, 123–5.
11. Speech of Auguste Beernaert, in Scott, *Proceedings of the Hague Peace Conferences*, 502–4.
12. Holquist, *Russian Empire*; Myles, '"Humanity", "Civilization" and "the International Community"', 310–34.
13. 2. Armee, AOK Kriegsfall B 1914/15, Subbeilage c) der Beilage 21, Oskar von Hranilović, 'Über Wesen, Ausrüstung und Kampfesart der Komitadschis', July 1914, Karton 2, Kriegsarchiv Wien (hereafter KAW), Neue Feldakten (hereafter NFA).
14. Nachläße, Nachlaß Oskar Potiorek, B/1503: 5, No. 74, Conrad to Potiorek, 21 July 1914 (KAW).
15. Lyon, 'A Peasant Mob', 481–502.

MILITARY OCCUPATIONS IN FIRST WORLD WAR EUROPE

16. 6. Armee, Telegram from *5. Armee-Etappenkommando* to *5. Armeekommando*, 'Serbische Grausamkeiten und Völkerrechtswidrigkeiten', 28 August 1914, Karton 13 (KAW, NFA).

17. Article 1, Chapter 1, Annex to the Convention (II) with Respect to the Laws and Customs of War on Land, The Hague, 29 July 1899, at http://www.icrc.org/ihl.nsf/FULL/150? OpenDocument. Only with the Geneva Conventions of 1949 were members of resistance movements in occupied territories considered belligerents; see Kalshoven and Zevgeld, *Constraints on the Waging of War*, 33–5.

18. 2. Armee, Oskar von Hranilović, 'Über Wesen, Ausrüstung und Kampfesart der Komitadschis', July 1914, Karton 2 (KAW, NFA).

19. 6. Armee, *5. Armeeoberkommando* to the War Ministry, AOK, and *6. Armeeoberkommando*, Op. No. 403/20, 26 August 1914, Karton 13 (KAW, NFA).

20. 15. Korps, *15. Korps* to *6. Armee*, Res. No. 10, 'Ausbildung der Truppen nach Beendigung der Mobilität', 29 July 1914, Karton 1893 (KAW, NFA).

21. Nachläße, Nachlaß Alexander Brosch von Aerenau, B/1441, Letter from Michael von Appel to Brosch von Aerenau, 10 August 1914 (KAW).

22. Gumz, *Resurrection and Collapse of Empire*, 62–104.

23. See the discussion on issues related to the laws in force in an occupied country in Scott, *Proceedings of the Hague Peace Conferences*, 507–15.

24. MS/1, WK: Carnegie-Stiftung, Hugo Kerchnawe, 'Wirtschaftliche Geschichte der Besatzung Serbiens', No. 21, 304–6 (KAW).

25. See, for example, the following three cases from Šabac: AOK-Qu.Abt., Gericht des Kreiskommandos Šabac to the AOK, 28 April 1916, Karton 2389 (KAW, NFA); AOK-Qu. Abt., Gericht des Kreiskommandos Šabac to the AOK, 1 May 1916, Karton 2389 (KAW, NFA); AOK-Qu.Abt., Gericht des Kreiskommandos Šabac to the AOK, 5 May 1916, Karton 2389 (KAW, NFA).

26. *5. Armeeoberkommando*, Op. No. 403/20, Beilage 1, 25 August 1914, Karton 13 (KAW, NFA).

27. 15. Korps, Befehle 1914/1916, *Oberkommando der Balkanstreitkräfte*, Res. No. 739, 5 November 1914 (KAW, NFA).

28. Liasse Krieg 32b, AOK to the Foreign Ministry, 'International Hilfe für Serbien', 15 November 1915, Karton 974, Haus, Hof und Staatsarchiv (hereafter HHStA), Politisches Archiv (hereafter PA); Liasse Krieg 32b, Private Letter from Wiesner to Burián, 20 November 1915, Karton 974 (HHStA, PA); Liasse Krieg 32b, Report from Wiesner to Burián, 'Hilfsaktion für Serbien', 20 November 1915, Karton 974 (HHStA, PA); Liasse Krieg 32a, Copy of Telegram from Conrad to Falkenhayn, 20 December 1915, Karton 973 (HHStA, PA).

29. Harrison and Broadberry, eds., *Economics of World War I*, 18–22.

30. Horne and Kramer, *German Atrocities*; De Schaepdrijver, *La Belgique et la Première Guerre Mondiale*; Engelstein, 'A Belgium of Our Own'; Holquist, Les violences de l'armée russe à l'encontre des Juifs en 1915'; Holquist, 'Role of Personality', 52–73; Prusin, *Nationalizing a Borderland*; Jonathan Gumz, *Resurrection and Collapse of Empire*.

31. Dülffer, *Regeln Gegen den Krieg?* 107–24.

32. *Belgrader Nachrichten*, 'Serbien auf der Wiener Kriegsausstellung', 28 August 1917.

33. AOK-Qu.Abt., AOK to MGG/S, 'Zwangsarbeit, Kriegsleistungen, gesetzliche Einführung in Serbien', 9 July 1917, Karton 2458 (KAW, NFA); AOK-Qu.Abt., 'M.V.S. Heranziehung der Bevölkerung zur Dienstleistung nach §52 der Haager Landkriegsordnung', 15 July 1917, Karton 2459 (KAW, NFA).

34. AOK-Qu.Abt., 'Bemerkung des Justizreferenten des AOK zu M.V. 308.559/S', 11 March 1918, Karton 2516 (KAW, NFA).

35. Vienna, Archiv der Republik, *Kommission zur Erhebung militärischer Pflichtverletzungen*, Testimony of Theoderich Sternat, 19 December 1919, B 4/19-31.

36. Kovács, *Untergang oder Rettung der Donaumonarchie?* vol. 1, 139.

37. K.u.k. Hof und Staatsdruckerei, Stenographische Protokolle des Herrenhauses des Reichsrates, 'Thronrede Seiner k. und k. Apostolischen Majestat des Kaisers, Karl I', 31 May 1917, Beilage 1, 2.

38. Eksteins, *Rites of Spring*.

39. Calder, *Britain and the Origins*, 108–44. Henry Wickham Steed, one of the most resolute opponents of the Habsburg Empire, complained that British Army officers around Haig saw war as 'a game to be won or lost according to the rules. To me it seemed a matter of life and death subject to one rule only – victory'. See Rothwell, *British War Aims*, 114.

40. For one of the few historical studies that takes into occupation's role in the broader international system, see Mazower, *Hitler's Empire*. Political science studies have tended to take a broader view of occupation, but often de-contextualize it and are more interested in finding predictive results from their examinations of the past. For two good examples, see Fazal, *State Death*; Edelstein, *Occupational Hazards*.
41. Even excellent historical works often handle international law in this way. See, for example, Kramer, *Dynamic of Destruction*, 24–27, 55.
42. Liulevicius, *War Land on the Eastern Front*.
43. von Hagen, *War in a European Borderland*, 95.
44. For recent works on this crisis of sovereignty in Russia and Eastern Europe, see Gerwarth and Horne, 'The Great War', 267–73; Sanborn, 'Genesis of Russian Warlordism', 195–213.
45. Weitz, 'From the Vienna to the Paris System', 1313–43.

References

Arendt, Hannah. *The Origins of Totalitarianism*. New York: Harcourt Brace, 1951.

Baranowski, Shelley. *Nazi Empire: German Colonialism and Imperialism from Bismarck to Hitler*. Cambridge: Cambridge University Press, 2011.

Benvenisti, Eyal. *The International Law of Occupation*. Princeton, NJ: Princeton University Press, 1993.

Best, Geoffrey. *Humanity in Warfare*. New York: Columbia University Press, 1993.

Calder, Kenneth J. *Britain and the Origins of the New Europe, 1914–1918*. Cambridge: Cambridge University Press, 1976.

De Schaepdrijver, Sophie. *La Belgique et la Première Guerre Mondiale*. Bern: P.I.E.-Peter Lang, 2004.

Dülffer, Jost. *Regeln gegen den Krieg? Die Haager Friedenskonferenzen von 1899 und 1907 in der Internationalen Politik*. Frankfurt: Ullstein, 1981.

Edelstein, David M. *Occupational Hazards: Success and Failure in Military Occupation*. Ithaca, NY: Cornell University Press, 2008.

Eksteins, Modris. *Rites of Spring: The Great War and the Birth of the Modern Age*. New York: Anchor Books, 1990.

Engelstein, Laura. "'A Belgium of Our Own': The Sack of Russian Kalisz, August 1914." *Kritika* 10 (2009): 441–73.

Fazal, Tanisha M. *State Death: The Politics and Geography of Conquest, Occupation, and Annexation*. Princeton, NJ: Princeton University Press, 2007.

Gerwarth, Robert, and John Horne. "The Great War and Paramilitarism in Europe, 1917–1923." *Contemporary European History* 19 (2010): 267–73.

Gumz, Jonathan E. *The Resurrection and Collapse of Empire in Habsburg Serbia, 1914–1918*. Cambridge: Cambridge University Press, 2009.

Harrison, Mark, and Broadberry, Stephen, eds. *The Economics of World War I*. Cambridge: Cambridge University Press, 2005.

Holquist, Peter. "The Role of Personality in the First (1914–1915) Russian Occupation of Galicia and Bukovina." In *Anti-Jewish Violence: Rethinking the Pogrom in East European History*, ed., by John Klier, 52–73. Bloomington, IN: Indiana University Press, 2011.

Holquist, Peter. "Les violences de l'armée Russe à l'encontre des Juifs en 1915: Causes et Limites." In *Vers la Guerre Totale: Le Tournant de 1914–1915*, ed., by John Horne, 191–219. Paris: Tallandier, 2010.

Holquist, Peter. The Russian Empire as Civilized State: International Law as Principle and Practice in Imperial Russia, 1874–1878, National Council for Eurasian and East European Research, 2004. http://www.ucis.pitt.edu/nceeer/2004_818-06g_Holquist.pdf

Horne, John, and Alan Kramer. *German Atrocities, 1914: A History of Denial*. New Haven, CT: Yale University Press, 2001.

Hull, Isabel V. *Absolute Destruction: Military Culture and the Practices of War in Imperial Germany*. Ithaca, NY: Cornell University Press, 2005.

Kalshoven, Frits, and Liesbeth Zevgeld. *Constraints on the Waging of War: An Introduction to International Humanitarian Law*. Cambridge: Cambridge University Press, 2011.

Knezevic, Jovana Lazic. "The Austro-Hungarian Occupation of Belgrade during the First World War: Battles at the Home Front." PhD diss., Yale University 2006.

MILITARY OCCUPATIONS IN FIRST WORLD WAR EUROPE

Koskenniemi, Martti. *The Gentle Civilizer of Nations: The Rise and Fall of International Law, 1870–1960*. Cambridge: Cambridge University Press, 2002.

Kovács, Elisabeth. *Untergang oder Rettung der Donaumonarchie?* Vol. 1, *Die österreichische Frage: Kaiser und König Karl I. (IV.) und die Neuordnung Mitteleuropas (1916–1922)*. Wien: Böhlau, 2004.

Kramer, Alan. *Dynamic of Destruction: Culture and Mass Killing in the First World War*. Oxford: Oxford University Press, 2007.

Liulevicius, Vejas Gabriel. *War Land on the Eastern Front: Culture, National Identity and German Occupation in World War I*. Cambridge: Cambridge University Press, 2000.

Lyon, James. "'A Peasant Mob': The Serbian Army on the Eve of the Great War." *The Journal of Military History* 61 (July 1997): 481–502.

Mazower, Mark. *Hitler's Empire: How the Nazis Ruled Europe*. New York: Penguin Press, 2008.

Mitrović, Andrej. *Serbia's Great War, 1914–1918*. West Lafayette, IN: Purdue University Press, 2007.

Myles, Eric. "'Humanity', 'Civilization', and 'the International Community' in the Late Imperial Russian Mirror: Three Ideas 'Topical for Our Days'." *Journal of the History of International Law* 4 (July 2002): 310–34.

Percy, Sarah. *Mercenaries: The History of a Norm in International Relations*. Oxford: Oxford University Press, 2007.

Phelps, Nicole Marie. "Sovereignty, Citizenship, and the New Liberal Order: US-Habsburg Relations and the Transformation of International Politics, 1880–1924." PhD diss., University of Minnesota 2008.

Prusin, Alexander. *Nationalizing a Borderland: War, Ethnicity, and Anti-Jewish Violence in East Galicia, 1914–1920*. Tuscaloosa: University of Alabama Press, 2005.

Rothwell, Victor. *British War Aims and Peace Diplomacy, 1914–1918*. Oxford: Clarendon Press, 1971.

Sanborn, Joshua. "The Genesis of Russian Warlordism: Violence and Governance during the First World War and the Civil War." *Contemporary European History* 19 (2010): 195–213.

Scheer, Tamara. *Zwischen Front und Heimat: Österreich-Ungarns Militärverwaltungen im Ersten Weltkrieg*. Frankfurt am Main: Peter Lang, 2009.

Schmitt, Carl. *The Nomos of the Earth in the International Law of the Jus Publicum Europaeum*. Trans. G.L. Ulmen. New York: Telos Press, 2003.

Schroeder, Paul. *The Transformation of European Politics, 1763–1848*. Oxford: Oxford University Press, 1994.

Scott, James, ed. *The Proceedings of the Hague Peace Conferences: The Conference of 1899 and 1907*. New York: Oxford University Press, 1921.

von Hagen, Mark. *War in a European Borderland: Occupations and Occupation Plans in Galicia and Ukraine, 1914–1918*. Seattle: University of Washington Press, 2007.

Weitz, Eric D. "From the Vienna to the Paris System: International Politics and the Entangled Histories of Human Rights, Forced Deportations, and Civilizing Missions." *American Historical Review* 113 (December 2008): 1313–43.

Misconceived *realpolitik* in a failing state: the political and economical fiasco of the Central Powers in the Ukraine, 1918

Wolfram Dornik[a] and Peter Lieb[b]

[a]LBI für Kriegsfolgen-Forschung, Graz (A); [b]Department of War Studies, Royal Military Academy Sandhurst

Translated from the German by Sophie De Schaepdrijver

The Brest-Litovsk Peace Agreement was supposed to be a grand solution. Germany and Austria-Hungary, under increasing domestic pressure, wanted to create facts on at least one front and demonstrate to the world at large their willingness to accept peace. In reality, the German Supreme Army Command's main goal was to bring large parts of Eastern Europe under German control and permanently weaken revolution-torn Russia. Since late 1917, Ukraine appeared to be the key to controlling the entire region: it was considered the 'breadbasket' of the former Russian Empire, it possessed heavy industry in the East and it offered access to the Black Sea. But the Brest Treaty proved to be brittle and the contracting states showed themselves to be either politically unstable (Ukraine) or unreliable (Bolshevik Russia). Additionally, Ukraine was not even remotely capable of fulfilling its economic pledges. Furthermore, the 'dictated peace' proved to the entente that there could be no negotiated peace with Germany and that fighting would have to continue until the capitulation of the Central Powers.

This article will analyse, first, the position of Ukraine within the Central Powers' foreign-policy and military-strategic conception until the invasion in early 1918; second, the occupation policies of 1918; and, third, the Ukrainians' own perception of the Central Powers. The Ukrainian 'failing state' exemplifies, with particular clarity, the Central Powers' strategic overstretch and their ill-considered policy in Eastern Europe at the end of the First World War. Finally, this essay will place the wartime conduct of the Central Powers in Ukraine into the larger scholarly discussion of the 'German Way of War'.

1. German-Habsburg policies vis-à-vis Ukraine, 1914 to early 1918

From the February Revolution of 1917, Ukraine took shape as an autonomous entity. In Kiev, a Central Council (*Zentralna rada*) was drawn from a broad cross section of society. Politically left-leaning, it also showed a strong nationalist bent, which led to frequent conflict with the Ukrainian Bolsheviks, as well as with those in Petrograd/Moscow. After the October Revolution, the Central Council permanently broke with the Bolsheviks and on 25 January 1918, declared Ukraine as an independent state. Earlier, in its quest for international recognition, the Central Council had sent its own delegation to Brest-Litovsk, and thereby stepped onto the stage of world politics. But foreign policy offices in Berlin and Vienna had no concept at hand as to how this key territory should be slotted into the political order of Eastern Europe.

Not that Ukraine was unknown. Since the turn of the century, the Ukrainian exiles had lobbied on the European stage for an independent Ukrainian state but these efforts had not impacted German or Austro-Hungarian foreign policy. Ukraine figured neither in Friedrich Neumann's 'Mitteleuropa' concept nor in the blueprints of other German-speaking intellectuals or of Hungarian or Polish ones. They either had their own designs on Ukrainian territory or considered the 'Little Russians' – as the Ukrainians were still primarily called in Russia, but also abroad – to be a part of the Russian Empire, even in an imagined post-war order.[1]

Austria-Hungary had long pursued a dichotomous policy vis-à-vis Ukrainians, cultivating their aspirations as a 'hearth of agitation against Russia',[2] while considering those living within the borders of the Habsburg Empire – a sizeable group – as a potential complicating factor. This split stance was evident in the Habsburg government's actions at the start of the war: on the one hand, plans to foster insurrection in the Russian Ukraine were discussed with Germany and the Ottoman Empire, the 'League for the Liberation of Ukraine' (LLU) was subsidized by the Foreign Ministry to the tune of millions of *Kronen*, and a separate legion of Ukrainians loyal to the crown was assembled out of the newly formed units of Sich Riflemen. On the other hand, in Galicia and Bukovina tens of thousands of 'Ruthenians' suspected of being 'Russophiles' were summarily shot or interned at Graz-Thalerhof camp. The civilian population was by the hundreds of thousands driven out of the areas of operations and the hinterland on the 'North-East Front', as the Eastern Front was named from the Viennese perspective. They landed in refugee camps, primarily in Lower Austria and Vienna, and were not even allowed to return to their hometowns after the Russian troops were driven out in 1917.[3]

Vienna continued this dichotomous policy until at least the winter of 1917/1918 in order to prevent jeopardizing the Polish administration of Galicia and the 'Austro-Polish Solution', viz. blueprints for a Polish State as a third constituent nation within the Habsburg Empire.[4] For fear of alienating the Polish national movement, cooperation with the LLU was officially discontinued, but unofficially its collaborators engaged in propaganda for Ukrainian independence in the camps that held Russian POWs. The Habsburg-loyal 'Ukrainian Legion', formed from Austro-Hungarian Ukrainians, fought on the Eastern Front throughout the entire First World War and cooperated later in the occupation of Russian Ukraine, but numbering fewer than 2500 men (and some women), it never achieved the influence of the Polish Legion. Emperor Karl attempted a cautious recognition of the Ukrainians by ending the internment of Ukrainians at Thalerhof camp and officially allowing the use of the term 'Ukrainian' instead of 'Ruthenian', a term that had been meant to thwart notions of a 'Greater Ukraine' spanning Russian and Austro-Hungarian populations and territory.[5]

For Germany, the situation was different. As no Ukrainian speakers lived in the Wilhelmine Empire, the question of Ukrainian nationality had no direct impact on German domestic policy. Still, since August of 1914, vague ideas about the future of that country had been circulating in business and political circles.[6] At the beginning of the war, some had briefly considered instigating insurrections in Ukraine; the project was quickly abandoned due to the military situation and financial bottlenecks. In the various official and unofficial War Aims Programmes of the German Imperial government, Ukraine never figured. Russian 'rule over the non-Russian vassal populations' was supposed to be broken, as stated in the 'September Program' of 1914, but it seems highly unlikely that Chancellor Theobald von Bethmann Hollweg understood Ukraine to be part of that goal. There was, then, no specific German-Ukrainian policy before 1917.[7]

MILITARY OCCUPATIONS IN FIRST WORLD WAR EUROPE

Only with the appearance of the Ukrainian Central Council's delegation in Brest-Litovsk in December 1917, Berlin's Ukrainian policy took concrete form. Under German pressure, this Kiev delegation was recognized as an independent negotiating partner. Berlin saw the young state as leverage for the expansion of its power in 'the East'. What was more, recognition and support of Ukraine could be used to force the Russian revolutionaries to accept the treaty. Events were indeed sped up: as the Bolsheviks drove the Central Council out of Kiev, the Ukrainian delegates hurriedly signed a peace agreement with the Central Powers on 9 February 1918. The Ukrainian Central Council had, parallel to the Brest negotiations, entered into talk of cooperation with the entente in Iaşi, and millions of British pounds had already changed hands. But Bolshevik pressure compelled the Council to opt for the Central Powers' concrete military support and break off the negotiations with the entente.

If Trotsky had hoped that the Central Powers would be blamed at home for their 'warmongering', he was mistaken: with the exception of the Independent Social-Democratic Party, German public opinion supported the agreement with Ukraine and the resumption of fighting from the Baltic to Ukraine. Berlin's strategy, in particular that of Ludendorff,[8] was successful, so that the military intervention of the Central Powers in Ukraine after the agreement of 9 February would not look like a conquest. Ukraine was encouraged to send official requests for help to the Central Powers, allowing them legally to march into an allied country. Vienna was less enthusiastic about the direct intervention into Ukraine, as the revival of military ambitions in Eastern Europe undermined the parallel secret negotiations between the young Emperor and the Entente.[9] Moreover, Vienna tried to use the state of emergency of the young Ukrainian state to its advantage to go back on an extremely awkward secret agreement signed between the Central Council's delegation and members of the Habsburg Foreign Ministry shortly before the signing of the Brest agreement. This so-called 'Crown Lands Protocol' promised the speedy formation of an autonomous Ukrainian territory (Crown Land) within the Habsburg Empire. This would undoubtedly have led to civil war in Galicia and the Bukovina. Already, the borders with Ukraine in the Cholm area, agreed upon at Brest, were unfavourably drawn in regard to the Polish population, which provoked protests and riots in the Polish occupation zones and Galicia. Foreign Minister Czernin hoped to use the Kiev Ukrainians' plight to reconsider the territorial allocation in Cholm and have the Crown Land Protocol – still a state secret – toned down or even abolished. Also, the Cisleithanian Imperial Council balked at renewed military action on the Eastern Front. Austria-Hungary, then, at first hesitated to join its German ally.

On 18 February 1918, the German advance into the East began on a broad front along the major railways. Within less than two weeks, Kiev was reconquered for the Central Council; by the end of April, the troops of the Central Powers advanced into the Crimea; and by May, they pushed into Rostov on the Don and the territory of the Don Cossacks; in the summer, there was even a military intervention in Georgia.[10] After initial hesitation, Austria-Hungary joined the invasion on 28 February 1918, not wanting to leave what looked like easy spoils to the German Empire. The main thrust of the Habsburg offensive was Odessa, considered a strategically valuable point that needed to be secured for the time after the war.

For all that, the invasion laid bare the political aimlessness of the German Empire and Austria-Hungary. Until May 1918, little thought was given to the limits of the troops' advance. Militarily, the undertaking was, for vast stretches, a leisurely stroll, as resistance increased only in the large industrial cities in the Northeast and East. Both powers were unaware of the wide-ranging political consequences of their invasion of Ukraine. But they *were* entangled in Ukrainian domestic politics.

2. The occupation policies of the Central Powers in the Ukraine, February 1918 to January 1919

In late spring 1918, Ukraine was fully under the control of the Central Powers. Fantastic prospects made the rounds in Vienna and Berlin. The Central Council's Brest promise to deliver one million tons of grain by the end of June led the mayor of hungry Vienna to rejoice over the 'Bread Peace'. Beyond that, the coal pits and the steel industry in the east of the country inspired great hopes. Odessa, the Crimea and Rostov on the Don were considered sally ports to economically and politically dominate the entire Black Sea region, indeed the Caucasus, possibly all of Central Asia. Great Britain already feared for its interests in Persia, Egypt and India.[11] Thoughts of annexation coursed through the mind of a few military men. Ludendorff wanted to send German settlers to the Crimea; some Austro-Hungarian commanders dreamed of a divided Ukraine, with the southern part under Vienna's influence guaranteeing the lucrative trade with Central Asia and bolstering Austro-Hungarian political influence over the Black Sea region.[12]

But Vienna was no longer in a position to execute Great Power politics or even to make demands. The Emperor Karl, having categorically rejected a joint military supreme commander in Ukraine under German leadership, had to see Austria-Hungary's influence being limited to the administration of the three provinces Podolia, Kherson and Yekaterinoslav (today Dnipropetrovsk). The Germans kept the Habsburg troops away from the political centre of power in Kiev, and even in Odessa the Austrians and Hungarians had to assert themselves against influential German administrators. The tension between Berlin and Vienna, simmering since the beginning of the war, culminated in Ukraine. Vienna had manoeuvred itself into a political dead end regarding Ukraine, as the Habsburg monarchy had not ratified the Brest agreement for fear of seeing one integral yet secret part of it implemented: the Crown Land Protocol, that massive menace to imperial ethnic cohesion. In Kiev, the Central Council insisted on its implementation. Meanwhile, members of the Habsburg Army, as well as a few unofficial Polish representatives, attempted from Odessa to steer an autonomous Austro-Hungarian course.[13]

But Germany only permitted such a course where it did not contradict its own interests. The influential Chief of Staff of Army Group Eichhorn-Kiew, Lieutenant General Wilhelm Groener, had since March systematically worked to place political, military and economic control of the land in the hands of German officials. Step by step, the Germans had established economic institutions, particularly the Imperial Economic Office in Kiev, a branch of the Imperial Economic Ministry. Alongside the army and the Foreign Office, the Economic Ministry attempted to influence Ukrainian policies, albeit with generally meagre success: the Central Council was unable to fulfil the grain shipments agreed upon in Brest. Groener angrily dismissed the Council as a 'governing club',[14] a 'clique of immature students and assorted youthful romantics and bad elements'.[15] In late April, Groener had the Council removed in a well-staged coup d'état, and replaced with a ruler supported by the major Ukrainian landowners. *Hetman* Pavlo P. Skoropadskyi corresponded more closely to the German image of a firm leader: he was a former Tsarist General, a major landowner, an anti-revolutionary and, most importantly, he was ready to compromise when it came to his own ideas about an independent Ukrainian nation.[16] Skoropadskyi always remained reserved towards Vienna; yet relations quickly improved. Under his rule the Crown Land Protocol was dropped, possibly because of his deep scepticism towards the Galician Ukrainians. He immediately repealed the Central Council's decrees on collectivization and redistribution. In addition, he pursued a policy of Ukrainization through the founding of a Ukrainian Academy of Science and the opening of Ukrainian schools and universities such as the ones in Kamianets-Podilskyi, Dnipropetrovsk, Simferopol or the Polytechnic University of Odessa. With the help of the occupation troops, he attempted to end Bolshevik action. The Central Powers, however, denied him an army of his own, feared to be politically and militarily unreliable. Only in the autumn of 1918 did Berlin and Vienna reconsider, but by then it was too late.

The installing of the Hetmanate, widely seen as a violation of Ukrainian sovereignty, with Skoropadskyi a puppet of the Central Powers, caused indignation. Large segments of the population had hoped that the foreign troops would end the state of confusion that had existed since March 1917. But the troops lost a lot of credit during their advance, which had occasioned chaotic requisitioning and violent battles with the Red Guards with attendant civilian suffering. The occupation forces were blamed for not having fulfilled hopes for political stability and economic upturn. The particularly heavy-handed requisitions by the Habsburg troops – to suppress resistance to requisitioning or other local protests, hostages were taken, villages shelled and houses burned – caused widespread discontent among the population as well as in the Ukrainian government and among its German allies.[17] In contrast, the German military tried, at least in theory, to limit violence against civilians in similar situations,[18] though it suppressed armed Bolshevik resistance very harshly.

In response to the wild requisitioning and the galloping inflation, the occupation powers and the Ukrainian government attempted to set prices, but since these fell far short of market value, farmers considered them as a form of *de facto* expropriation. This discontent fostered sympathy for Bolshevism, which in addition was able to rely on robust networks of workers and intellectuals, particularly in the cities and centres of industry. Protest actions up until the summer included a large-scale railroad strike that briefly disrupted exports to the Central Powers.

It should be noted at this point that in rural Ukraine, peasant social and political loyalty traditionally centered on local networks and societal hierarchies and not on the state. Already the Tsarist government had exercised only limited power in the villages and had experienced huge difficulties in enforcing law and order. The turbulences of the First World War and the Civil War exacerbated this. As a result, the power basis in the countryside often laid in the hands of warlords and their followers, impoverished peasants who did not shrink from robbing and terrorizing other peasants. A culture of everyday violence emerged.[19] In many parts of the country, the summer of 1918 saw larger revolts, like the one in June in the territory of Smjela, south of Kiev. These insurrections were due to social problems and often sustained by Bolshevik efforts. They reached a high point on 30 July when a social revolutionary shot the Supreme Commander of the German troops, Field Marshal Hermann von Eichhorn.[20] Still, the occupation powers were able, using a carrot and stick policy, to prevent the spread of revolt; at the same time they could not fundamentally change the pre-war state of affairs in the countryside.[21]

In May, Germany assumed complete control over the economy: the Berlin agreement of 18 May compelled Austria-Hungary to give up control of the critical grain output in the 'Ukraine, the rest of the formerly Russian Empire, in Rumania and in the Bessarabian territory occupied by Rumania' to Germany 'until the new harvest' (i.e. until August).[22] Only through the joint institutes, the 'German-Austro-Hungarian Economic Center' and the 'Ukrainian Nutritional Council' could Vienna now attempt to pursue its interests.[23]

In regard to the combating of revolts, the Austro-Hungarian occupation forces were brought into line with the German ones step by step. After the Skoropadskyi coup, the Army Group Eichhorn-Kiew tended to work with rather than against Ukrainian authorities, relying on the Ukrainian administration and local security forces to round up suspects. Defiance, harassment or even small armed actions were to be punished, at first, by contributions in kind; only in larger armed revolts would weapons come into play. The Austro-Hungarian occupation officials followed Groener's concept, but reluctantly. The Habsburg military mistrusted the Ukrainians and were unfamiliar with cooperative procedures in occupation situations. Against armed insurgents, they conceived of no mercy; in contrast to the German modus operandi, court martial measures against alleged insurgents seem to have been rare: few documents attest to them, whereas there are many reports of suspects killed while purportedly fleeing. In May and June, the numbers of killed 'suspected robbers' or 'Bolshevik murderers' exploded.[24] These methods seemed to be sanctioned from on high: Emperor Karl enjoined the Austro-Hungarian troops in March to 'requisition with no remorse, even with violence'.[25] In May 1918, the young emperor appointed General Alfred Krauß, a known hardliner, as military supreme commander in Ukraine and provided him with near-dictatorial powers.[26]

At the same time, there were built-in limits to violence in the modus operandi of the Habsburg troops as well. As Jonathan Gumz has argued, the Habsburg Army's code of honour rested on 'conservative international values such as dynastic legitimacy, the sanctity of treaties [. . .], and a measured but significant respect for international law'.[27] Moreover, the Habsburg military saw itself as representing a culturally distinguished state intent on ending revolutionary or national chaos and on integrating parts of Ukraine into the Habsburg sphere in the long run. Military leaders frequently referred to colonial precedent. Alfred Krauß, for one, in the Spring of 1918 referred to colonial Egypt and India as examples.[28] Such a long-term view of domination entailed limits: military leaders did not order mass killings of civilians, let alone of women and children, and did not pursue starvation policies.[29]

Also, dynamics in the field gradually limited violence against civilians. One of the reasons Groener was able to bring his Austro-Hungarian allies in line was pacification: after the railroad strike was broken by replacing the strikers with military railroad operators in early August, Ukraine became almost a 'rest area' for the troops stationed there.[30] Groener wrote to his wife in early October that 'in the Ukraine it is currently so peaceful and quiet that it would be possible to enjoy a comfortable life, were it not that the uncertainty in the other combat zones and from Berlin itself extend their shadows all the way here'.[31] The German generals commanding the Army Corps came to the same conclusion. During a meeting in October, they judged internal developments satisfactory and expected further improvement.[32]

From the Ukrainian perspective, however, the situation looked vastly different. Crucially, the occupation did not improve the economic situation. Blame was placed on the occupation forces. This was partly correct: oft-arbitrary requisitionings of foodstuffs, especially the Habsburg troops' early, chaotic appropriations between February and April 1918, were not conducive to economic confidence. It was true that the Supreme Commander of the Second Army, Field Marshall Eduard von Böhm-Ermolli, stipulated that payment of requisitioned goods, in receipts if no money was available, and the use of military violence only as a last resort since, as he stated, 'otherwise the entire operation in Ukraine is worthless'.[33] Though this relatively moderate approach was one of the reasons for Böhm-Ermolli's replacement in May 1918, his successor Krauß by and large followed the same line on requisitions. Still, Austro-Hungarian military violence never fully ceased until the end of the occupation.

Interestingly the occupation troops failed to establish any censorship, and the *Hetman* did not have the power to implement it. Vienna and Berlin did attempt to achieve some measure of influence over reporting through press efforts of their own, which ranged from providing journalists with information to outright bribery.[34] It did not stop Ukrainian newspapers from reporting violence against civilians, and this with the *imprimatur* of both successive Ukrainian governments – the Central Council as well as the Hetmanate – which exploited such reports for their own political ends. The veracity of these reports cannot be ascertained due to the inaccessibility of archives from 1919 onwards; certainly, the 'imperialist' troops of Germany and 'Austria' were accused of infringements by left newspapers without closer examination. Into the 1920s, when the Soviet regime continued this argumentation, this would serve as justification for the difficult industrial and food situation in the country. The Central Powers attempted to counter this with a targeted propaganda policy. The Ukrainian Legion, in particular, was portrayed as embodying the positive attitude of Austria-Hungary towards the Ukrainians. Its very existence and its cultural activities in its different postings were held up as proof of Ukrainians' cultural freedoms in the Habsburg monarchy. Even that failed to sway public opinion; nevertheless, the population remained mostly quiescent after the summer.[35]

But from September, with the Central Powers under tremendous military pressure and the Habsburg Empire beginning to collapse internally, increasing numbers of troops had to be withdrawn from Ukraine and by mid-October many Austro-Hungarian units began to dissolve and make for home on their own. Almost at the last minute, the Germans attempted to drastically redefine their Ukrainian policy. 'Democratization' and 'Ukrainization' were now the watchwords. With German assistance the Hetmanate was to be endowed with a large Ukrainian army to ensure its protection against the Bolshevik threat within and without. In that way, the Germans hoped to maintain their influence in Eastern Europe through indirect rule and to stop the revolutionary tide. But it was too late. Bolsheviks and representatives of the mostly left-wing, anti-Bolshevik Directorate struggled for power in Kiev. The Hetman had no power base left and was forced to retreat to Berlin along with the German troops. Full-scale struggles between 'Reds', 'Whites', 'Greens' and local warlords broke out.[36] The poorly planned and even more poorly executed French–Greek intervention in Southern Ukraine from December 1918 till March 1919 could not change this. Only from the late 1920s were the communists able to bring Ukraine largely under their control.[37]

3. Results and consequences of the occupation

On 11 November 1918 the German empire capitulated in Compiègne. But the retreat of the Central Powers from Ukraine would take a while longer. After the failed occupation few Germans wished for their troops to remain in the country, but the entente obliged troops to temporarily remain at their posts to stop the advancing revolutionary forces. Hence, the last German units did not leave the country until March 1919. Even the retreat of the Austrians and Hungarians dragged on until January 1919. Although the Habsburg monarchy was disintegrating and troops had flooded homewards since September 1918, the senior officers had to remain in Odessa and Kiew, even without their men, and acquit themselves of their missions: the repatriation of prisoners of war, the disentangling of economic interests and the liquidation of remaining military materials.[38]

All in all, the Ukrainian undertaking ended in political and military disaster for both Berlin and Vienna. Not a single aim was achieved. Economically, too, the occupation was a complete failure. As the Central Council had failed to deliver, the occupiers had set in place a system of economic organizations, jointly administered by the Central Powers and the Ukrainian authorities, and delivery contracts for single product groups. As a result, thousands of carts of livestock, horses, oilseeds, fodder, eggs, bacon, sheep, poultry, preserves, butter, cheese, diverse raw materials and other spoils made their way to the Central Powers; yet the entire amount only reached half a million tons by the end of the occupation. One million tons of grain had been expected by the end of June 1918;

by the end of the occupation, no more than 130,000 tons had been delivered. Over half of the grain went to Austria-Hungary; the German Empire received barely 50,000 tons. Even the Ottoman Empire and Bulgaria received small contingents. This disillusioning yield was made worse by the fact that Germany, in particular, saw itself forced to deliver coal to Ukraine (23,500 wagons) to keep the railroad running and avoid further unrest. Even the ailing Habsburg state delivered around 2000 wagons of mineral-oil products as well as enamelware, agricultural machines, scythes and other industrial and medical products.

Additionally, there were the millions of *Reichsmarks* in occupation costs for Austria-Hungary and the German Empire (Germany alone paid 125 million *Reichsmark* per month) to prop up and support the failing state. German banks handed out loans in the amount of one billion *Reichsmark* over the summer, which were never paid back.[39] German economic and financial expenditures stood in no relationship to the output. The German Imperial Treasury drily stated in October 1918, 'Under these circumstances an immediate start to the gradual evacuation of the Ukraine [...] must be considered desirable from the perspective of the Imperial financial administration.'[40]

For the Ukrainians themselves the occupation did not bring about the desired long-term stabilizing effect. The troops of the Central Powers provided a brief respite from civil war but did not bring a lasting stabilization. The countryside, which was inadequately controlled by the occupation troops, remained beset by unrest; some of it wrought the occupation troops' requisitions.

But was the First World War a catastrophe for the region comparable to what would come afterwards? Interwar Soviet propaganda and historiography would spread the image of a brutal plundering of the land through 'imperialist' German and 'Austrian' troops, but the actual catastrophe occurred in the 1920s and 1930s. The local famine and supply difficulties of 1918 were mostly limited to urban areas and could be traced to the collapse of commerce and of the infrastructure. The occupation-era economic organizations had an equalizing effect. Particularly the 'Ukrainian Nutritional Council', a joint Ukrainian-Central Powers body, endeavoured to regulate agricultural production and distribution down to the communal level. These institutions allowed swift reactions to supply difficulties.

To sum up, while the occupation of Ukraine was hardly a phase of peace and harmony, compared to the preceding revolutionary year and to the era from November 1918 on, it was a phase of relative calm, 'which nonetheless – and this must be stressed – was ensured by the bayonets of the allied troops'.[41] From our present point of view, the events that followed – the brutal Sovietization, the collectivization, the famine of 1932/1933 (*'Holodomor'*), the Stalinist purges, the destructive campaign of Nazi Germany against the Soviet Union and the Soviet re-conquest of Ukraine, including the expansion of the territory by East Galicia and North Bukovina – certainly allow the events of 1918 to be seen in a milder light. And, of course, the nadir of early twentieth-century violence on Ukrainian soil was reached between 1941 and 1944, with the destruction of the Ukrainian Jews, the planned or at least accepted famine of the Ukrainian population, the abduction of over one million young Ukrainians (particularly women) for slave labour, the murder of millions of Soviet prisoners of war – among them hundreds of thousands of Ukrainians – the division of society in the fight for Ukrainian territory and the triple-fronted destruction during the conquest, the partisan struggle and the German retreat.[42]

4. The German Military and a 'German Way of War' in Ukraine?

For all the differences between the occupations of 1918 and those of 1941–1944, there were, from a military perspective, two constants. Both times Bolshevism was the enemy;

both times, partisan warfare broke out. How did the German military behave in both cases? Did Imperial Germany possess a specific military culture characterized by the unconditional suppression of any form of civilian resistance – a 'German Way of War'?[43] Was, to borrow Michael Geyer's words, 'premeditated use of violence against civilians', which 'shifted the burden of war onto the local population in a system of violent extortion', already a hallmark of German warfare in Ukraine in 1918?'[44]

Ukraine in 1918 was the theatre of one mass crime committed by the German military on the battlefield unparalleled even in comparison to the Second World War: the shooting of some 2000 captured Bolsheviks on 12 June after an unsuccessful amphibious operation near Taganrog. Already during the battle the Germans had taken no prisoners. The initiative for the execution order came from the local commander, Colonel Arthur Bopp. However, the primary sources and secondary literature seem to indicate that if there were any civilians among these victims, their number must have been small.[45] One should note that armed Bolsheviks did not offer the Germans in Ukraine in 1918 any quarter either. During the invasion in February the German troops had not received any concrete orders regarding the treatment of captured Bolsheviks, but after reports of Bolshevik violence, in particular the killing of hundreds if not thousands of Russian officers in Kiev alone,[46] the standing orders changed. Armed Bolsheviks were to be shot. The Habsburg troops received similar orders in the spring of 1918. Additionally, as the German Empire recognized the Central Council and not the Bolsheviks as the Ukrainian government, armed Bolsheviks in Ukraine were considered francs-tireurs. By contrast, in the Baltic and Belarus, the Germans did take prisoners among the Red Guardsmen.[47]

The killing of Bolshevik prisoners was definitely designed to spread terror, as stated in a report by the First Bavarian Cavalry Brigade after the breakthrough to the Crimea in April 1918. The systematic shooting of prisoners 'had the effect of instilling great fear [...] in the enemy, as all residents unanimously admitted'. As a result, 'once defeated, Bolsheviks no longer gather to resist'.[48] The Bavarian Cavalry Division announced in its 20 April 1918 order of the day: 'Now onwards to the complete destruction of these hateful bands, whom we must consider not as soldiers, but as robbers and as murderous incendiaries.'[49] It should be noted that the Germans definitely attempted to differentiate between armed and unarmed Bolsheviks, i.e. civilians. Insurgents could only be shot if they were caught in the act. Those captured later were court-martialled. Proper evidentiary procedure was followed or at least attempted, since 'a German court' could 'convict nobody [...] whose guilt had not been proven'.[50] This theoretically reined in the capriciousness of individual commanders. However, what constituted 'armed Bolshevik fighters' was nowhere defined. They rarely possessed clearly recognizable uniforms and mostly fought in civilian garb, with armbands and individual elements of uniforms. The ubiquity of military materiel after the dissolution of the Tsarist Army did not make the situation any clearer. Also, there were youths and women among the Bolshevik fighters, which further blurred the line between combatants and non-combatants for the occupying troops. This widened possibilities of blunders and trespasses against civilians.

That efforts were nevertheless made to keep a strict distinction between armed combatants and uninvolved civilians emerges clearly in the suppression of revolts in the summer of 1918. Initially, the Germans burnt down houses, but soon they realized that such measures were counterproductive. Bans were issued on the shelling of villages. 'Harshness' was to be avoided to prevent 'the well-disposed from having to suffer for the acts of the odd hostile minority'. The Royal Bavarian 15th Reserve Infantry Brigade decreed that 'peaceful inhabitants' were 'in every matter to be spared and protected'.[51] Additionally, even the *taking* of hostages was forbidden, let along the *shooting* of hostages. A tried and tested means of punishment for defiant villages were fines, in kind or money. While this still entailed the collective responsibility of the population, the German occupation troops in large measure abstained from *violent* collective measures against the population in Ukraine in 1918.[52]

Their Austro-Hungarian allies were rather harsher in the repression of insurrections and mostly wary of cooperating with Ukrainian officials. When in the middle of June the Germans briefly followed a harder line in combating insurrections, the Habsburg liaison to the German Army Group Eichhorn-Kiew, Captain Klemens Waldbott, commented, somewhat gloatingly: 'now they apply drastic measures too, perhaps too late'.[53] By contrast, the Habsburg military record does not evince a large-scale crime against Bolsheviks like the one at Taganrog. The Austro-Hungarian military neither had the power nor the desire to overstep the mark: in Ukraine, as in Serbia, it remained within certain traditional military norms, as noted earlier.[54] This seemingly contradictory position may be linked to the Austro-Hungarian military's self-image, with its strong anti-revolutionary and anti-liberal attitude and scepticism regarding civilian authority and democratic participation[55] (which, incidentally, it shared with the German army).

In sum, the measures by the German military to win over and secure rule over Ukraine seem to have been twofold, at least in principle: a ruthless, even brutal procedure against armed insurgents on the one hand, and on the other a moderate treatment of unarmed civilians. There can be no talk of a focused military campaign against the civilian population in Ukraine in 1918; no 'German Way of War' emerged. Austro-Hungarian troops, in contrast, do not seem to have adopted a pitiless no-quarter policy against Bolsheviks, but displayed less constraint against civilians. It should be noted that Western armies at the time were no gentler in the fight against insurgents: the British in Mesopotamia in 1920 resorted to far harsher measures against the civilian population. In Mesopotamia the burning of large swathes of land was part of the strategy, while the Germans in Ukraine in 1918 utilized this measure only selectively and ultimately gave it up altogether.[56]

The example of Ukraine in 1918, then, cannot serve as a link between a putative 'German Way of War' in Imperial Germany and the crimes of the Wehrmacht. But the German conduct of war in Ukraine in 1918 does reveal one continuity: lethal anti-Bolshevism. The massacre in Taganrog in June 1918 was an exception in terms of magnitude, but captured Bolsheviks were rarely spared during the invasion in the spring or the fight against insurgency in the summer. In that sense Ukraine in 1918 was already a war of ideology – and for both sides.

Acknowledgements

The authors would like to thank Sophie De Schaepdrijver for her critical suggestions on the text.

Notes

1. Flasch, *Die geistige Mobilmachung*; Naumann, *Mitteleuropa*; Remer, *Ukraine im Blickfeld*.
2. Bachmann, *Herd der Feindschaft*.
3. Wolfram Dornik and Peter Lieb, 'Die Ukrainepolitik der Mittelmächte während des Ersten Weltkrieges', chap. 1.c in Dornik et al., *Die Ukraine*, 99–105; Dornik, 'Ukraincy v avstro-vengerskich vojskach'.
4. See also Batowski, 'Die Polen', 550–3; Gaul, 'The Austro-Hungarian Empire', 205–7.
5. Hoffmann et al., *Thalerhof 1914–1936*, 95–124.

MILITARY OCCUPATIONS IN FIRST WORLD WAR EUROPE

6. Borowsky, *Deutsche Ukrainepolitik*; Baumgart, *Deutsche Ostpolitik*; Wolfram Dornik and Peter Lieb, 'Die Ukrainepolitik der Mittelmächte während des Ersten Weltkrieges', chap. 1.c in Dornik et al., *Die Ukraine*, 97–9; Remer, *Ukraine im Blickfeld*.
7. Dornik and Lieb, 'Die Ukrainepolitik der Mittelmächte während des Ersten Weltkrieges', chap. 1.c in Dornik et al., *Die Ukraine*, 93–9; Golczewski, *Deutsche und Ukrainer*, 197–239; Fedyshyn, *Germany's Drive*; Baumgart, *Deutsche Ostpolitik*. Some authors claim the opposite: Fischer, *Griff*; Borowski, *Deutsche Ukrainepolitik*; Remer, *Ukraine*; Grelka, *Die Ukrainische*.
8. Nebelin, *Ludendorff*, 371–80.
9. Dornik and Lieb, 'Die Ukrainepolitik der Mittelmächte während des Ersten Weltkrieges', chap. 1.c in Dornik et al., *Die Ukraine*, 105–13; Golczewski, *Deutsche und Ukrainer*, 187–92.
10. Wolfram Dornik and Peter Lieb, 'Die militärischen Operationen', chap 3.a in Dornik et al., *Die Ukraine*, 203–14.
11. Brinkley, 'Allied Policy and French Intervention', 326–28; Lowe and Dockrill, *The Mirage of Power*, 310–20.
12. Wolfram Dornik and Peter Lieb, 'Die Besatzungsverwaltung', chap. 3.b in Dornik et al., *Die Ukraine*, 267–70; Kamenetsky, 'German Colonization Plans', 95–8.
13. Ibid., 263–73.
14. Bundesarchiv–Militärarchiv (BA–MA,) N 46/172. Groener to Ludendorff, 23 March 1918.
15. Baumgart, *Brest-Litovsk*, 348.
16. For the Ukrainian perspective, see the memoirs of Skoropadskyi, an exciting read if not always a reliable source: Rosenfeld, ed., *Skoropads'kyj*.
17. See, for example, the incident near Jampil (Podolia) in late May, or in Kanizh in mid-June: Dornik and Lieb, 'Die militärischen Operationen', chap. 3.a in Dornik et al., *Die Ukraine*, 234–37.
18. See, for example, Bayrisches Hauptstaatsarchiv, Kriegsarchiv (BayHStA-KA), Etappenkommandantur 54, Bd. 22. Militärbezirk Kiew. XXVII. Res.Korps. Ia Nr. 1100. 13 April 1918. BayHStA-KA, 15. Res.Inf.Brig., Bd. 7. Militärbezirk Kiew. XXVII. Res.Korps Ia Nr. 1370. 28 April 1918.
19. Schnell, *Räume des Schreckens*.
20. Borys, *The Sovietization of Ukraine*, 139–50; Dornik and Lieb, 'Die militärischen Operationen', chap 3.a in Dornik et al., *Die Ukraine*, 225–39; Wolfram Dornik and Peter Lieb, 'Die wirtschaftliche Ausnutzung', chap. 3.c in Dornik et al., *Die Ukraine*, 306f.; Vasyl' Rasevyč, 'Die Sicht von innen – Besatzungsalltag', chap 3.d in Dornik et al., *Die Ukraine*, 330–6.
21. The primary sources and the academic literature about the experience of the occupied population are both scarce for 1918. Vasyl' Rasevyč, 'Die Sicht von innen – Besatzungsalltag', chap 3.d in Dornik et al., *Die Ukraine*, 325–41. Schnell, *Räume des Schreckens*.
22. ÖStA (Österreichisches Staatsarchiv), KA (Kriegsarchiv), NFA (Neue Feldakten), AOK (Armeeoberkommando), Kt. (Karton) 470, Dok. Nr. (Dokument-Nummer) 1634, 'Neuer Berliner Vertrag', 25 May1918.
23. Dornik and Lieb, 'Die wirtschaftliche Ausnutzung', chap. 3.c in Dornik et al., *Die Ukraine*, 293–308.
24. ÖStA, KA, FA, NFA, Höhere Heeres- und Armeekommanden/Armeegruppenkommando, 2. Armee, Op. Armeekommando, Kt. 305, 1918 Situations- und Tagesmeldungen.
25. Kaiser Karl in a handwritten letter to the commander of the k.u.k. 2nd Army, Eduard Freiherr von Böhm-Ermolli, on 31 March 1918: '... die Requirierungen haben rücksichtslos, eventuell mit Gewalt zu erfolgen': ÖStA, KA, FA, AOK, Op. Abt., Op. Geh. Akten, Kt. 468, Document 1372.
26. Krauß, *Die Ursachen unserer Niederlage*, 253f.
27. Gumz, *Resurrection*, 16–23.
28. ÖStA, KA, NFA, AOK, Kt. 471, Dok. Nr. 1684, 'Ukraine Bericht', 6 June 1918.
29. See on this also the paper of Wolfram Dornik, *A Colonial School of Violence? Austro-Hungarian Experiences of the First World War in Eastern Europe*, which will be published in the proceedings of the conference of the International Society for First World War Studies in Innsbruck, 2011.
30. Dornik and Lieb, 'Die militärischen Operationen', chap 3.a in Dornik et al., *Die Ukraine*, 225–39.
31. Baumgart, *Brest-Litovsk*, 442.
32. BayHStA-KA, Etappenkommandantur 54, Bd. 22. 18. Kavallerie Brigade. I. Nr. 70 per.geheim v. 28 October 1918.

MILITARY OCCUPATIONS IN FIRST WORLD WAR EUROPE

33. ÖStA, KA, NFA, HHkmdo (Höhere Heereskommanden), Akmdo/AG-Kmdo (Armeekommanden/Armeegruppen-Kommanden), 2. Armee, Op. Akmdo (Operatives Armeekommando), Kt. 308, Duplikat des Befehls der Qu. Abt. (Quartierabteilung) des AOK Nr. 121.055, 9 April 1918.

34. Wolfram Dornik and Peter Lieb, 'Die Besatzungsverwaltung', chap. 3.b in Dornik et al., *Die Ukraine*, 278–80.

35. Wolfram Dornik and Peter Lieb, 'Die Besatzungsverwaltung', chap. 3.b in Dornik et al., *Die Ukraine*, 273–8; Dornik and Lieb, 'Die wirtschaftliche Ausnutzung', chap. 3.c in Dornik et al., *Die Ukraine*, 281–93; Rasevyč, 'Die Sicht von innen – Besatzungsalltag', chap 3.d in Dornik et al., *Die Ukraine*, 325–41.

36. For the different parties of the civil war, see Hannes Leidinger, 'Zeit der Wirren: Revolutionäre Umwälzungen und bewaffnete Auseinandersetzungen im ehemaligen Zarenreich 1917–22', chap 1.a in Dornik et al., *Die Ukraine*, 29–60.

37. Georgiy Kasianov, 'Die Ukraine zwischen Revolution, Selbständigkeit und Fremdherrschaft', chap 2.a in Dornik et al., *Die Ukraine*, 131–79 (insbesondere ab 161); Bogdan Musial, 'Die Ukrainepolitik des bolschewikischen Russlands', chap. 4.b in Dornik et al., *Die Ukraine*, 367–89.

38. Dornik and Lieb, 'Die militärischen Operationen', chap 3.a in Dornik et al., *Die Ukraine*, 239–46.

39. Dornik and Lieb, 'Die wirtschaftliche Ausnutzung', chap. 3.c in Dornik et al., *Die Ukraine*, 317–23; Golczewski, *Deutsche und Ukrainer*, 323–32; Haj-Nyžnyk, *Finansova polityka*, 78f.

40. The National Archives (TNA), GFM 6/99. Der Staatssekretär des Reichsschatzamts (Graf Roedern) IV.A.6347 v. 22.10.1918. An den Herrn Chef des Generalstab des Feldheeres.

41. Baumgart, *Brest-Litovsk*, 33. Subtelny's assessment is also positive: he calls this time a 'relatively calm hiatus imposed by the German occupation': Subtelny, *Ukraine*, 355–9.

42. Musial, 'Ukrainepolitik des bolschewikischen Russlands', chap. 4.b in Dornik et al., *Die Ukraine*, 379–88; Kasianov, 'The Great Famine'; Snyder, *Bloodlands*.

43. Hull, *Absolute Destruction*, 159–81 and 226–62 and especially Geyer, *War and Terror*. A critical stance regarding a German specificity in colonial warfare is taken by Kuß in *Deutsches Militär*. John Horne and Alan Kramer were the first scholars to mention a specific culture of violence in the German Army and coin the term 'German Way of War': Horne/Kramer, *German Atrocities*, 161 and 170. Alan Kramer's latest monograph, however, cautiously distances itself from the idea of a German military *Sonderweg*, with specific reference to Hull's postulate of 'destruction': Kramer, *Dynamics*, 341–50. It should be noted that the term 'German Way of War' was launched to refer to an operational, not a military-cultural specificity: Citino, *German Way of War*.

44. Geyer, *War and Terror*, 66, 61.

45. Dornik and Lieb, 'Die militärischen Operationen', chap 3.a in Dornik et al., *Die Ukraine*, 221–5; Nachtigal, 'Krasnyj Desant'.

46. Dornik and Lieb, 'Die militärischen Operationen', chap 3.a in Dornik et al., *Die Ukraine*, 217–8.

47. For the German troops, see: BayHStA-KA, 15. Res.Inf.Brig., Bd. 7. Korps Knoerzer. Abt. Ib Nr. 528 v. 24 March 1918. Besondere Anordnungen (Zusammenfassung der bisher erlassenen wichtigsten Bestimmungen). For the Austro-Hungarian troops, see: ÖStA, KA, AdTK (Archiv der Truppenkörper), FAReg (Feldartillerie-Regiment) Nr. 59, Kt. 832, Abfertigung 57, 9 May 1918; ÖStA, KA, AdTK, FABrig (Feldartillerie-Brigade) Nr. 59, Kt. 4131, Dok. Nr. 307, 'Verhalten der Zivilbevölkerung gegenüber', 20 August 1918. For the situation in the Baltics and in Belarus, see BayHStA-KA, 2. Landwehr Division, Bd. 40. Generalkommando VI. A.K. Ib Nr. 850. 16 March 1918, Besondere Anordnungen Nr. 3: Behandlung ehem. russ. Soldaten und roter Gardisten.

48. BayHStA-KA, Kav.Div., Bd. 19. 1. bayer. Kavallerie Brigade, Kommandeur, 20 May 1918, Erfahrungen aus den Operationen und Kämpfen gegen die Bolschewisten in Taurien und in der Krim in der Zeit vom 16.4. bis 2 May 1918. The divisional report also admitted that no prisoners had been taken: BayHStA-KA, Kav.Div., Bd. 18. Kaiserl. Deutsches Gouvernement Sewastopol Ia Nr. 120 v. 13 May 1918, Betr.: Bericht über die Tätigkeit der B.K.D. von Bierislawa bis zur Besetzung von Feodosia. See also the letter by the commanding general of 52nd Army Corps, General Robert Kosch, to his wife, 21 April 1918, in file BA-MA, N 754/10: 'Well, it's to be hoped that the defeat at Pjerjekop [Perekop, Crimea, PL], where the Bavarians pretty much slaughtered all, will have given them [the Bolsheviks, PL] a salutary fright.'

49. BayHStA-KA, 29. InfReg, Bd. 3. BayKavDiv. Divisions-Tagesbefehl, 20 April 1918.

50. BayHStA-KA, 15. Res.Inf.Brig., Bd. 7. Bez.Komdtr. Smiela, 10 June 1918, Merkblatt; BayHStA-KA, 4. Kav.Brig., Bd. 4, Gruppe Tannstein, Nr. 3020/I v. 11 September 1918, Gerichtliches Verfahren gegen Landeseinwohner.

MILITARY OCCUPATIONS IN FIRST WORLD WAR EUROPE

51. BayHStA-KA, 15. Res.Inf.Brig., Bd. 7. K.Bayr. 15. Res.Inf.Brigade, Nr. 4460 v. 15 July 1918, Merkblatt für Unterweisung von Führern und Mannschaften für ihr Verhalten im besetzten Gebiet und bei Unternehmungen.
52. See also Lieb, *A Precursor*.
53. See also the relevant report from Waldbott from 15 June 1918: ÖStA, KA, AOK, Op. Abt., Op. Geh. Akten, Kt. 472, Documents 1707 and 1710.
54. Gumz, *Resurrection*. Stephan Lehnstaedt (Warsaw) is currently working on a comparison of German and Austro-Hungarian occupation policies in Poland during the First World War. His first findings confirm that one cannot speak of a harsher German occupation regime when compared to Austria-Hungary. Lehnstaedt, 'Das Militärgeneralgouvernement'.
55. Allmayer-Beck, 'Die bewaffnete Macht in Staat und Gesellschaft', 1–11.
56. Lieb, 'Suppressing Insurgencies'.

References

Allmayer-Beck, JohannChristoph. "Die bewaffnete Macht in Staat und Gesellschaft." In *Die Habsburgermonarchie 1848–1918, Volume 5:* Die bewaffnete Macht, edited by Adam Wandruczka, and Peter Urbanitsch, 1–141. Vienna: Verlag der Österreichischen Akademie der Wissenschaften, 1987.

Bachmann, Klaus. *Ein Herd der Feindschaft gegen Rußland. Galizien als Krisenherd in den Beziehungen der Donaumonarchie mit Rußland (1907–1914).* Vienna, Munich: Verlag für Geschichte und Politik and R. Oldenbourg Verlag, 2001.

Batowski, Henryk. "Die Polen." In *Die Habsburgermonarchie 1848–1918.* Volume 3: Die Völker des Reiches, Part 1, edited by Adam Wandruczka, and Peter Urbanitsch, 522–54. Vienna: Verlag der Österreichische Akademie der Wissenschaften, 1980.

Baumgart, Winfried. *Deutsche Ostpolitik 1918. Von Brest-Litowsk bis zum Ende des Ersten Weltkrieges.* Vienna, Munich: Oldenbourg, 1966.

Baumgart, Winfried, ed. *Von Brest-Litowsk zur deutschen Novemberrevolution. Aus den Tagebüchern, Briefen und Aufzeichnungen von Alfons Paquet, Wilhelm Groener und Albert Hopman. März bis November 1918.* Göttingen: Vandenhoek und Ruprecht, 1971.

Borowsky, Peter. *Deutsche Ukrainepolitik 1918 unter besonderer Berücksichtigung der Wirtschaftsfragen.* Lübeck, Hamburg: Matthiesen, 1970.

Borys, Jurij. *The Sovietization of Ukraine 1917–1923: The Communist Doctrine and Practice of National Self-Determination.* Edmonton: Canadian Institute of Ukrainian Studies Press, 1980.

Brinkley, GeorgeA. Jr.. "Allied Policy and French Intervention in the Ukraine, 1917–1920." In *The Ukraine, 1917–1921: A Study in Revolution*, edited by Taras Hunczak, 323–51. Cambridge: Harvard University Press, 1977.

Dornik, Wolfram, Georgiy Kasianov, Hannes Leidinger, Peter Lieb, Alexey Miller, Bogdan Musial, and Vasyl Rasevyč. *Die Ukraine zwischen Selbstbestimmung und Fremdherrschaft 1917–1922.* Graz: Leykam Verlag, 2011.

Fedyshyn, Oleh F. *Germany's Drive to the East and the Ukrainian Revolution 1917–1918.* Utopia, NJ: Rutgers University Press, 1971.

Fischer, Fritz. *Griff nach der Weltmacht. Die Kriegsziele des kaiserlichen Deutschland 1914/15.* Düsseldorf: Droste, 1961.

Flasch, Kurt. *Die geistige Mobilmachung. Die deutschen Intellektuellen und der Erste Weltkrieg.* Berlin: Alexander Fest Verlag, 2000.

Gaul, Jerzy. "The Austro-Hungarian Empire and Its political Allies in the Polish Kingdom." In *Karl I. (IV.), der Erste Weltkrieg und das Ende der Donaumonarchie*, edited by Andreas Gottsmann, 203–22. Vienna: Verlag der Österreichische Akademie der Wissenschaften, 2007.

Geyer, Michael. "War and Terror: Some Timely Observations on the German Way of Waging War." In *War and Terror in Historical and Contemporary Perspective*, edited by Michael Geyer, 47–69. Washington, DC: American Institute for Contemporary German Studies, The Johns Hopkins University, 2003.

Golczewski, Frank. *Deutsche und Ukrainer 1914–1939.* Paderborn: Ferdinand Schöningh, 2010.

Grelka, Frank. *Die ukrainische Nationalbewegung unter deutscher Besatzungsherrschaft 1918 und 1941/42.* Wiesbaden: Harrassowitz, 2005.

Gumz, Jonathan. *The Resurrection and Collapse of Empire in Habsburg Serbia, 1914–1918.* Cambridge: Cambridge University Press, 2009.

Haj-Nyžnyk, P. *Finansova polityka urjadu Ukraïns'koï Deržavy Het'mana Pavla Skoropads'koho (29 kvitnja – 14 hrudnja 1918 r.).* Kiev: Drukarnja SPD Šerbenok S.G., 2004.

Hoffmann, Georg, Nicole-Melanie Goll, and Philipp Lesiak. *Thalerhof 1914–1936. Die Geschichte eines vergessenen Lagers und seiner Opfer.* Herne: Gabriele Schäfer Verlag, 2010.

Horne, John, and Alan Kramer. *German Atrocities 1914: A History of Denial.* New Haven, CT/ London: Yale University Press, 2001.

Hull, Isabel V. *Absolute Destruction: Military Culture and the Practices of War in Imperial Germany.* Ithaca, NY: Cornell University Press, 2004.

Kamenetsky, Ihor. "German Colonization Plans in Ukraine during World Wars I and II." In *German-Ukrainian Relations in Historical Perspective*, edited by Hans-Joachim Torke and John-Paul Himka, 95–109. Edmonton/Toronto: Canadian Institute of Ukrainian Studies, 1994.

Kasianov, Georgiy. "The Great Famine of 1932–1933 (Holodomor) and the Politics of History in Contemporary Ukraine." In *Postdiktatorische Geschichtskulturen im Süden und Osten Europas. Bestandsaufnahme und Forschungsperspektiven*, edited by Stefan Troebst, 619–41. Göttingen: Wallstein Verlag, 2010.

Kuß, Susanne. *Deutsches Militär auf kolonialen Kriegsschauplätzen: Eskalation von Gewalt zu Beginn des 20. Jahrhunderts.* Berlin: Ch. Links Verlag, 2010.

Kramer, Alan. *Dynamic of Destruction: Culture and Mass Killing in the First World War.* Oxford: Oxford University Press, 2007.

Krauß, Alfred. *Die Ursachen unserer Niederlage. Erinnerungen und Urteile aus dem Weltkrieg.* Vienna/Munich: Lehmann, 1923.

Lehnstaedt, Stephan. "Das Militärgeneralgouvernement Lublin: Die "Nutzbarmachung" Polens durch Österreich-Ungarn im Ersten Weltkrieg." *Zeitschrift für Ostmitteleuropa-Forschung* 61 (2012): 1–26.

Lieb, Peter. "Suppressing Insurgencies in Comparison: The Germans in the Ukraine, 1918, and the British in Mesopotamia 1920." *Small Wars & Insurgencies* 23 (2012): 627–47.

Lieb, Peter. *A Precursor of Modern Counter-Insurgency Operations? The German Occupation of the Ukraine in 1918.* Working Papers in Military History and International History, No. 4, Salford, European Studies Research Institute, University of Salford, 2007.

Lowe, C. J., and M. L. Dockrill. *The Mirage of Power, Volume 2: British Foreign Policy 1914–22, Volume IV: Foreign Politics of the Great Powers.* London/ Boston, MA: Routledge & Kegan Paul, [1972] 2002.

Nachtigal, Reinhard. "Krasnyj Desant: Das Gefecht an der Mius-Bucht. Ein unbeachtetes Kapitel der deutschen Besetzung Südrusslands 1918." *Jahrbücher für Geschichte Osteuropas* 53 (2005): 221–46.

Naumann, Friedrich. *Mitteleuropa.* Berlin: Reimer, 1915.

Nebelin, Manfred. *Ludendorff. Diktator im Ersten Weltkrieg.* Munich: Siedler Verlag, 2010.

Remer, Claus. *Die Ukraine im Blickfeld deutscher Interessen. Ende des 19. Jahrhunderts bis 1917/18.* Frankfurt/Main et al. Lang, 1997.

Rosenfeld, Günter, ed. *Pavlo Skoropads'kyj. Erinnerungen 1917 bis 1918.* Stuttgart: Steiner, 1999.

Schnell, Felix. *Räume des Schreckens. Gewalträume und Gruppenmilitanz in der Ukraine, 1905–1933.* Hamburg: Hamburger Editionen, 2012.

Snyder, Timothy. *Bloodlands: Europe between Hitler and Stalin.* New York: Basic Books, 2010.

Subtelny, Orest. *Ukraine. A History.* Toronto: University of Toronto Press, 2009.

Index

abuse of power 12–13
Albania 40
Appel, Michael von 101
Arbeitsscheu ('workshyness') 3–4, 42, 43, 55
Aschauer, Philip 87
Austro-Hungarian Empire 1, 3, 40, 87; occupation of Serbia 97–110; policy towards Ukraine 111–13
Auxiliary Service Law (*Hilfsdienstgesetz*) 43, 55

Balkans 3
Baltic countries *see* Ober Ost
Barensfeld, Adolf Rhemen von 104
Baucq, Philippe 29
Becker, Annette 1, 5, 29
Belgium 1, 2, 3; *Deutsches Industriebüro* 42; German labour policy 39–50; underground press 23–38
Benn, Gottfried 44
Beseler, Hans Hartwig von 53, 55, 66, 68–71, 73–4, 75–6
Bethmann Hollweg, Theobald von 65, 83, 112
Bildung 69, 70
Bissing, Moritz von 4, 42, 43
black market 88, 90
'Bochartes' 14, 15
Böhm-Ermolli, Eduard von 116
Bolshevism 111, 113, 116, 118–19, 120
Bopp, Arthur 119
Bosnian Annexation Crisis 100
Brendel, Heiko 5
Brest-Litovsk Peace Agreement 111, 113, 114
Brudziński, Józef 70, 72, 74
Brussels Declaration (1874) 99, 100
Buerbaum, Ernest 30
Buerbaum, Jozef 25, 27
Bulgaria 40
Burián, István 103

Ca et Là 31
Catholic underground press 27–8
Cavell, Edith 29
censorship 2

Central Purchasing Agency (ZEG) 82
Chickering, roger 89
Civil Workers Battalions (*Zivil-Arbeiter-Bataillone*) 44, 55–6, 57
coercive labour *see* forced labour
collaboration 9, 13–14
Commission for Relief in Belgium 8, 41
Committee for Feeding Northern France (CANF) 8
Congress Poland 66, 69
conquest 3
culture de l'occupé 11, 12, 13, 15, 16
Czernin, Ottakar von 105

Dangiulescu, Janku 90
De Vlaamsche Leeuw 26, 28
De Vlaamsche Wachter 31
De Vrije Stem 26, 28, 30, 31
de-nationalization 3
Debruyne, Emmanuel 5
denunciations 9, 11, 14
depoliticization 101
deportations 39–50
Deutsche Arbeiterzentrale 53–4
Deutsches Industriebüro 42
Die Ostmark 71
Droogstoppels 25, 26, 28, 30
Duisberg, Carl 41, 43
Dülffer, Jost 103

eastern occupied territories *see* Ober Ost
Eichhorn, Hermann von 115
Entente 39, 40, 44
Erzberger, Matthias 75
espionage 14, 29
Etappengebiet 41, 43–4

Flamenpolitik 26, 27, 31
food 81–95; black market 88, 90; Central Purchasing Agency (ZEG) 82; consumption 88–91; expropriation of 87–8; gifts 4, 86–7, 90; organization of production 83–6; rationing 89; shortages 91, 102–3; unauthorized trading 90

INDEX

forced labour 3–4; Belgium and Northern France 39–50; Civil Workers Battalions (*Zivil-Arbeiter-Bataillone*) 44, 55–6, 57; Jews 53, 56, 58; lessons from 57–8; Poland and Lithuania 51–63; POWs 85–6; women 43; workshyness (*Arbeitsscheu*) 3–4, 42, 43, 55

France 1, 2, 4; German labour policy 39–50; Nord region 7–21, 39–50

Frank, Hans 57–8

Frank, Liborius 101, 102

Franz Ferdinand, Archduke of Austria, assassination of 100, 101

Geist 68, 69

genocide 58

Germany 1, 3; labour policy in Belgium and Northern France 39–50; labour policy in Poland and Lithuania 51–63; military occupation of Ukraine 111–13, 118–20

Grégoire, Henri 31

Groener, Wilhelm 81, 114, 116

Gromaire, Georges 12

Gumz, Jonathan 4, 116

Habsburg Empire *see* Austro-Hungarian Empire

Hague Conference (1899) 100

Hague Convention 100, 104

Handelsman, Marceli 72, 75

Hannsen, Hans Peter 82

Herbert, Ulrich 46

Het Nachtlichtje 28

Hilfsdienstgesetz (Auxiliary Service Law) 43, 55

Hindenburg, Paul von 40, 43, 53, 54–5, 105

Hindenburg Program 40, 43

Hoetzendorff, Franz Conrad von 98, 100, 102–3, 104

homosexuality 12

Hoover, Herbert 8

Hubich, Wilhelm 88, 90

Hugenberg, Alfred 43

Hull, Isabel 2, 100

Hutten-Czapski, Bogdan Graf von 70, 72, 73, 74

informing 8

internal siege 1

Isenburg-Birstein, Franz-Josef von 56

Italy 40

Jacoby, Julie 5

Jewish labour 53, 56, 58

Kerchnawe, Hugo 102

Kostanecki, Antoni 74

Krasiński, Zygmunt 71

Krauss, Alfred 116

Kriegsverrat 30

Kries, Wolfgang von 68, 69–70

La Belgique 25

La Soupe 25

La Vedette 25, 27

labour camps 1, 44

labour policy *see* forced labour

L'Âme Belge 26, 28, 30

L'Antiprussien 30

'latitudinarian suspicion' 2

Lava, Gustaaf 30

Le Bruxellois 25

Le Bulletin 25

Le Flambeau 31

Le Révolté 27

League for the Liberation of Ukraine 112

Lelewel, Joachim 72

Les Dernières Nouvelles 25

Les Petites Nouvelles 27

Les Vidanges 30–1

Libre Belgique 25, 28, 29, 30, 32

Lithuania *see* Ober Ost

Liulevicius, Vejas 106

Lloyd George, David 105

Ludendorff, Erich 40, 43, 53, 54–5, 56–7, 83, 85, 105, 114

'Ludendorffian turn' 31

Mackensen, August von 65

Manteuffel, Tadeusz 67

massacres 1

mauvaise conduit 7–21; abuse of power 12–13; collaboration 9, 13–14; definition 9–10; denunciations 9, 11, 14; punishment 15–16; sexual misconduct 9, 10–12

men: abuse of power 12–13; commerce with the enemy 14; denunciations 14

Mercier, Cardinal 26, 44

Michaelis, George 81, 89

Mick, Christoph 5

Mikułowski-Pomorski, Józef 74

Mitrany, David 87

Montenegro 24, 40

moral-patriotic framework 3

Nabulsi, Karma 29

Nazi ideology 57–8

Neumann, Friedrich 112

newspapers *see* underground press

Nivet, Philippe 5, 10, 13–14

Nord region 7–21; abuse of power 12–13; collaboration 9, 13–14; denunciations 9, 11, 14; *Etappen* 7–8, 43; forced labour 39–50; *mauvaise conduit* 9–10; punishment 15–16; sexual misconduct 9, 10–12

norms of war 97–111

INDEX

Notstandsarbeiten 41
Nowaczyński, Adolf 71

Ober Ost 3, 24, 51, 66, 67, 85, 106; Civil
    Workers Battalions (*Zivil-Arbeiter-
    Bataillone*) 55–6, 57; forced labour 54–6;
    Germany labour policy, 1914–1916 53–4;
    grain requirements 89; maintenance of
    coercion 56–7; self-governance 56–7
Oberbefehlshaber Ost see Ober Ost
Operationsgebiet 41, 43–4
Opfer-Klinger, Björn 5
Ossietzky, Carl von 32
Ostmarkenverein 75
Ottoman Empire 40

Paris Peace Treaty 45
Paris system 107
Paszkowski, Wilhelm 71, 73
Patrie 27
Percy, Sarah 98
Piłsudski, Józef 72
Poland 1, 2, 3, 24, 42; Congress Poland 66,
    69; German labour policy 51–63; Warsaw
    University 65–79; *see also* Ober Ost
Polish Socialist Party 72
political movements 66
post-war revenge 16
Potiorek, Oskar 102
POWs *see* prisoners of war
prison camps 1
prisoners of war (POWs): food rations 89; use
    as labour force 85–6
Proctor, Tammy 5
profiteering 9
prostitution 11
punishment 15–16; post-war revenge 16

Rathenau, Walter 43
realpolitik 111–24
resistance 2, 5, 29
resources, withholding of 2
respectability, reinforcement of 15–16
Revue de la Presse 28, 30
Revue Hebdomadaire de la Presse Française
    25
Romania 1, 2, 4, 39, 40, 81–95;
    Darlehenskassen 86; food consumption
    88–91; food rationing 89; labour shortages
    84–5; malnutrition 91; organization of food
    production 83–6; planning for occupation
    82–3; plundering 87; pretend burials of grain
    2, 87; prisoners of war 85–6; wheat exports
    82
Rommel, Erwin 86
Russian Empire: February Revolution 72–3;
    German occupation 52
Russo-Turkish War (1877–1878) 100

Satirische Zeitung 31
Scaripa, Nicolae 90
self-mobilization 24
Serbia 2, 3, 24, 40; depoliticization of
    101; food shortages 102–3; Hajduk law
    104; Komitadjis (guerrillas) 101, 104;
    Majestätsbeleidigung 102, 105; military law
    102; occupation by Austro-Hungary 97–110;
    Standrecht 102
sexual misconduct 9; as betrayal 12;
    prostitution 11
Siemieński, Józef 71, 75
Sklarz, Leon 51
Skoropadskyi, Pavlo P. 114–15
Snoeck, Gustave 27
Spoerer, Mark 58
spying 14, 29
Steed, Henry Wickham 108
Stinnes, Hugo 43
Straussenberg, Arz von 98
strikes 2
student activism 72–5
Stürgkh, Karl Graf von 101, 104
Suck, Leopold 88, 90
Sursum Corda 23–38
Svoljšak, Petra 5

Tisza, István 104
Transylvania 81
Trotsky, Leon 113

Ukraine 1, 2, 3, 4, 111–24; Brest-Litovsk Peace
    Agreement 111, 113, 114; consequences
    of occupation 117–18; German military
    measures 118–20; German-Habsburg
    policies 111–13; Hetmanate 114–15, 116–17;
    League for the Liberation of Ukraine 112;
    occupation by Central Powers 114–17
underground press 23–38; Catholic input
    27–8; *Kriegsverrat* 30; monthly output 30;
    suppression of 29–30; *see also individual
    publications*

Van Doren, Eugène 23
Van Doren, Maria 23–4
Van Ypersele, Laurence 5
Velburg, Gerhard 84, 86, 87–8, 90
volunteers 14–15; punishment of 15–16

Waldbott, Klemens 120
war culture 8
Warsaw University 65–79; *Bratnia Pomoc*
    (Fraternal Aid) 72, 73; deceptive stability
    (1915–1917) 71–2; establishment of 67–71;
    Lelewel Society 72, 75; second occupation
    (1939–1945) 75–6; student strike 72–5
Wegner, Larissa 5
Weinberg, Gerhard 75

INDEX

Weitz, Eric 107
Whitlock, Brand 29
women: 'Bochartes' 14, 15; forced labour 43; sexual misconduct 10–12
workshyness (*Arbeitsscheu*) 3–4, 42, 43, 55

Zievereer-Excelsior 28
Zimmerman, Arthur 85
Zivil-Arbeiter-Bataillone (Civil Workers Battalions) 44, 55–6, 57
Zweig, Arnold 56